SEVENTH GRADE TECHNOLOGY

A COMPREHENSIVE CURRICULUM

SIXTH EDITION

Part Eight of the SL Technology Curriculum

Version 6.3 2020

Visit the companion website at Ask a Tech Teacher for more resources to teach technology

For permission to use material from this text or product, contact us by email at:
info@structuredlearning.net

ISBN 978-1-942101-29-1

Printed in the United States of America

Introduction

The educational paradigm has changed—again. Technology has become granular to learning, blended into educational standards from Kindergarten on, like these that expect students to:

- *demonstrate sufficient command of* **keyboarding** *to type at least three pages in a single sitting*
- **evaluate different media** *[print or digital]*
- **gather information** *from print/digital sources*
- *integrate and evaluate* **information presented in diverse media** *and formats*
- **interpret information** *presented visually, orally, or quantitatively [such as interactive Web pages]*
- *make* **strategic use of digital media**
- *use* **print/digital glossaries/dictionaries** ...
- *use information from* **images and words in print/digital** *text*
- *communicate with a* **variety of media**
- **use text features and search tools** *(e.g., key words, sidebars,* **hyperlinks***) to locate information*

But how is this taught?

With the nine-volume **Structured Learning Technology Curriculum**. Aligned with Common Core Standards* and National Educational Technology Standards, and using a time-proven method honed in classrooms, students learn the technology that promotes literacy, critical thinking, problem-solving, and decision-making through project-based work. The purpose is not to teach step-by-step tech skills (like adding borders, formatting a document, and creating a blog). There are many fine books for that. What this curriculum does is guide you in providing the **right skills at the right time**.

Just as most children can't learn to read at two, or write at four, they shouldn't be required to place hands on home row in kindergarten or use the Internet before they understand the digital risks and responsibilities. The Structured Learning curriculum makes sure students get what they need at the right age and with proper scaffolding. The end result is a phenomenal amount of learning in a short period of time.

For skills you don't know, visit our Help blog, Ask A Tech Teacher. There's always someone there who can help.

●   ●   ●

"New technologies have broadened and expanded the role that speaking and listening play in acquiring and sharing knowledge and have tightened their link to other forms of communication. Digital texts confront students with the potential for continually updated content and dynamically changing combinations of words, graphics, images, hyperlinks, and embedded video and audio."

—CCSS

●   ●   ●

●   ●   ●

"Use of technology differentiates for student learning styles by providing an alternative method of achieving conceptual understanding, procedural skill and fluency, and applying this knowledge to authentic circumstances."

—CCSS

●   ●   ●

What's in the SL Technology Curriculum?

The SL Curriculum is project-based and collaborative with wide-ranging opportunities for students to show their knowledge in the manner that fits their communication and learning style. Each grade level includes topics to be woven into 'most' 21st-century lesson plans:

- *keyboarding—more than typing*
- *digital citizenship—critical with the influx of internet-based and online learning*
- *problem-solving—to encourage independence, critical thinking*
- *vocabulary—decode unknown words in any subject quickly*

For more on this, see *"4 Things Every Teacher Must Teach and How"* at the end of Lesson 1.

Besides these four topics, here's a quick overview of what is included in the curriculum:

- *list of assessments and images*
- *articles that address tech pedagogy*
- *Certificate of Completion for students*
- *curriculum map of skills taught*

- *monthly homework (3rd-8th only)*
- *posters*
- *Scope and Sequence of skills taught*
- *step-by-step weekly lessons*

Each weekly lesson includes:

- *assessment strategies*
- *class warm-up and exit ticket*
- *Common Core and ISTE Standards*
- *differentiation strategies*
- *educational applications*
- *essential question and big idea*

- *examples, rubrics, images, printables*
- *materials/preparation required*
- *problem solving for lesson*
- *steps to accomplish goals*
- *time required to complete*
- *vocabulary used*

Throughout the text are online resources to extend lessons, enrich learning, and differentiate your teaching. Google the name to find it or visit the Ask a Tech Teacher resources pages for options. *Figure 1a-b* shows what's at the beginning and end of each lesson:

Figure 1a-b—What's included in each lesson

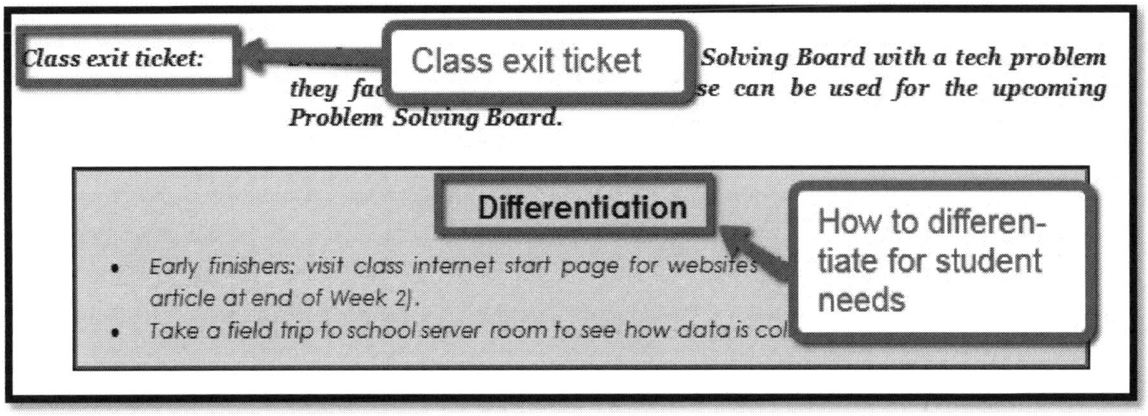

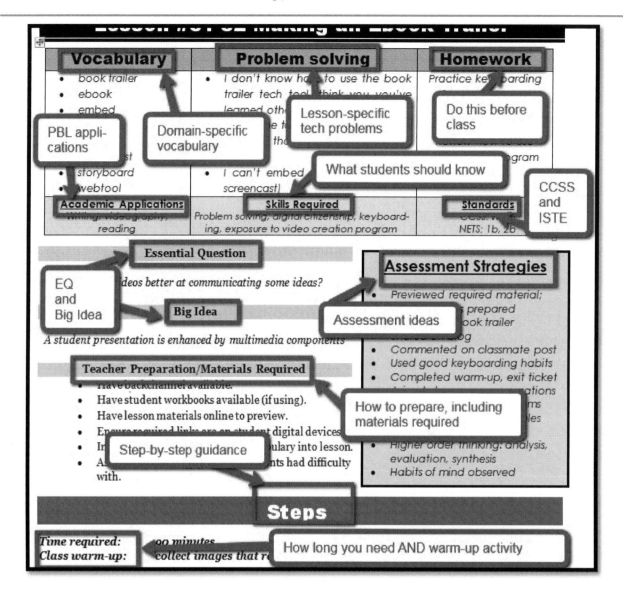

Who Needs This Book

You are the Tech Specialist, Coordinator for Instructional Technology, IT Coordinator, Technology Facilitator or Director, Curriculum Specialist, or tech teacher—tasked with finding the right project for a classroom. You have a limited budget, less software, and the drive to do it right no matter roadblocks.

Or you are a grade-level teacher, a tech enthusiast with a goal this year—and this time you mean it—to integrate the wonders of technology into lessons. You've seen it work. Others in your PLN are doing it. And significantly, you want to comply with state/national requirements and/or IB guidelines that weave technology into the fabric of inquiry.

You are a homeschooler. Even though you're not comfortable with technology, you know your children must be. You are committed to providing the tools s/he needs to succeed. Just as important: Your child WANTS to learn with these tools!

How do you reach your goal? With this curriculum. Teaching children to strategically and safely use technology is vital to being a functional member of society—and should be part of every curriculum. If not you (the teacher), who will do this? To build **Tomorrow's Student** (*Figure 2*) requires integration of technology and learning. We show you how.

Figure 2—Tomorrow's student

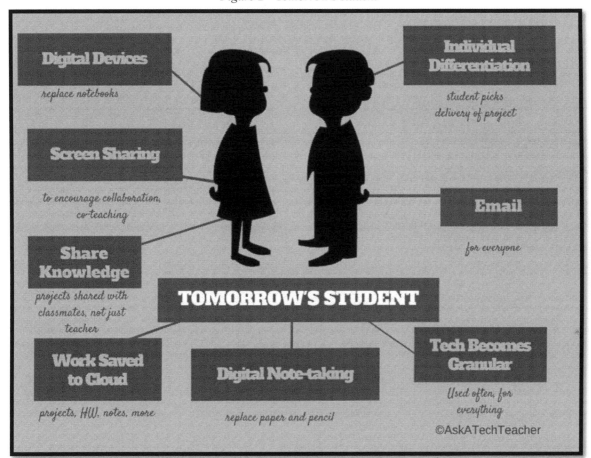

How to Use This Book

You can use this curriculum on its own—as a teacher manual—or in conjunction with the companion student workbooks (sold separately through Structured Learning). Contact Zeke at admin@structuredlearning.net for free start-up training.

If there is a skill students don't get, circle back on it, especially when you see it come up a second or third time through the course of the K-8 curricula. By the end of 8th grade, students have a well-rounded tech toolkit that serves their learning needs and prepares them for college and/or career.

The curriculum map (*Figure 3*) shows what's covered in which grade. Units taught multiple years reflect increasingly less scaffolding and more student direction. Here's how to use it:

- Determine what skills were covered earlier years. Expect students to transfer that knowledge to this new school year. Review the topics and skills, but don't expect to teach.
- For skills covered prior years, confirm that was done. If not (for whatever reason), when you reach lessons that require the skills, plan extra time.

Figure 3—Curriculum Map—K-8

	Mouse Skills	Vocabulary - Hardware	Problem-solving	Platform	Keyboard	WP	Slide-shows	DTP	Spread-sheet	Google Earth	Search/ Research	Graphics/	Co-ding	WWW	Games	Dig Cit
K	☺	☺	☺	☺	☺					☺		☺	☺	☺		☺
1	☺	☺	☺	☺	☺	☺	☺	☺	☺	☺		☺	☺	☺		☺
2		☺	☺	☺	☺	☺	☺	☺	☺	☺		☺	☺	☺		☺
3		☺	☺	☺	☺	☺	☺	☺	☺	☺	☺	☺	☺	☺		☺
4		☺	☺		☺	☺	☺	☺	☺	☺	☺	☺	☺	☺		☺
5		☺	☺		☺	☺		☺	☺	☺	☺	☺	☺	☺		☺
6		☺	☺	☺	☺	☺	☺	☺	☺	☺	☺	☺	☺	☺		☺
7		☺	☺	☺	☺				☺	☺	☺	☺	☺	☺	☺	☺
8		☺	☺	☺	☺				☺	☺	☺	☺	☺	☺	☺	☺

Here are hints on using this curriculum:

- This curriculum uses the 'flipped classroom' approach. Homework prepares students for the class lesson so class time is spent on enrichment. Homework materials can be shared via the class website, blog, wiki, class internet start page, and/or videos. The last can be done via 10-15 minute informal videos providing an overview, your expectations, and where to find resources. Prepare your video with the free Screencast-o-matic or an inexpensive recording program of your choice and then upload to YouTube/Vimeo/TeacherTube. You can find options on Ask a Tech Teacher's resource pages under 'Screenshots/Screencasts'.
- A number of lessons are mixed throughout the year:

    #3 Keyboarding
    #4 Problem Solving
    #5 Digital Citizenship

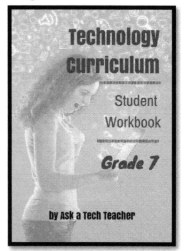

Figure 1--Student workbook

- 'Academic Applications' provide suggestions on how to blend lessons into your curriculum.
- Invest in student digital workbooks (sold separately through Structured Learning LLC), a student-centric companion to the teacher guide. Here are reasons why:

- o *Full-color projects at student fingertips with examples and directions (licensing varies based on plan).*
- o *Workbooks can be annotated.*
- o *Students work at their own pace.*

- Units focus on strategies useful throughout a student's learning day. Collaborate with grade-level teachers on cross-curricular planners that involve technology.
- Most lessons start with a warm-up to get students into tech and you to finish a prior class.
- 'Teacher Preparation' often includes chatting with the grade-level team. Why?

- o *tie tech into their inquiry*
- o *offer websites for early-finishers that address their topics*

- Some lessons offer several activities that meet goals outlined in the Essential Question and Big Idea. Pick what works best for your student group.
- Check off completed items on the line preceding the step so you know what to get back to when you have time. If you have the ebook, use Acrobat, Kami, iAnnotate, Notability or another annotation tool that works for your devices.
- Look for these icons to guide teaching:

- *indicates video*

- *indicates work with a partner*

- *indicates an article*

- *indicates a poster (in Appendix)*

- *indicates workbook material*

- Use as much technology as possible in your class. Encourage students to do the same whether it's a smartphone timing a quiz, a video of activities posted to the class website, or an audio file with student input. If you treat tech as a tool in daily activities, so will students.
- Always use lesson vocabulary. Students gain authentic understanding by your example.
- Expect students to direct their own learning. You are a 'guide on the side', a facilitator not lecturer. Learning is accomplished by both success and failure.
- Expect students to be risk takers. Don't rush to solve their problems. Ask them to think how it was done in the past. Focus on problems listed in the lesson but embrace all that come your way. This scaffolds critical thinking and troubleshooting when you won't be there to help.
- Don't expect free time while students work. Move among them to provide assistance and observations on their keyboarding, problem-solving, and vocabulary decoding skills.

- Encourage student-directed differentiation. If the Big Idea and Essential Question can be accommodated in other ways, embrace those.
- If you have the digital book, zoom in on posters, rubrics, lessons to enlarge as needed.
- Lessons expect students to develop 'habits of mind' (*Figure 5*). Read more about Art Costa and Bena Kallick's discussion of these principles in the article at the end of Lesson #1. In a sentence: Habits of Mind ask students to engage in learning, not simply memorize.

Figure 5—Habits of Mind

- Every effort has been made to accommodate varied digital devices. Project samples are often on multiple platforms. If the activity is impossible on your digital device (i.e., iPads don't have mouses; software doesn't run in Chromebooks), focus on the **Big Idea and Essential Question**—the skill taught and its application to inquiry. Adapt instructions as you follow steps.

More Help

Need more help? Visit the companion website, Ask a Tech Teacher©, run by teachers using the curriculum. Here, you'll find:

- *free lesson plans*
- *targeted websites*
- *free tech tips and weekly newsletters*
- *free training videos on tools used in lesson plans*
- *great apps to include on iPads, digital devices*

Finally, here are useful pieces to extend this curriculum, available at Structured Learning LLC:

- *Student workbooks—(sold separately) allow students to be self-paced*
- *Digital Citizenship curriculum— if this is a focus (sold through Structured Learning LLC)*
- *Keyboarding Curriculum— if this is a focus (sold through Structured Learning LLC)*

Copyrights

About the Authors

Ask a Tech Teacher is a group of technology teachers who run an award-winning resource blog. Here they provide free materials, advice, lesson plans, pedagogical conversation, website reviews, and more to all who drop by. The free newsletters and articles help thousands of teachers, homeschoolers, and those serious about finding the best way to maneuver the minefields of technology in education.

*Throughout this text, we refer to Common Core State Standards and a license granted to "...copy, publish, distribute, and display the Common Core State Standards for purposes that support the CCSS Initiative. Copyright 2010. National Governors Association Center for Best Practices and Council of Chief State School Officers. All rights reserved.

Table of Contents

Scope and Sequence

Lessons

#1	Introduction	#12	Internet Search/Research
#2	Digital Tools in Class	#13-16	Robotics
#3	Keyboarding	#17-20	Coding/Programming
#4	Problem Solving	#21	Gamification of Education
#5	Digital Citizenship	#22-24	Web Comm. Tools
#6	Word Processing Options	#25-28	Differentiated Learning
#7	Spreadsheets	#29-30	Writing/Publishing an Ebook
#8-9	Google Earth	#31-32	Making an Ebook Trailer
#10-11	Online Image Legalities		

Arranged by theme:

Basics

#1	Introduction
#2	Digital Tools in Class
#3	Keyboarding
#6	Word Processing Options
#7	Spreadsheets

Logical Thinking

#4	Problem Solving
#13-16	Robotics
#17-20	Coding/Programming
#21	Gamification of Education

Digital Citizenship

#1	Intro
#2	Digital Tools in Class
#5	Digital Citizenship
#10-11	Online Image Legalities
#12	Internet Search/Research
#22-24	Web Communication Tools

Writing

#6	*Word Processing Options*
#8-9	*Google Earth*
#12	*Internet Search/Research*
#25-28	*Differentiated Learning*
#29-30	*Writing/Publishing an Ebook*
#31-32	*Making an Ebook Trailer*

Problem Solving

#4	*Problem solving*
#17-20	*Coding/Programming*
#21	*Gamification of Education*
#25-28	*Differentiated Learning*

Articles

Article 1—Habits of Mind vs. CC vs. IB 30
Article 2—Class Warm-ups and Exit Tickets 32
Article 3—4 Things Every Teacher Must Teach and How 33
Article 4 7 Ways to Assess Student Knowledge 35
Article 5—Which Class Internet Start Page is Best 62
Article 6—13 Ways Blogs Teach Common Core 64
Article 7 ""How to integrate web tools into the classroom" 66
Article 8 ""8 Things My Blog Taught Me" 68
Article 9 "13 Ways Twitter Improves Education" 70
Article 10—5 Ways to make classroom keyboarding fun 86
Article 11—How to Prepare Students for PARCC/SBA Tests 88
Article 12—How to Teach Students to Solve Problems 98
Article 13—5 Must-have Skills for New Tech Teachers 100
Article 14—Let Students Learn From Failure 102
Article 15—11 Ways Twitter improves education 114
Article 16—Will texting destroy writing skills? 116
Article 17—How to Thrive as a Digital Citizen 117
Article 18——14 Factors to Consider for Tech Report Cards 142
Article 19 3 Websites to Gamify Your Math Class 187
Article 20 Minecraft in School 189

Appendix

Posters
Certificates

Table of Images

Figure 1a-b—What's included in each lesson 5

Figure 2—Tomorrow's student 8

Figure 3—Curriculum Map—K-8 9

Figure 4—Student workbook 9

Figure 5—Habits of Mind 10

Figure 6a-b—Which image represents 'technology'? 25

Figure 7—Class rules 27

Figure 8—How to hold a mouse 38

Figure 9a-d—Digital devices and their parts 39

Figure 10a—Parts of iPad; 10b—Chromebook 39

Figure 11a—iAnnotate; 11b—Notability; 11c—Adobe Acrobat 40

Figure 12a-d—Avatars 41

Figure 13a-b—Backchannel devices 41

Figure 14a-c—Student blogs 42

Figure 15a—Blogging rules; 15b—blogging rubric 43

Figure 16—Class Internet start page 44

Figure 17a—Class start page in Symbaloo; 17b—Portaportal; 17c—LiveBinders ... 44

Figure 18a-b—Note-taking tools—word processing and Notability 45

Figure 19—Collaborative notes in Google Spreadsheets 46

Figure 20a—Evernote; 20b—Twitter 46

Figure 21a—Wiki; 21b—Google Drive 47

Figure 22—Homework dropbox 47

Figure 23—Email Etiquette 48

Figure 24—Gmail sample 48

Figure 25a—Evidence Board; 25b—Badge 49

Figure 26—What is a flipped classroom? 49

Figure 27a-b—Homework samples 50

Figure 28—Google Apps 50

Figure 29a—Screenshot to explain log-in; 29b—screencast to explain the use of screencasts ... 51

Figure 30—Student website rubric 52

Figure 31—Why learn to keyboard 74

Figure 32a—Keyboarding posture; 32b—position 74

Figure 33—Keyboarding hand position 75

Figure 34—Keyboarding technique checklist 75

Figure 35—Shortkeys 77

Figure 36a-e—Project-based learning and keyboarding 77

Figure 37a—iPad shortkeys; 37b—Chromebook shortkeys; 37c—PC shortkeys; 37d—Internet shortkeys ... 78

Figure 38—Important keys on keyboard 79

Figure 39a—Blank keyboard quiz for PCs; 39b—for Chromebook 80

Figure 40—Problem solving quotes 91

Figure 41—How to solve a problem 92

Figure 42—Common tech problems 93

Figure 43a-b—Problem-solving Board sign-ups 93

Figure 44—Problem-solving Board rubric 94

Figure 45—Common tech problems 97

Figure 46—Personal responsibility quote 106

Figure 47—Digital Citizenship topics 107

Figure 48a—Netiquette Rules; 48b—Digital pyramid 112

Figure 49a-c—Word processing examples 1st-5th grade 120

Figure 50—Compare-contrast: Productivity tools 121

Figure 51—Tools on toolbars 122

Figure 52a-c—Examples of outlines in word processing programs 122

Figure 53a—MS Word; 53b—Google Docs 123

Figure 54—Twitter novel sample 124

Figure 55—Serialized novel by Conrad 125

Figure 56a-c—Comic samples 127

Figure 57—Decoding a comic strip 127

Figure 58a-d—Writing with Art K-6 128

Figure 59a-f—DTP project from 2nd-6th grade 129

Figure 60a-b—Compare-contrast report covers 130

Figure 61a-d—Writing with slideshows 131

Figure 62a-b—Writing with spreadsheets 131

Figure 63a-b—Drawing with spreadsheets 132

Figure 64a-f—Projects with spreadsheets 132

Figure 65a-b—Two formulas 137

Figure 66a-b—Formula unpacked 138

Figure 67a-e—Prior Google Earth projects 144

Figure 68—Google Earth: Siege of Vicksburg 145

Figure 69a—Mini tour placemark; 69b—tour list 145

Figure 70a—Placemark dialogue box in GE; 70b—in Google Maps 146

Figure 71a—Overlay in ScribbleMaps; 71b in GE 147

Figure 72—Digital law—rephrased 151

Figure 73—Copyright protections on browsers 151

Figure 74—Two copyrighted images 152

Figure 75a-b—Creative Commons licensing 153

Figure 76a-b—Student drawing used without permission 153

Figure 77—Real or a hoax? 154

Figure 78a-b: Add or remove pieces from a photo 154

Figure 79a-c—Real or hoax pictures? 155

Figure 80—Internet research 158

Figure 81—What are the parts of a website? 159

Figure 82—Research skills 160

Figure 83a-b—Robotic pieces 166

Figure 84a-b—Programming robot 167

Figure 85a-b—Finding robot program 167

Figure 86a-b—Completed robots 168

Figure 87a-b—Blogs about robotics 168

Figure 88a-b—Bot Battles 169

Figure 89—Bot tournament 169

Figure 90a-b—What programming feels like vs. what it is 172

Figure 91a-e—Coding from previous years 172

Figure 92—Scratch program page 173

Figure 93a-b—Scratch script and result 174

Figure 94—Scratch tools I 175

Figure 95—Scratch tools II 175

Figure 96a-b—Scratch remix 175

Figure 97a-d—Scratch projects 176

Figure 98—Scratch embed 176
Figure 99a-b—Blogs about programming 176
Figure 100—Scratch rubric 177
Figure 101—Wolfram/Alpha widget 177
Figure 102a-b—Wolfram/Alpha completed widget; 102c—embedded in blog 178
Figure 103a—Visual organizers in 1st grade; 103b—2nd;103c—3ʳᵈ; 103d—4ᵗʰ; 103e—6ᵗʰ ... 197
Figure 104—Differentiated communication with ScribbleMaps 197
Figure 105—A chart to visually represent info 198
Figure 106a-e—More visual organizers in K-6 198
Figure 107—Mindmap for project 198
Figure 108a—Timeline using Google Draw; 108b-Data communication using Voki 199

Table of Assessments

1—Parts of the computer 54
2—Parts of the smartphone 55
3—Parts of an iPad 56
4—Chromebook parts 57
5—Student blogging agreement 58
6—Blog grading rubric 59
7—Website grading rubric 60
8—Digital portfolio rubric 61
9—Keyboarding quiz 81
10—Important Keys 82
11—Blank keyboard quiz 83
12—Chromebook blank keyboard quiz 84
13—Keyboarding Challenge 85
14a-b—Problem solving authentic data 94
15—Problem-solving Board 95
16—Problem-solving Presentation Assessment 96
17—Compare-contrast productivity tools 121
18—Evaluate writing options 129
19—Word processing summative 135
20—Spreadsheet summative 139
21—Spreadsheet summative 141
22—Civil War Google Earth assessment 148
23—Google Earth tour storyboard 149
24—Awesome Robotics Award 170
25—Am I Ready? 194
26—Web-based Communication Tools 195

GRADE 6-8 TECHNOLOGY SCOPE AND SEQUENCE

Aligned with ISTE (International Society for Technology in Education) and Common Core State Standards
Check each skill off with I (Introduced), W (Working on), or M (Mastered)
Organized by ISTE Standards 1-7

	Empowered Learner	6	7	8
	Use technology and digital media strategically and capably (CCSS C&CR profile)	W	M	M
	Are familiar with the strengths and limitations of various technological tools and mediums and can select and use those best suited to communication goals (CCSS C&CR Profile)	W	M	M
	Strategize personal learning			
	Understand how inquiry contributes to creative and empowered learning	W	W	M
	Understand how technology contributes to classroom and personal learning	W	M	M
	Understand how higher order thinking skills are buttressed by technology	W	M	M
	Select between available options, choosing one best suited to learning	W	M	M
	Compare-contrast available tools, determining which is best suited to need	W	M	M
	Know how to use available digital tools (i.e., calendars, blogs, annotation tools)	M	M	M
	Be responsive to varied needs of task-audience-purpose	M	M	M
	Interact, collaborate, publish with peers employing a variety of digital media	W	M	M
	Develop cultural understanding by engaging with learners of other cultures	W	M	M
	Seek feedback to demonstrate learning			
	Add comments to class blogs, forums, discussion boards, webtools	M	M	M
	Work in groups collaboratively and productively	M	M	M
	Transfer knowledge			
	Scaffold learning year-to-year and lesson-to-lesson	M	M	M
	Transfer understanding of one digital tool or device to others	M	M	M
	Use familiar tech tools (like Google Earth's ruler) to solve real-world problems	M	M	M
	Hardware			
	Know parts of digital devices and how to connect them	M	M	M
	Can troubleshoot hardware	M	M	M
	Operating Systems (PC, Mac, Chromebook, iPads)			
	Know how to find files, add more, and save to network file folder and/or cloud	M	M	M
	Know how to drag-drop (or copy-paste) within a doc and between folders	M	M	M
	Know how to use tool tips (hover over icon) and right-click menus	M	M	M
	Can troubleshoot operating systems	M	M	M
	Online Tech for Classroom Management			
	Understand school technology	W	M	M
	Understand Cloud for transferring school work to home	M	M	M
	Know how to annotate a PDF or online document	W	M	M
	Know how to share out classwork (including homework)	I	W	M

Askatechteacher©

	Know how to use online vocabulary decoding tools quickly and efficiently	M	M	M
	Keyboarding			
	Know how to practice keyboarding on internet sites and software	M	M	M
	Strive to achieve grade-appropriate keyboarding speed and accuracy goal	M	M	M
	Practice touch typing	M	M	M
	Compose at keyboard by creating classroom-based projects	M	M	M
	Understand speed difference between handwriting and keyboarding	M	M	M
	Select shortkeys instead of toolbar tools when appropriate	M	M	M
	Use correct posture, elbows at sides	M	M	M
	Know parts of keyboard--keys, numbers, F keys, arrows, Esc	W	M	M
	Word Processing			
	Know when to use a word processing program, both software and online tools	W	M	M
	Use classroom principles of grammar, spelling when word processing on computer	M	M	M
	Know basic page layout--heading, title, body, footer	W	M	M
	Know how to use the thesaurus	M	M	M
	Know how to format a document—i.e., add header, footer, border, cover page, embedded link	W	M	M
	Can troubleshoot word processing	W	M	M
	Google Earth			
	Display familiarity with tools for moving around world	M	M	M
	Run a tour of placemarks around the planet	W	M	M
2	**Digital Citizen**			
	Gather relevant information from print and digital sources, assess credibility of source, and integrate the information while avoiding plagiarism. (CCSS C&CR Writing Anchor Standards)	I	W	M
	Internet privacy and safety			
	Know how to configure privacy settings	I	W	M
	Understand cyberbullying, use of passwords	M	M	M
	Understand digital footprint and online presence	I	W	M
	Understand how online entities track student activity online	I	W	M
	Understand the appropriate use of the 'digital neighborhood'	M	M	M
	Legal use of online materials			
	Discuss copyright law, fair use, intellectual property, rights and obligations of the digital world	W	M	M
	Discuss plagiarism and how to cite sources	W	M	M
	Digital Netiquette			
	Understand etiquette in the digital neighborhood	M	M	M
	Digital Citizenship			
	Understand what a 'digital citizen' is	M	M	M
	Exhibit a positive attitude toward technology that supports collaboration and learning	M	M	M
	Demonstrate personal responsibility for lifelong learning	M	M	M
	Exhibit leadership for digital citizenship--set the standard for classmates	M	M	M
	Interactions online			

	Address digital commerce	I	W	M
	Use safe, responsible and ethical behavior on the internet	M	M	M
	Discuss social media	I	W	M
	Discuss digital rights and responsibilities	M	M	M
	Recognize irresponsible and unsafe practices on the internet	I	W	M
	Know how online comments follow same rules as speaking and listening	I	W	M
3	**Knowledge Constructor**			
	Use the internet to build strong content knowledge (CCSS C&CR profile)	M	M	M
	Use technology to produce and publish writing and collaborate with others (CCRA.W.6)	M	M	M
	Use technology and digital media strategically and capably (CCSS C&CR profile)	M	M	M
	Comprehend as well as critique. (CCSS C&CR profile)	W	M	M
	Value evidence (CCSS C&CR profile)	W	M	M
	Compare-contrast documents across varied digital media (CCSS Anchor Standards)	W	M	M
	Gather relevant information from multiple digital sources (CCRA.W.8)	W	M	M
	Assess credibility of digital sources used for research (CCSS Anchor Standards)	W	M	M
	Integrate and evaluate information from diverse media (CCRA.R.7)	W	M	M
	Make strategic use of digital media to express information (CCRA.SL.5)	W	M	M
	Use electronic menus and links to locate key facts (RI/)	W	M	M
	Effective online research strategies			
	Use screenshots to collect information	W	M	M
	Locate, organize, analyze, evaluate, and synthesize information from a variety of sources	M	M	M
	Evaluate and select information sources and digital tools based on task	W	M	M
	Know how to search effectively and efficiently, limit search as needed, and use Ctrl+F	I	W	M
	Know how to effectively use LMS systems and the Cloud	I	W	M
	Technology as knowledge curator			
	Evaluate the accuracy, perspective, relevancy of information, media, data or other resources	I	W	M
	Curate information from digital resources using a variety of tools and methods that demonstrate meaningful connections or conclusions (such as outlines, mindmaps).	I	W	M
	Present information in a manner suited to task, audience, and purpose (i.e., infographics, graphic organizers, Google Earth)	M	M	M
	Build knowledge by exploring real-world issues, developing ideas, and pursuing solutions using online learning programs	M	M	M
	Online collaborative environments			
	Use blogs for journaling and tracking project progress	W	M	M
	Incorporate text, images, widgets to better communicate ideas	W	M	M
	Know how to use Discussion boards and forums	I	W	M
4	**Innovative Designer**			
	Respond to demands of audience, task, purpose, and discipline (CCSS C&CR profile)	M	M	M
	Use glossaries or dictionaries to clarify meaning of key words and phrases (CCSS.L.K.4)	M	M	M
	Gather, comprehend, evaluate, synthesize, and report on information in order to answer questions or solve problems, (CCSS Key Design Consideration)	W	M	M
	Draw on information from multiple print or digital sources, demonstrating the ability to locate an answer to a question quickly or to solve a problem efficiently (CCSS. RI.5)	I	W	M

		Reason abstractly and quantitatively (CCSS. Math.Practice.MP2)	M	M	M
		Use appropriate tools strategically (CCSS. Math.Practice.MP5)	M	M	M
		Attend to precision (CCSS. Math.Practice.MP6)	M	M	M
	Design Process				
		Use tools such as mindmaps and brainstorming to organize ideas and solve problems	I	W	M
		Use presentation tools like graphic organizers, Infographics, screencasts, videos, and trailers to share in-depth topical ideas and solve authentic problems in a variety of creative ways	I	W	M
		Use templates and patterns to create new designs (like shapes, letters)	M	M	M
		Select and use digital tools (such as comics) to plan and manage a design process that considers design constraints and calculated risk	M	M	M
		Develop, test and refine prototypes as part of a cyclical design process	W	M	M
		Able to tolerate ambiguity, persevere, with a capacity to work with open-ended problems.	M	M	M
		Use established patterns and design processes in solving common tech problems	M	M	M
		Recognize the part 'failure' plays in solving problems	M	M	M
	Decision Making				
		Identify and define authentic problems and questions for investigation	M	M	M
		Collect, analyze data to identify solutions and make informed decisions	M	M	M
		Able to debug programs using sequencing, if-then thinking, logic, or other strategies	M	M	M
		Able to evaluate which program is right for which task	M	M	M
	Slideshows				
		Know when and how to use presentation tools as software and online tools	W	M	M
		Understand how to deliver a professional presentation	W	M	M
		Can troubleshoot presentation tools	M	M	M
	Graphics				
		Use drawing software and web-based tools efficiently	M	M	M
		Know how to create and annotate screenshots to share information	M	M	M
	Desktop publishing				
		Can identify parts of the desktop publishing screen	W	M	M
		Know when to use a desktop publishing program to share information	W	M	M
		Know how to plan a publication	I	W	M
		Can troubleshoot publishing tools	W	M	M
	Screencasts, Videos				
		Know how to create screencasts, videos, and trailers to share information	I	W	M
		Know how to upload screencasts , videos, and trailers to easily-accessible locations for peers	I	W	M
		Know how to use the design process to prepare screencasts	I	W	M
5	**Computational Thinker**				
		Gather, comprehend, evaluate, synthesize, and report on information to conduct original research in order to answer questions or solve problems, (CCSS Key Design Consideration)	M	M	M
		Draw on information from multiple sources, demonstrating the ability to locate an answer to a question quickly or to solve a problem efficiently (CCSS. RI.5)	M	M	M
		Make sense of problems and persevere in solving them (CCSS. Math.Practice.MP1)	M	M	M

	Reason abstractly and quantitatively (CCSS. Math.Practice.MP2)	M	M	M
	Construct viable arguments and critique the reasoning of others (CCSS. Math.Practice.MP3)	M	M	M
	Model with mathematics (CCSS. Math.Practice.MP4)	M	M	M
	Use appropriate tools strategically (CCSS. Math.Practice.MP5)	M	M	M
	Attend to precision (CCSS. Math.Practice.MP6)	M	M	M
	Look for and make use of structure (CCSS. Math.Practice.MP7)	M	M	M
	Look for and express regularity in repeated reasoning (CCSS. Math.Practice.MP8)	M	M	M
Critical Thinking				
	Understand how to identify, define authentic problems, questions	M	M	M
	Know how to use digital tools available including calendars, blogs, websites, annotation tools	M	M	M
	Always attempt to solve a problem before asking for teacher assistance	M	M	M
	Know how to research and develop an argument (such as for a debate)	I	W	M
	Know how to use programs not yet learned	M	M	M
	Know why a particular digital tool is suited to a specific need	M	M	M
	Know how to analyze data and use it to facilitate problem-solving and decision-making.	I	W	M
Problem solving				
	Identify, define, and solve authentic problems, questions for investigation	M	M	M
	Know how to access work from anywhere in the school	M	M	M
	Know how to solve common hardware problems	M	M	M
	Know what to do if computer doesn't work	I	W	M
	Can trouble shoot a non-working program	I	W	M
	Can break problems into component parts, extract key information, and develop descriptive models to understand complex systems or facilitate problem-solving.	I	W	W
Programming				
	Understand technology contributes to higher-order thinking	W	M	M
	Understand the cause-effect relationship inherent in actions	W	M	M
	Eagerly experiment with programming tools	M	M	M
	Understand how automation works; use algorithmic thinking to develop a sequence of steps to create and test automated solutions. (i.e., timelines, brainstorming)	W	W	W
	Able to debug programs using sequencing, if-then thinking, logic, or other strategies	W	W	W
Robotics				
	Contribute to project teams to produce original works or solve problems		I	W
	Build, program, debug a robot		I	W
	Trouble shoot simple problems		I	W
	Use sensors to monitor the environment and able to measure distances with robots		I	W
Spreadsheets				
	Process and sort data, report results by collecting data and reporting it	I	W	M
	Know how to publish spreadsheet through a widget to blog and/or website	I	W	M
	Can troubleshoot spreadsheets	I	W	W
6 **Creative Communicator**				

Use technology and digital media strategically and capably (CCSS C&CR profile)	W	M	M
Use technology to produce and publish writing and collaborate with others (*ELA-LITERACY.CCRA.W.6*)	M	M	M
Explore digital tools to produce and publish writing (CCSS.ELA-Literacy.W)	M	M	M
Explore digital tools to collaborate with peers (CCSS.ELA-Literacy.W)	M	M	M
Use multimedia to aid comprehension (CCSS.ELA-Literacy.W)	W	M	M
Ask and answer questions from information presented (CCSS.ELA-Literacy.SL)	M	M	M
Include audio recordings and multimedia to enhance main ideas (CCSS.ELA-Literacy. SL)	W	M	M
Integrate and evaluate information presented in diverse media and formats, including visually, quantitatively, and orally (*CCSS.ELA-LITERACY.CCRA.SL.2*)	M	M	M
Use multimedia to organize ideas, concepts, info (CCSS.ELA-Literacy.WHST)	M	M	M

Blogs

Interact, collaborate, publish with peers employing a variety of digital media	W	M	M
Develop cultural understanding and global awareness by engaging learners of other cultures	W	M	M

Digital Tools

Communicate ideas effectively to multiple audiences using a variety of media and formats including visual organizers, infographics, comics, Twitter (where appropriate), and more	W	M	M
Use web-based communication tools to share unique and individual ideas	W	M	M
Learn a variety of tools that address varied communication styles (from written to visual to video) by teaching them to classmates	W	M	M
Know how to use models and simulations to explore complex systems and issues	W	M	M
Develop cultural understanding by engaging with learners of other cultures	M	M	M

Digital Storytelling, Debate

Work collaboratively to develop a persuasive argument (such as for a debate)	M	M	M
Participate in a virtual field trip that tells the story of a student's experience	M	M	M

Speaking and Listening

Engage in impromptu speaking such as the Evidence Board	I	W	W
Present well-prepared presentations such as slideshows or debate, knowing how to use multimedia props	W	M	M
Engage in short presentations such as the Presentation Boards	I	W	M
Interact, collaborate, and publish with peers or others employing a variety of digital media	W	M	M

7 Global Collaborator

Understand other perspectives and cultures. (CCSS C&CR profile)	M	M	M
Respond to the demands of audience, task, purpose, discipline. (CCSS C&CR Profile)	M	M	M
Use digital tools to connect with learners from a variety of backgrounds and cultures, engaging with them in ways that broaden mutual understanding and learning	M	M	M
Explore local and global issues and use collaborative technologies to investigate solutions	M	M	M

Collaborate with Others

Use collaborative technologies to work with others, including peers, experts or community members, to examine issues and problems from multiple viewpoints.	I	W	M
Contribute constructively to project teams to work effectively toward a common goal.	I	W	M
Use blogs, forums, Discussion Boards to collaborate and share	I	W	M
Work in groups to teach technology skills to others	I	W	M

Askatechteacher©

Lesson #1 Introduction

Vocabulary	Problem solving	Homework
• Back-up • Digital • Digital citizen • Right-click menu • Save-as • Save early/often • Select-do • Technology • Webtool	• What's the difference between 'save' and 'save-as' • What's a quick way to ** (shortkey) • How do I annotate student workbook (check Digital Tools Lesson) • I don't have a flash drive (how else can you back up files?) • I can't do my keyboarding homework at home (come to afterschool club)	Test accounts that will be used for this class
Academic Applications	**Required skills**	**Standards**
General, problem solving, critical thinking	keyboarding, digital citizenship, tech problem solving, and digital devices; comfort with tech	CCSS: Anchor Standards NETS: 1a, 1b

Essential Question

How do I use technology to share with classmates?

Big Idea

Students use tech to enhance their education

Teacher Preparation/Materials Required

- Have student workbooks available (if using).
- Have a list of class rules from last year.
- Have Exit Ticket class poll ready.
- Have class syllabus (or use this table of contents).
- Ensure required links are on digital devices.
- Integrate domain-specific tech vocabulary into lesson.
- Know whether you need extra time to complete lesson.
- Have info on afterschool Keyboard Club and Help time.
- Something happen you weren't prepared for? No worries. Show students how you fix the emergency without a meltdown and with a positive attitude.

Assessment Strategies

- Previewed required material; came to class prepared
- Annotated workbook (if using)
- Completed exit ticket
- Joined classroom conversations
- [tried to] solve own problems
- Decisions followed class rules
- Left room as s/he found it
- Higher order thinking: analysis, evaluation, synthesis
- Habits of mind observed

Steps

Time required: 45 minutes
Class warm-up: None

_____Homework listed on this lesson is assigned the week before you start unit.

_____Tour classroom to familiarize students with room. Where are the tech devices that will assist students? Printer? Class announcements? Evidence Board? What else?

_____What does 'technology' mean at your school? Do students understand 'tech in education'? How have they used it? Is it *Figure 6a* or *Figure 6b*?

Figure 6a-b—Which image represents 'technology'?

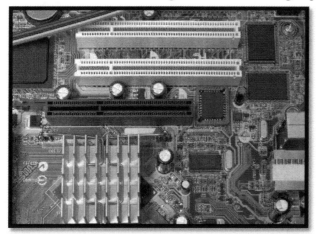 

_____Success in 7th grade tech is predicated on student enthusiasm for learning, transfer of knowledge, and evidence of problem-solving skills. Students will often 'pick which program works best' or 'devise a plan to accomplish goals' or 'teach themselves'.

_____Discuss student tech background, what they know and want to know, and difficulties they see taking this class. Discuss your expectations.

_____Understand domain-specific technology language pursued two ways:

- *Students use correct 'geek speak' words during class, as do you. Tech words students don't know will be added to a virtual wall or a similar collection spot.*
- *Every time students find a word they don't understand, decode it—use the class dictionary tool, ask friends, or ask teacher. Don't skip over it.*

_____Discuss the focus of 7th grade technology:

1. **Think critically:**

   - *which program, tools and strategies work best for what activity*
   - *devise solutions to problems based on past knowledge*
   - *trouble-shoot; find alternatives*
   - *work collaboratively to draw on everyone's knowledge*
   - *understand what you do and don't know, and the difference*
   - *research answers effectively, efficiently, and ethically*

2. **Employ problem-solving skills:**

   - *use available tools to solve a problem*
   - *critically think about a problem; ignore chaff; focus on pertinent details*
   - *present information in a way others understand*
   - *make sense of data*

3. Transfer knowledge:

- *...to other parts of academic and social life*
  - *publish and share online to collaborate and seek constructive criticism*
  - *create a digital portfolio accessible from many locations*
  - *link information to others*

4. Be a good digital citizenship:

- *learn to thrive in the digital world*
- *learn fundamentals of research, search, social media, and communication*
- *understand rights and responsibilities inherent to digital world and those who inhabit it*

5. Learn fundamental tech skills:

- *learn to type faster than you can think*
- *know how word processing in many programs*
- *use spreadsheets to turn data into information*
- *make presentations that are effective, responsive to audience, and interesting*
- *understand tech hardware and how to trouble shoot when needed*
- *learn about digital devices needed to thrive in the learning community*
- *know what online tools are available and what they can be used for*

_____Review class syllabus and goals. Use *Table of Contents* and *Scope and Sequence* if desired. This year, class is less about tech skills and more about higher order thinking. Briefly review each theme in the *Table of Contents*. 'Sell" it as exciting and useful:

- ***Basics**—Why is keyboarding important? Why is it important to understand tech terminology? How can understanding hardware help students use tech efficiently and with fewer problems? How does selecting the right tool (word processing or spreadsheet) affect how you communicate?*
- ***Logical thinking**—How can technology teach critical thinking? How can robotics, programming, and games show how to recognize/solve problems?*
- ***Digital citizenship**—How can the vast amount of time students spend on the internet be more productive? What are the rights and responsibilities students must consider before crossing the digital boundary? How do students effectively— and legally—use internet resources? What are some of the tools available?*
- ***Writing**—How can students use technology to effectively communicate? Besides word processing, what options are available? How can students research online? How can students write, publish, and market an ebook?*
- ***Problem Solving**—How can technology help students solve real-world problems? How can students learn to critically think?*

_____Review class rules (see *Figure 7* and full-size sample at end of lesson). Collect more rules from students that will make class productive, efficient, and fair for all students, such as:

- *Save early, save often, about every ten minutes.*
- *No food or drink around digital devices.*
- *Respect the work of others and yourself.*
- *Keep your body to yourself—don't touch neighbor's digital device.*
- *No excuses; don't blame people or computer.*
- *Help neighbor with words, not by doing.*
- *When collaborating, build on others' ideas as you clearly express your own.*
- *As a general rule: Select first, then do. You can't do the latter without the former.*

_____If using workbooks, students can handwrite their suggested rules into the PDF.

_____Students will learn to be good digital citizens (see Lesson on *Digital Citizenship*).

_____Students will use a wide range of web tools (see lesson on *Digital Tools*).

_____Let students know that you are open to alternative suggestions on tools to use for class projects. For example, if you suggest Wordle, a student can request Tagxedo. Approve the change if the tool fulfills class guidelines. Expect them to use **evidence** to build their case, **compare-contrast** their tool to your suggestions, and **draw logical conclusions**.

_____Offer an after school **Keyboarding Club** two days a week for students who can't do their homework at home. Limit it to 45 minutes.

_____Offer **after-school help** on Keyboarding Club days for those who need assistance with tech or a project involving tech. Request student volunteers to assist. Collaborate with your school's STAR program, where volunteering is part of class requirements.

_____Homework is completed prior to class, to prepare students for in-class activities. More on this 'flipped classroom' approach in lesson on *Digital Tools in Class*.

_____Students try to solve tech problems before requesting help.

_____Show how to check grades online.

_____Discuss student responsibility to make up missed classes. Show where you post lessons.

_____Discuss privacy. Do not share log-ins. Have students save login info wherever it is secure. More on this in another lesson.

_____Discuss how you will assess student work. For ideas, see the article at the end of this lesson, *"7 Ways to Assess Student Knowledge"*.

_____For more on *"Class Warm-ups and Exit Tickets"*, see article at lesson end.

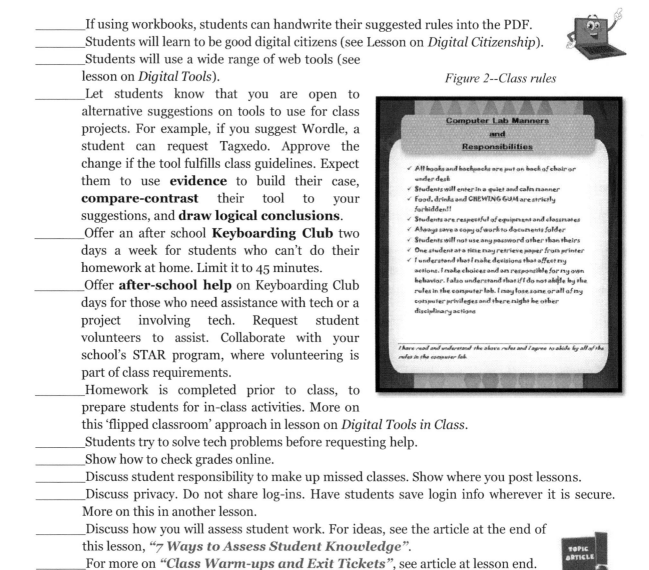

Figure 2--Class rules

Class exit ticket: *Display on class screen a poll created (in Google Forms or similar) and embedded into class website/wiki/blog. It lists 7th grade tech topics. Students vote on which they think will be the most fun, most useful, or most exciting to learn. Leave poll open until next class.*

Differentiation

- *Add homework due date to class online calendar for each month.*

Computer Lab Manners

and

Responsibilities

Assignments / Homework

- Check class website each day.
- Read and respond to communications at least once a day.
- If an assignment is not completed in class, turn it in remotely from home by 6:00 pm the same day with no penalty.
- Late assignments are 10% off for each day late.

Behavior in the Lab

- Keep an open mind that *something new will be learned* each day.
- Have clean hands; keyboards are shared by everyone.
- No food or drinks allowed in lab
- When helping other students, use words. Do not take over their computer.

Posting emails

- Always enter subject of email
- Start each email with a greeting. (e.g. Hi Mrs. *** or Dear Mr. ***)
- Use correct punctuation. Start each sentence with a capital; end with a period.
- Proofread email and check spelling every time.
- Show insight and intelligence when responding to a class discussion or commenting on a post.
- CC anyone mentioned in an email. That's polite
- Don't share private information in emails. They aren't secure!
- Don't be rude in emails. They aren't private.
- Don't use capitals—THIS IS SHOUTING

Habits of Mind vs. Common core vs. IB

Pedagogic experts have spent an enormous amount of time attempting to unravel the definition of 'educated'. It used to be the 3 R's—reading, writing, and 'rithmetic. The problem with that metric is that, in the fullness of time, those who excelled in the three areas weren't necessarily the ones who succeeded. As long ago as the early 1900's, Teddy Roosevelt warned:

""C students rule the world."

It's the kids without their nose in a book that notice the world around them, make connections, and learn natively. They excel at activities that aren't the result of a GPA and an Ivy League college. Their motivation is often failure, and taking the wrong path again and again. As Thomas Edison said:

""I have not failed. I've just found 10,000 ways that won't work."

Microsoft founder, Bill Gates, and Albert Einstein are poster children for that approach. Both became change agents in their fields despite following a non-traditional path.

In the face of mounting evidence, education experts accepted a prescriptive fact: student success is not measured by milestones like 'took a foreign language in fifth grade' or 'passed Algebra in high school' but by how s/he thinks. One curated list of cerebral skills that has become an education buzzword is Arthur L. Costa and Bena Kallick's list of sixteen what they call Habits of Mind (Copyright ©2000):

1. *Persisting*
2. *Managing impulsivity*
3. *Listening with Understanding and Empathy*
4. *Thinking Flexibly*
5. *Thinking about Thinking*
6. *Striving for Accuracy*
7. *Questioning and Posing Problems*
8. *Applying Past Knowledge to New Situations*
9. *Thinking and Communicating with Clarity and Precision*
10. *Gathering Data through All Senses*
11. *Creating, Imagining, Innovating*
12. *Responding with Wonderment and Awe*
13. *Taking Responsible Risks*
14. *Finding Humor*
15. *Thinking Interdependently*
16. *Remaining Open to Continuous Learning*

Together, these promote strategic reasoning, insightfulness, perseverance, creativity, and craftsmanship.

But they're not new. They share the same goals with at least three other widely-used education systems: 1) Common Core (as close as America gets to national standards), 2) the International Baccalaureate (IB) program (a well-regarded international curriculum, much more popular outside the US than within), and 3) good ol' common sense. Below, I've listed each Habit of Mind with a brief explanation of what that means (in italics). I then point out connections to Common Core, the IB Program, and the common sense your grandma shared with you. The result is a compelling argument that education is less a data download and more a fitness program for our brains.

Persisting

Stick with a problem, even when it's difficult and seems hopeless.

Winston Churchill said, "Never, never, in nothing great or small, large or petty, never give in..." The same decade, Albert Einstein said:

> *"It's not that I'm so smart, it's just that I stay with problems longer."*

The Common Core is not a curriculum, rather a collection of forty-one overarching Standards in reading, writing, language, math, and speaking/listening that shape a student's quest for college and career. Sprinkled throughout are fundamental traits that go beyond the 3R's and delve deeply into the ability of a student to think. The math standards require students learn to 'persevere in solving problems'.

The IB Program has twelve attitudes that are fundamental to every learner: *appreciation, empathy, commitment, enthusiasm, confidence, independence, cooperation, integrity, creativity, respect, curiosity, and tolerance.* Students exhibiting the attitude of commitment persist in their own learning, persevere no matter the difficulties.

Managing Impulsivity

Consider options. Think before speaking.

Among his endless words of wisdom, Benjamin Franklin said:

> *"It is easier to suppress the first desire than to satisfy all that follow it."*

Common Core Standards tell us to 'Use appropriate tools strategically'.

Besides the twelve attitudes listed above, the IB Program names ten traits that profile a learner: *inquirer, knowledgeable, thinker, communicator, principle, open-minded, caring, a risk-taker, balanced, and reflective.* Students who are reflective give thoughtful consideration before acting.

For the rest of the article, visit Ask a Tech Teacher

Class Warm-ups and Exit Tickets

Warm-ups are given at the beginning of class to measure what students remember from prior lessons or know about a subject before jumping into a unit. They inform teachers how to optimize time by teaching what students need to learn, not wasting time on what students already know. They are a couple of minutes, can be delivered via a Discussion Board, blog comments, a Google Form, or many other methods.

Exit tickets are similar, but assess what students learned **during** the lesson. In this way, teachers know if they should review material, find a different approach to teaching a topic, or students are ready to move on. Like Warm-ups, Exit tickets are a few minutes, and delivered in a wide variety of creative methods.

Polls

Polls are quick ways to assess student understanding of the goal of your daily teaching. It measures student learning as much as lesson effectiveness. Polls are fast—three-five minutes—are anonymously graded and shared immediately with students. It lets everyone know if the big idea of the lesson is understood and if the essential questions have been answered.

These can be graded, but are usually used formatively, to determine organic class knowledge before moving on to other topics.

Tools: Socrative, PollDaddy, Google Forms
Time: a few minutes
Method: Formative assessment

Virtual Wall

Ask students a question and have them add their answer to a virtual wall.

Virtual walls are also great ideas for reviewing a subject prior to a summative assessment. Have each student post an important idea they got from the unit with significant required details.

Tools: Padlet, Linoit
Time: a few minutes
Method: Formative assessment

Article 3—4 Things Every Teacher Must Teach and How

4 Things Every Teacher Must Teach and How

Teaching technology is not sharing a new subject, like Spanish or math. It's exploring an education tool, knowing how to use computers, IPads, the Internet, and other digital devices to serve learning goals. Sure, there are classes that teach MS Word and C++, but for most schools, technology is employed strategically and capably to achieve all colors of education.

Which gets me to the four subjects every teacher must teach, whether s/he's a math teacher, science, literacy, or technology. In today's education world, all of us teach—

- *vocabulary*
- *keyboarding*
- *digital citizenship*
- *research*

They used to be taught in isolation—*Fridays at 8:20, we learn vocabulary*—but not anymore. Now they must be blended into all subjects like ingredients in a cake, the result—college or career for the 21st-century student. Four subjects that must be taught—and thanks to technology, CAN be with ease. Let me explain.

Vocabulary

Common Core requires that:

> ***Students constantly build the transferable vocabulary they need to access grade level complex texts. This can be done effectively by spiraling like content in increasingly complex texts.***

Does that sound difficult? Think back to how you conquered vocabulary. As an adult, you rarely meet words you can't understand—unless you're chatting with William F. Buckley—and if you do, you decode it by analyzing prefixes, suffixes, roots, context. Failing that, e-dictionaries are available on all digital devices.

Teach your students to do the same:

- first: try to decode the word using affixes, root, context
- second: research meaning

You might think that will grind the academic process to a halt, but truth, in age-appropriate texts, there are likely less than five unknown words per page. What you don't want to do is have students write down words for later investigation. That becomes a chore, cerebral excitement leeched like heat to a night desert sky. Much better to stop, decode, and move on.

As students work on a project in my classes, I see neighbors ask for help with a mysterious word (students are welcome to chat during class about academic topics), screens light up as students use the online dictionary to discover meaning, and words appear on the class screen as part of the backchannel Twitter stream. Seconds later, a definition will appear—someone's contribution. If it's wrong, invariably a student will correct it. Rarely, I jump in.

Don't believe this works? Try it out.

Keyboarding

For years, I taught keyboarding as a separate activity. We warmed up class with 10-15 minutes of keyboarding augmented by 45 minutes a week of keyboard homework. I've revised my thinking. Since keyboarding benefits all classes, I make all teachers—including the librarian—my partners in this effort. I go into classrooms and show students the broad strokes of keyboarding posture, good habits, skills that will enable them to type fast and accurately enough to eventually—maybe third or fourth grade—use the keyboard without slowing down their thinking. That's a big deal and worth repeating—

> *To be organic, students must be able to keyboard without thinking of their fingers, fast enough that they keep up with their thoughts.*

That's about 25 words per minute. *Really?* Yes really. Sure, we think fast, but ruminating over a class question, essay, report is much [much] slower. 25-35 words per minute suffice.

I start students with mouse and keyboard familiarity in kindergarten and 1st grade, introduce the concept of hands and fingers in 2nd, and start speed and accuracy in 3rd. By 5th grade, they're good. This works because now, keyboarding is integrated across all classes, anytime students use a digital device with a keyboard. Now, all teachers pay as much attention to HOW students use the keyboard as WHAT is produced, focusing on:

- good posture
- hands on home row (by 3rd grade)
- elbows at sides
- paper (if using one) to the side of keyboard

- eyes on screen (by 4th grade)
- no flying fingers or hands
- paced rhythm

Parents, too, are my partners. I communicate the same requirements to them with the hope they'll reinforce these at home. A reminder that assessments are often online gets their attention.

For more, visit Ask a Tech Teacher

Article 4 7 Ways to Assess Student Knowledge

7 Ways to Assess Student Knowledge

This is always challenging, isn't it? Finding evidence that students have learned what you taught, that they can apply their knowledge to complex problems. How do you do this? Rubrics? Group projects? Posters? None sound worthy of the Common Core educational environ—and too often, students have figured out how to deliver within these guidelines while on auto-pilot.

Where can we find authentic assessments that are measurable yet student-centered, promote risk-taking by student and teacher alike, are inquiry-driven, and encourage students to take responsibility for his/her own learning? How do we assess a lesson plan in a manner that insures students have learned what they need to apply to life, to new circumstances they will face when no teacher is at their elbow to nudge them the right direction?

Here are some of my favorite approaches:

Anecdotally

I observe their actions, their work, the way they are learning the skills I'm teaching. Are they engaged, making their best effort? Do they remember skills taught in prior weeks and apply them? Do they self-assess and make corrections as needed?

Transfer of knowledge

Can students transfer knowledge learned in my class to other classes and/or other parts of their life? Do I hear fun stories from parents and teachers about how students used something learned? Do the students themselves share a snippet about how they 'helped mom use Google Maps to find...?"

Teach others

Are students comfortable flipping learning and becoming the teacher? There's a hierarchy of learning that goes like this:

1. *Student doesn't listen*
2. *Student doesn't believe*
3. *Student tries it once*

4. *Student remembers it*
5. *Student shows it to others*
6. *Student teaches others*

Like Maslow's Hierarchy of Needs, the highest praise is that students teach the skill to others. That's learning.

I encourage it in my classes by having the lab open during recess and lunch, but with students as helpers. I only take 1-2 and always have more offers than I need.

Verbalize

Can students use the right words to share answers? No umms, no hand motions, no giggles. Can they take a deep breath and share their knowledge in a few succinct sentences? This works well on a Discussion Board which I use as a summative for vocabulary and problem-solving tests. I set up a discussion board, ask each student to add a problem or vocabulary word we covered, and then comment on a classmate's. They can then use this resource during the test. We've done it a few times and students have figured out if they blow off the Discussion Board part of the assessment, everyone suffers. Friends don't have the study guide, or worse, the answer's wrong because classmates didn't take the time to write it correctly.

Portfolio

I like portfolios, but today, that means digital. Collect all student work onto wikis, digital lockers, Box.net, via embed widgets or screen shots or the original software. Keep it in the cloud where students, teachers, even parents can access it. That's transparency. No one will wonder what grade the student earned

Summarize knowledge

But not in an essay. Use knowledge to create a magazine, an Animoto video, a Puzzlemaker crossword. It's the 'use' part of assessment that's most important. Can students use the knowledge or does it just sit in a mental file folder?

Oral presentations

This can be summative, formative, informational, or informal. It can be a quick answer to questions in the classroom, coming up to the class screen and solving a problem, teaching classmates how to solve a problem during class, or preparing a multimedia presentation to share with others online or in person. It includes much more than an assessment of learning. It judges a student's presentation skills, ability to talk to people—life skills fundamental.

In the end, the choice of assessment depends upon the goal of teaching. Which works best for you?

Lesson #2 Digital Tools in Class

Vocabulary	Problem solving	Homework
• Annotation • App • Backchannel • Benchmark • Blog • Chrome • Cloud • Digital portfolio • Digital tools • Domain-specific • Hashtag • Linkback • PDF • Plagiarism • Template	• I'm too young for Twitter (use class account) • Avatar didn't show in my blog (ask a neighbor how they did it) • My work disappeared (Google Apps automatically saves; or, Ctrl+Z) • Teacher isn't around and I need help (ask for peer support, or use student forum) • Just give me a handout (Sorry, we learn through experience and collaboration) • Can't find annotation tool (ask friend) • I'm not fast enough decoding vocabulary (keep at it—it gets easier) • I forgot my Evidence (you'll have a chance every month)	Preview tech tools. Know how to log in from home/school (if appropriate) Prepare for hardware quiz Practice keyboarding for 45minutes, 15 minutes at a time
Academic Applications	**Required skills**	**Standards**
Writing, research, publishing, online safety	blogging, digital notetaking, PDFs, hardware, avatars, email, problem solving, digital citizenship, keyboarding	CCSS: WHST.6-8.7-9 NETS: 1b, 4b

Essential Question

How do I use technology to pursue my education?

Big Idea

Students become aware of how tech enhances educational goals

Teacher Preparation/Materials Required

- Have lesson materials online to preview upcoming unit.
- Have Internet start page prepared (if using).
- Have back channel available.
- Have copies (if required) of hardware assessment.
- Have student accounts for digital tools.
- Have Evidence Board and badges prepared.
- Post links to training videos on digital tools (if using)
- Have copies of blogging agreement (if necessary).
- Integrate domain-specific tech vocabulary into lesson.
- Know whether you need extra time to complete lesson.
- Know which tasks weren't completed last week and whether they are necessary to move forward.
- Something happen you weren't prepared for? Show students how you fix the emergency without a meltdown and with a positive attitude.

Assessment Strategies

- Previewed required material; came to class prepared
- Annotated workbook (if using)
- Completed warm-up, exit ticket
- Joined classroom conversations
- [tried to] solve own problems
- Decisions followed class rules
- Left room as s/he found it
- Higher order thinking: analysis, evaluation, synthesis
- Habits of mind observed

Steps

Time required: *90 minutes; 10 minutes set aside for hardware quiz*
Class warm-up: *Test digital tool accounts while waiting for class to start*

_____Homework listed on this lesson will be assigned the week before starting this unit—so students are prepared for the flipped classroom.

_____Any questions from preparatory homework? Expect students to review upcoming unit and come to class with questions.

_____Discuss results of interest poll (Exit Ticket from *Lesson #1*).

_____Discuss digital tools in general terms. What are they? How are they different from software and/or apps? Which ones have students used? Why have they become mainstays in education? See if students come up with ideas such as:

- *to facilitate collaborative work*
- *to enable students easily publish and share a project with classmates*
- *to make communication with multiple audiences easier*
- *to enable use of a wide variety of media and formats*
- *to encourage cultural understanding and global awareness*
- *to provide options (for example: for communication—email, forums, blogs)*
- *to provide access from anywhere with an internet connection*

_____This *Digital Tools* unit has three expected learning outcomes:

- *introduce digital tools used in 7ᵗʰ grade*
- *acclimate students to the concept that tech tools enable differentiation, collaboration, sharing, and publishing*
- *show how to employ them in student educational endeavors*

_____Discuss digital citizenship in broad strokes. Remind students of rights and responsibilities inherent to the digital community. You focus on it in another lesson and return to it every time students use internet.

_____Before reviewing digital tools to be used during this class, have neighbor's check each other's mouse hold (see *Figure 8*):

Figure 8—How to hold a mouse

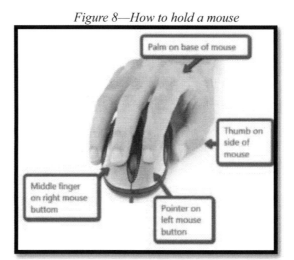

_____Review your school's digital device. Students should know the basic parts and whether they're input or output. *Figures 9a-d* are assessments at the end of this Lesson. These can be filled out in student workbooks or as formative assessments during classtime. *Figures 10a-b* are sample completed worksheets by students.

Figure 9a-d—Digital devices and their parts

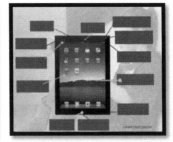
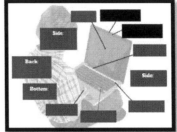

_____If necessary, review with students. For example, if you use iPads, ask where the headphones are on this device? Or the mouse? How about the USB Port? Ask students where the iPad microphone is on, say, the PC or Chromebook. How about the charging dock?

Figure 10a—Parts of iPad; 10b—Chromebook

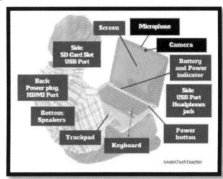

_____Discuss how understanding hardware helps to solve tech problems.

_____The following tools are discussed in this Lesson. Pick those that your students use and add others you have:

- *annotation tool*
- *avatars*
- *backchannel devices*
- *blogs*
- *class calendar*
- *class Internet start page*
- *class Twitter account*
- *class website*
- *digital note-taking*
- *digital portfolios*

- *dropbox*
- *email*
- *Evidence Board*
- *Flipped classroom*
- *Google Apps*
- *Journaling*
- *screenshots and screencasts*
- *student websites*
- *student workbooks*
- *vocabulary decoding tools*

_____Adapt them to your digital devices (Chromebooks, PCs, iMac, iPads, or other).

Student workbooks

_____If using the PDF student workbooks that go along with this curriculum, introduce them now. Show how they open in the digital device, how to access links, find rubrics and project samples, and take notes using the annotation tool. Students access links within the PDF, see full-color images, circle back to review concepts or forward to preview upcoming lessons.

Annotation Tool and Screenshots

_____If using student workbooks, show students how to annotate their copy with the note-taking tool used in your school such as iAnnotate (*Figure 11a*), Notability (*Figure 11b*), or Adobe Acrobat (free—*Figure 11c*).

Figure 11a—iAnnotate; 11b—Notability; 11c—Adobe Acrobat

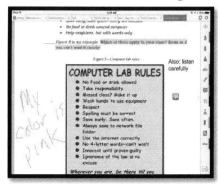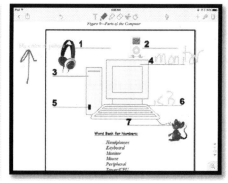

_____If students share the PDF (for example, it's loaded on a digital device that multiple students use), show how to select their own color that's different from other students.

_____Include a discussion of screenshots. Often, students will annotate a page (say, a rubric) and then save a screenshot of it to their digital portfolio. Depending upon your digital device, you'll use a screenshot tool like one of these:

- **Windows**: *the Snipping Tool*
- **Chromebook:** *hold down the control key and press the window switcher key*
- **Mac**: *Command Shift 3 to do a full screenshot and Command Shift 4 for a partial*
- **Surface tablet**: *hold down volume and Windows button at the same time*
- **iPad**: *hold Home button and power button at same time*
- **Online**: *a screenshot tool like Jing or Snagit*

Avatars

_____Students can create a profile picture with an avatar creator like (Google for address, or use one from Ask a Tech Teacher resource pages—*Figures 12a-d* are examples):

- *Animal yourself*
- *Monster yourself*
- *Pickaface*

- *Pixton*
- *Storyboard That!*
- *Voki yourself*

Figure 12a-d—Avatars

_____These can be used in student wikis, websites, or any digital platform that requires a profile picture. Use them to reinforce a discussion of digital privacy and safety.

Backchannel Devices

_____The 'backchannel' is classroom communication that isn't from the presenter. 'Backchannel devices' encourage students to share their thoughts and ideas, even questions, while a lesson is going on. Typically, the comments show up on the class screen, shared with all classmates, likely anonymously. Students read and respond. Teacher uses them to be informed when students get/don't get a topic s/he is covering.

_____Popular backchannel options are:

- *Google Docs*
- *JamBoard*
- *Padlet_— a virtual wall; Figure 13a*
- *Socrative_— a closed virtual; Figure 13b*
- *Twitter — a virtual stream organized by hashtags; private or public*

Figure 13a-b—Backchannel devices

_____Why use backchannels? Here are a few reasons:

- *you know what engages students and extend those ideas*
- *you hear from shy students who need a classroom voice*
- *gregarious students can ask as much as they want without dominating class*

_____Introduce to students, demo, and test on this lesson. Student feedback will inform whether you teach all or some of the digital tools.

Blogs

_____Blogs are short online articles with the purpose of sharing ideas and garnering feedback. In 7th grade, you are particularly interested in the facility to:

- o *engage effectively in collaborative discussions with diverse partners*
- o *build on others' ideas*
- o *express their own ideas clearly*

_____Review the article at lesson end on *"13 Ways Blogs Teach Common Core"*.
_____*Figures 14a-c* are examples of student blogs. Notice how posts incorporate text and screenshots:

Figure 14a-c—Student blogs

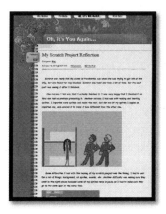  

_____Student blogs teach writing skills, how to use evidence to support arguments (in both posts and comments), and perspective-taking. They are student-directed, but you approve both posts and comments until students get used to the rules that apply to online conversations.
_____Blogs reflect student personalities with colors, fonts, widgets. What students include will help you better understand how they learn and how to reach them academically.
_____In general, student blogs require:

- • *titles that pull reader in*
- • *tone/voice that fits this type of writing and intended audience*
- • *linkback(s) to evidence that supports statements*
- • *at least one media to support each article (picture, video, sound)*
- • *understanding of target audience*
- • *understanding of purpose--how is it different from tweets? Essays? Poetry?*
- • *citations—authors name, permission, linkbacks, copyright where required*
- • *occasional teamwork*
- • *pithy content*
- • *correct spelling and grammar with no slang*

_____Before beginning, students sign an agreement similar to *Seventh Grade Blogging Rules (Figure 15a*—full size at the end of the lesson). Ask them to discuss the agreement with parents and bring it to school before the next class. If you're using workbooks, students can sign the copy in there, take a screenshot, and email that to you.

Figure 15a—Blogging rules; 15b—blogging rubric

_____Students can create blogs in Edublogs, Class Blogmeister, Blogger (Google for addresses; Blogger comes with Google Apps). They can be public or private.

_____Discuss blogging netiquette—similar to email etiquette:

- *be polite*
- *use good grammar and spelling*
- *don't write anything everyone shouldn't read (school blogs are private, but get students used to the oxymoron of privacy and the Internet)*

_____Remind students to practice good keyboarding as they type the entry.

_____Once a month, have students post an article that discusses an inquiry topic. Additionally, students should visit and comment on five classmate blogs.

_____Student comments aren't always appropriate? Set account so you approve comments before they're live. And, chat about how supportive comments contribute to the conversation.

_____Occasionally throughout the year, use the Student Blogs Rubric (*Figure 15b*—full-size assessment at the end of the lesson) to assess student progress.

Class Calendar

_____Class calendars can be through Google Apps or another tool that works for your student group. Show students how to access it and how it's updated to reflect class activities.

_____If students will be editing, demonstrate how to do this by adding upcoming homework.

_____Encourage students to contribute responsibly to class calendar.

_____If using Google Apps, students can embed calendar into blogs, websites, and/or wiki pages.

Class Internet Start Page

_____A class Internet start page is a website that comes up when the student opens the Internet. It organizes critical content in a single location and curates links students will use.

_____Include what students visit daily (i.e., guidelines, calendar, 'to do' list, typing websites, research locations, sponge sites, calculator) as well as information specific to current project.

_____Mine (*Figure 16*) also includes pictures of interest, RSS feeds, weather, a graffiti wall, and class pet. Yours will be different.

Figure 16—Class Internet start page

_____Use Protopage.com_*(Figure 16)*, Ighome, or a collection site like Symbaloo_*(Figure 17a)*, Portaportal_*(Figure 17b)*, LiveBinders *(Figure 17c)*, class Diigo account, or class Evernote account (Google names for address).

Figure 17a—Class start page in Symbaloo; 17b—Portaportal; 17c—LiveBinders

_____Remind students that any time they visit the Internet, they do so safely and legally. This will be discussed in depth in another lesson.

_____See article at the end of this lesson, ***Class Internet Start Page***.

Class Twitter account

_____Twitter is a natural in the 7th-grade classroom. It is hip. Students want to check their stream to see what's up. Because tweets must be concise, they are an excellent way to teach writing.

_____Like blogs and wikis, Twitter feeds are used to:

- *engage collaboratively with diverse partners*
- *review key ideas*
- *present findings with descriptions, facts, and details*
- *Pose questions that elicit elaboration*
- *acknowledge information from others*

_____Set up a private class twitter account for announcements, group questions, discussions, and collaboration. Use #hashtags to organize themes like #homework, #class, #questions, and whatever works for your student group.

_____Most blog and website activity can also be tweeted, so it's a great redundancy for getting news where it needs to go.

Class website

_____Class websites serve as a general resource collection for class information.

_____Create this using the same tool that students will use for their student blog or website.

Digital Note-taking

_____Why take notes (from Common Core):

- *determine central ideas*
- *provide an accurate summary*
- *identify key steps*
- *cite text evidence to support analysis*
- *analyze structure used to organize text*
- *analyze author's purpose*

_____Here are five digital note-taking methods for students:

Figure 18a-b—Note-taking tools—word processing and Notability

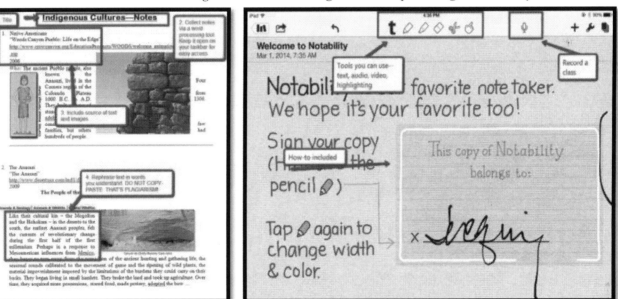

- *Word processing program (for any digital device) – Figure 18a*
- *Notability (for iPads) – Figure 18b*
- *Google Apps – (for any digital device) — Figure 19*

Figure 19—Collaborative notes in Google Spreadsheets

- *Evernote/OneNote (for most digital devices) — Figure 20a*
- *Twitter (for most digital devices) — Figure 20b*

Figure 20a—Evernote; 20b—Twitter

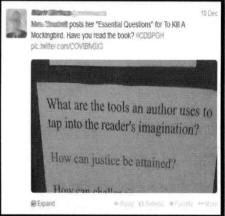

Digital portfolios

_____Discuss how students use Digital Portfolios (also known as digital lockers or digital binders):

- *store work (in Cloud) required in other classes or at home*
- *interact, collaborate, and publish with peers, experts, or others*
- *edit or review work in multiple locations*
- *submit class assignments*

_____There are a variety of approaches to digital portfolios that satisfy some or all of the above uses: 1) folders on school network, 2) fee-based programs from companies such as Richer Picture, 3) cloud-based storage like Dropbox or Google Apps *(Figure 21b),* and 4) online collaborative sites (Google for address).

_____Occasionally, use the *Assessment* at the end of this lesson to review student progress.

Figure 21a—Wiki; 21b—Google Drive

Drop-box

_____If your school has this option, review it with students. If you don't, show students how they will be expected to submit classwork and homework.

_____An assignment dropbox can be created through the school Learning Management System (LMS), email, Google Apps (through 'share' function) or even a Discussion Board.

_____If you have Google Apps, create a Homework dropbox like *Figure 22*:

- *Each student creates a folder called 'Homework' that is shared with you.*
- *To submit work to you, copy it to that folder so you can view and comment.*

Figure 22—Homework dropbox

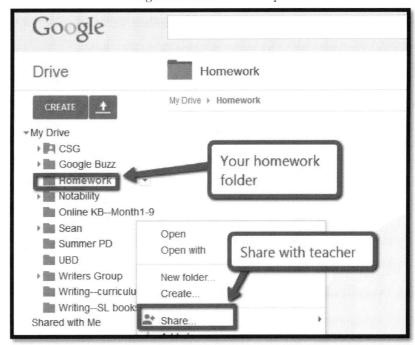

Email

_____Use web-based account such as Gmail (comes with GSuite).

_____Review email etiquette (*Figure 23*—full-size poster in Appendix):

- *Use proper writing conventions.*
- *CC anyone mentioned.*
- *Make 'Subject line' topic of email.*
- *Answer swiftly.*
- *Re-read before sending.*
- *Don't use all caps—THIS IS SHOUTING.*
- *Don't attach unnecessary files.*
- *Don't overuse high priority.*
- *Don't email confidential information.*
- *Don't email offensive remarks.*
- *Don't forward chain letters or spam.*
- *Don't open attachments from strangers.*

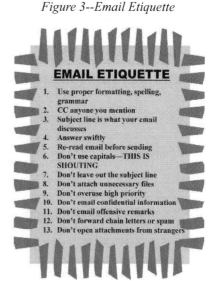

Figure 3--Email Etiquette

_____If you use GSuites (with Gmail activated), review email. Show how to control settings so students don't get spam.

_____Clarify terms like 'high priority', 'chain letters', and 'CC'.

_____Let students (and parents) know that the email program they use at home may not match the instructions you've provided. Ask parents to show students how to use the home-based email.

_____Why is correct grammar/spelling important in email and not so much with texting? Hint: Consider this Common Core standard: *Produce clear and coherent writing in which development, organization, and style are appropriate to task and audience.*

_____Email addresses are often required for online tools.

_____Discuss 'spam'. What is it? Why is it sent? What should students do when spam shows up in their email?

_____Discuss how email can be used to back-up important documents (by emailing a copy to themselves or creating a draft email with doc attached and stored in 'Draft' file).

_____When students get an email, follow this checklist:

- *Do you know sender?*
- *Is email legitimate? For example, does the 'voice' sound like sender?*
- *Is sender asking for personal information? Legitimate sources never do.*
- *Is there an attachment? If so, don't open it.*

Figure 24—Gmail sample

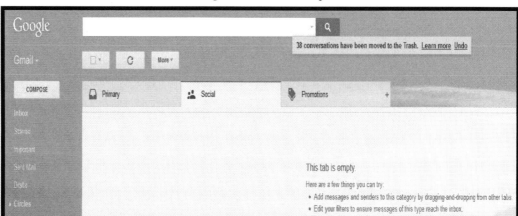

Evidence Board

_____The Evidence Board (*Figure 25a*) is a bulletin board that celebrates student transfer of knowledge from tech class to home, friends, or other educational endeavors.

_____About once a month, students share how they use tech skills outside of your class. They will make a ten-second presentation to class, fill out a badge (like *Figure 25b*), and post it on the Evidence Board by their class. By year end, you want this collection to encircle the classroom.

Figure 25a—Evidence Board; 25b—Badge

Flipped Classroom

_____What is a flipped classroom (see *Figure 26* and *Figure 27b*)? In the Flipped Classroom, teachers record their lectures for consumption by students outside of class, and then dedicate class time to project-based learning that supports the homework. This approach allows students to ask questions of their teacher or collaborate with peers *as they're doing the work*, rather than struggling with it at home and asking for help the next day.

_____Show students where they'll find their homework (probably on the class website or blog, or pushed out through Google Classroom) and model how they will complete it.

_____Likely, it will include several pieces:

Figure 4--What is a flipped classroom?

FLIPPED CLASSES PUTS RESPONSIBILITY FOR EDUCATION IN THE HANDS OF STUDENTS. TEACHERS INFUSE HOMEWORK WITH SCALABLEAND AUTHENTIC RESOURCES. STUDENTS UNPACK BY DIFFERENTIATING FOR THEIR LEARNING STYLES—INDIVIDUALLY OR IN GROUPS. THEY SHOW EVIDENCE OF WHAT THEY'VE LEARNED DURING CLASS, TEACHER SCAFFOLDING WHERE NECESSARY.

- *summary video prepared by you*
- *reading material from ebooks or online sources*
- *hands-on work such as keyboard practice*
- *preparatory steps required to participate in the classtime project*

_____Tools you might use for the summary video include (search Google for websites):

- *YouTube channel*
- *Periscope*
- *Vialogues*
- *Touchcast*

_____Tools you might use to collect homework materials for students are:

- Google Classroom
- Google Apps

Figure 27a-b—Samples of homework assignment

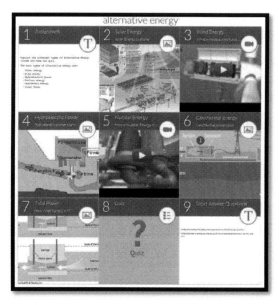 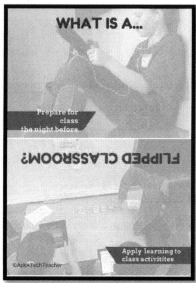

Google Apps

_____To access Google Apps requires a Google account. *Figure 28* is an example of what the Google Drive might look like:

Figure 28—Google Apps

_____There are many resources available for teaching how to use Google Apps.
_____Give students time to explore Google Drive before moving on.
_____The most popular apps—and the ones students will use the most—are:

- *Google Docs—for word processing projects*
- *Google Slides—for slideshow presentations*
- *Google Spreadsheets—for the analysis of data using spreadsheets*
- *Google Draw—for visual representation of information*

Screenshots and Screencasts

_____Review detail under 'Annotation and Screenshots'.

_____Students will use screenshot (still images) tools, apps, or add-ons (depending upon your digital device), as well as screencasts (videos) to record information from their screen. More on this in the lesson on *Screenshots and Screencasts*.

Figure 29a—Screenshot to explain log-in; 29b—screencast to explain the use of screencasts

 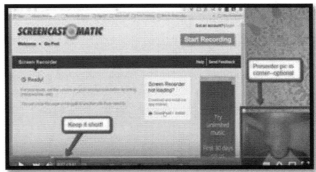

Student website

_____Most teachers will select either blogs or websites for students, depending upon their goal:

- *Blogs are more interactive and time-sensitive.*
- *Websites more fully cover a topic and new posts don't push older out of the way.*

_____Like blogs, websites are a great way to encourage reflection, organization, logical thinking, and are a perfect place to embed sharable projects, i.e., Tagxedos and Animotos.

_____Websites are available with Google Apps. If your school doesn't have Google Apps, free websites can be created at Weebly, Wix, or blog accounts like Wordpress (Google for addresses).

_____Websites should reflect student personalities with colors, fonts, and layout. In general:

- *website and article titles pull reader in*
- *articles review what readers can expect, provide evidence with supporting links, and include a summary of content*
- *tone/voice fits this type of writing and intended audience*
- *links connect to evidence and links work*
- *at least one media is provided to support each article (picture, video, sound)*
- *posts understand target audience. How are blogs different from essays?*
- *writing purpose is clear. How is that different from tweets? Essays? Poetry?*
- *citations are included as needed*
- *occasional teamwork is exhibited*

_____Occasionally (several times a grading period), assess websites based on the criteria in *Figure 30* (full-size assessment at end of lesson):

Figure 30—Student website rubric

Evaluation scale:

Exemplary:	32-36 points
Proficient:	28-31 points
Partially Proficient or Incomplete:	< 28 points (resubmit)

CRITERIA	Exemplary	Proficient	Partially	Incomplete	POINTS
Relevance of Content to Students and Parents	**9 points** • Content has useful information • Content is clear, concise; points readers to up to date resources. • Content is updated frequently	**6 points** • Content points readers to quality resources, is informative • Resources are clearly described so readers can navigate easily	**3 points** • Content points to unrelated information. • Resources are not clearly described so readers cannot navigate easily.	**0 points** • Resources pointed to are inaccurate, misleading or inappropriate • Annotations are missing, do not describe what is found	
Use of Media	**6 points** • Media enhance content and interest. • Creativity enhances content	**4 points** • Most media enhance content. • Most files show creativity	**2 points** • Some media don't enhance content. • Some use of creativity is evident to enhance content.	**0 points** • Media are inappropriate or detract from content.	
Fair Use Guidelines	**6 points** Fair use guidelines are followed with proper citations.	**4 points** Fair use guidelines are frequently followed; most material is cited.	**2 points** Sometimes fair use guidelines are followed with some citations.	**0 points** Fair use guidelines are not followed. Material is improperly cited.	
Links	**3 points** All links are active and functioning.	**2 points** Most links are active	**1 point** Some links are not active.	**0 points** Many links are not active.	
Layout and Text Elements	**3 points** • Fonts are easy-to-read • Use of bullets, italics, bold, enhances readability. • Consistent format throughout	**2 points** • Sometimes fonts, size, bullets, italics, bold, detract from readability. • Minor formatting inconsistencies exist	**1 point** • Text is difficult to read due to formatting	**0 points** • Text is difficult to read with misuse of fonts, size, bullets, italics, bold • Many formatting tools are misused	
Writing Mechanics	**3 points** No grammar, capitalization, punctuation, spelling errors	**2 points** Few grammar, capitalization, punctuation, and spelling errors	**1 point** 4+ errors in grammar, capitalization, punctuation, and spelling	**0 points** More than 6 grammar/ spelling/ punctuation errors.	
				TOTAL POINTS	**/30**

Vocabulary Decoding Tools

_____Show students how to access the native apps or webtools on their digital devices that can be used to decode vocabulary students don't understand. Depending upon the device, these will be on the homepage, the browser toolbar, a shortkey, or a right click. Show students how to quickly look up words from any of their classes rather than skipping over content that includes the word. Let them practice with several of the words in this lesson's *Vocabulary* list.

_____Options include:

- *right click on word in MS Word and select 'Look up'*
- *right click in Google Apps (i.e., Google Docs) and select 'research'*
- *use an online resource like Dictionary.com*
- *use a browser app or plug-in*

_____A note: Every chance you get, use technology to facilitate teaching. Lead by example. Students will see you use tech quickly and facilely and follow your good example. They want to use tech. Don't discourage them!

Class exit ticket: ***Students send a well-constructed email, tweet, or comment to a classmate and reply to one they receive appropriately.***

Differentiation

- *Explore inside computer.*
- *See article at end of Lesson on **Internet Start Pages**.*
- *For more Google Apps, try these:*

  - *Maps: Explore, create and collaborate with mapping tools.*
  - *Scholar: Research and analyze sources from books, websites, other.*
  - *Tour Builder: Use Google Earth to create an online tour of anywhere in world.*
  - *Translate: Translate any text.*
  - *YouTube EDU: View educational content.*

"In theory, there is no difference between theory and practice. But, in practice, there is."

- Jan L.A. van de Snepscheut

Assessment 1—Parts of the computer

HARDWARE—PARTS OF THE COMPUTER

Student name: _____

Name each part of computer hardware system and whether it's INPUT or OUTPUT. Spelling must be correct to get credit

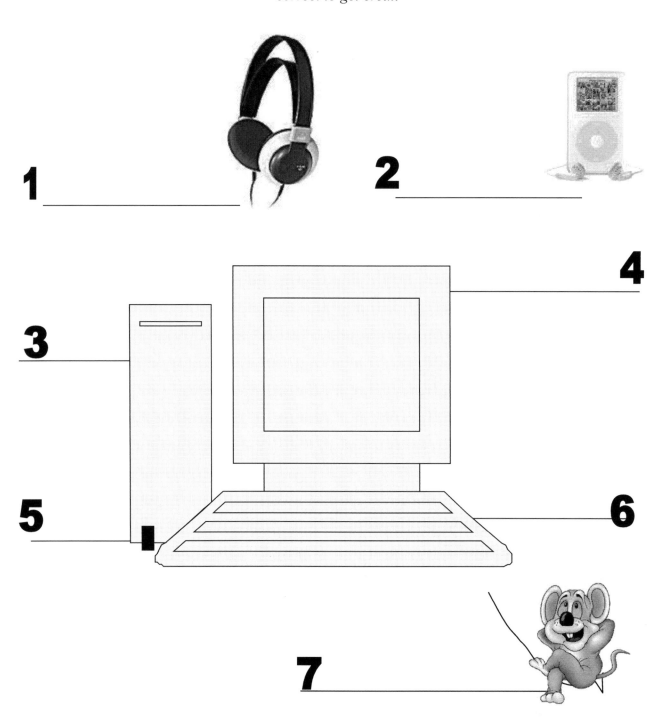

1 _____

2 _____

4 _____

3 _____

5 _____

6 _____

7 _____

Assessment 2—Parts of the smartphone

HARDWARE—PARTS OF THE SMARTPHONE

Adapt this to your needs

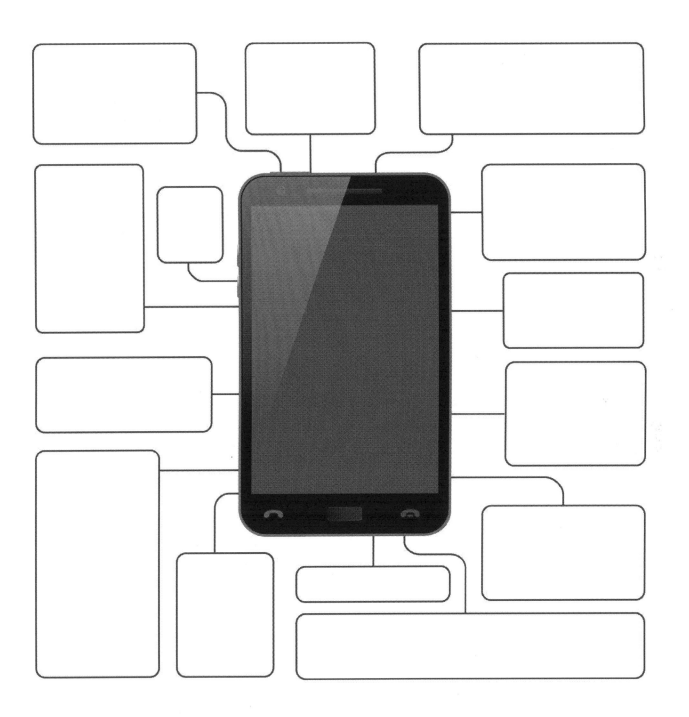

Parts of an iPad

©AskATechTeacher

Parts of a Chromebook

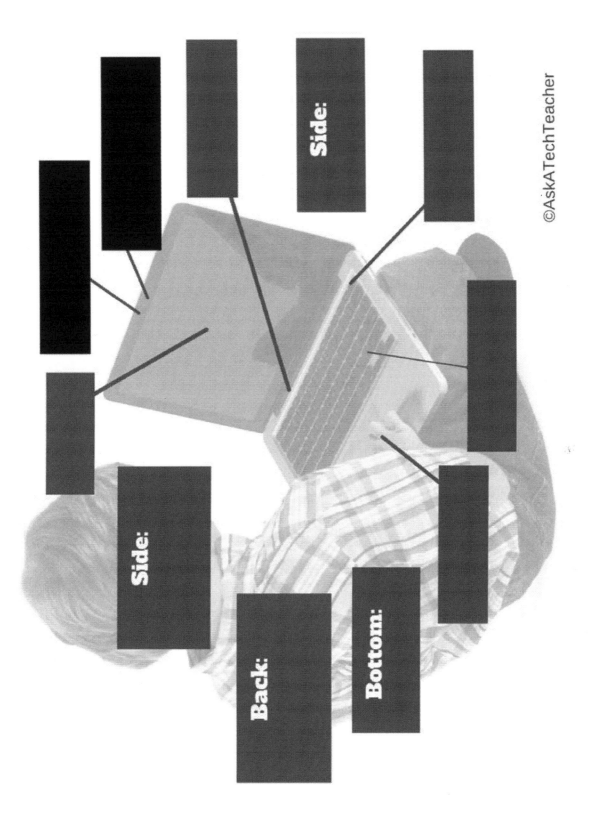

©AskATechTeacher

Side:

Side:

Back:

Bottom:

Seventh Grade Blogging Rules

1. I will not give out any information more personal than my first name
2. I will not plagiarize; instead I will expand on others' ideas and give credit where it is due.
3. I will use language appropriate for school.
4. I will always respect my fellow students and their writing.
5. I will only post pieces that I am comfortable with everyone seeing.
6. I will use constructive/productive/purposeful criticism, supporting any idea, comment, or critique I have with evidence.
7. I will take blogging seriously, posting only comments and ideas that are meaningful and that contribute to the overall conversation.
8. I will take my time when I write, using formal language (not text lingo), and I will try to spell everything correctly.
9. I will not bully others in my blog posts or in my comments.
10. I will only post comments on posts that I have fully read, rather than just skimmed.
11. I will not reveal anyone else's identity in my comments or posts.

Any infraction of the Blogging Rules may result in loss of blogging privileges and an alternative assignment will be required.

Student Signature _____ Date _____

Assessment 6—Blog grading rubric

Student Blog Rubric

Adapted from University of Wisconsin-Stout

Evaluation scale:

Exemplary:	32-36 points
Proficient:	28-31 points
Partially Proficient or Incomplete:	< 28 points (resubmit)

CRITERIA	Exemplary	Proficient	Partial	Incomplete	POINTS
Relevance of Content to Students and Parents	**9 points** ▪ Content has useful information ▪ Content is clear, concise; points readers to up to date resources. ▪ Blog is updated frequently	**6 points** ▪ Content points readers to quality resources, is informative ▪ Resources are clearly described so readers can navigate easily	**3 points** ▪ Content points to unrelated info. ▪ Resources are not clearly described so readers cannot navigate easily.	**0 points** ▪ Resources pointed to are inaccurate, misleading or inappropriate ▪ Annotations are missing, do not describe what is found	
Use of Media	**6 points** ▪ Media enhance content and interest. ▪ Creativity enhances content	**4 points** ▪ Most media enhance content. ▪ Most files show creativity	**2 points** ▪ Some don't enhance content. ▪ Some creativity enhances content.	**0 points** ▪ Media are inappropriate or detract from content.	
Fair Use Guidelines	**6 points** Fair use guidelines are followed with proper citations.	**4 points** Fair use guidelines are frequently followed; most material is cited.	**2 points** Sometimes fair use guidelines are followed with some citations.	**0 points** Fair use guidelines are not followed. Material is improperly cited.	
Links	**3 points** All links are active and functioning.	**2 points** Most links are active	**1 point** Some links are not active.	**0 points** Many links are not active.	
Layout and Text Elements	**3 points** ▪ Fonts are easy-to-read ▪ Use of bullets, italics, bold, enhances reading. ▪ Consistent format	**2 points** ▪ Sometimes fonts, size, bullets, italics, bold, detract from readability. ▪ Minor formatting inconsistencies	**1 point** ▪ Text is difficult to read due to formatting	**0 points** ▪ Text is difficult to read with misuse of fonts, size, bullets, italics, bold ▪ Many formatting tools are misused	
Writing Mechanics	**3 points** No grammar, capitalization, punctuation, spelling errors	**2 points** Few grammar, capitalization, punctuation, and spelling errors	**1 point** 4+ errors in grammar, caps, punctuation, and spelling	**0 points** More than 6 grammar/ spelling/ punctuation errors.	
				TOTAL POINTS	/30

Assessment 7—Website grading rubric

Student Website Rubric

Adapted from University of Wisconsin-Stout

Evaluation scale:

Exemplary:	32-36 points
Proficient:	28-31 points
Partially Proficient or Incomplete:	< 28 points (resubmit)

CRITERIA	Exemplary	Proficient	Partially	Incomplete	POINTS
Relevance of Content to Students and Parents	**9 points** • Content has useful information • Content is clear, concise; points readers to up to date resources. • Content is updated frequently	**6 points** • Content points readers to quality resources, is informative • Resources are clearly described so readers can navigate easily	**3 points** • Content points to unrelated information. • Resources are not clearly described so readers cannot navigate easily.	**0 points** • Resources pointed to are inaccurate, misleading or inappropriate • Annotations are missing, do not describe what is found	
Use of Media	**6 points** • Media enhance content and interest. • Creativity enhances content	**4 points** • Most media enhance content. • Most files show creativity	**2 points** • Some media don't enhance content. • Some creativity is evident.	**0 points** • Media are inappropriate or detract from content.	
Fair Use Guidelines	**6 points** Fair use guidelines are followed with proper citations.	**4 points** Fair use guidelines are frequently followed; most material is cited.	**2 points** Sometimes fair use is followed with some citations.	**0 points** Fair use guidelines not followed. Mat'l improperly cited.	
Links	**3 points** All links are active and functioning.	**2 points** Most links are active	**1 point** Some links are not active.	**0 points** Many links are not active.	
Layout and Text Elements	**3 points** • Fonts are easy-to-read • Use of bullets, italics, bold, enhances reading. • Consistent format throughout	**2 points** • Sometimes fonts, size, bullets, italics, bold, detract from readability. • Minor formatting inconsistencies exist	**1 point** • Text is difficult to read due to formatting	**0 points** • Text is difficult to read with misuse of fonts, size, bullets, italics, bold • Formatting tools misused	
Writing Mechanics	**3 points** No grammar, capitalization, punctuation, spelling errors	**2 points** Few grammar, capitalization, punctuation, and spelling errors	**1 point** 4+ errors in grammar, capitalization, punctuation, and spelling	**0 points** More than 6 grammar/ spelling/ punctuation errors.	
				TOTAL POINTS	/30

Assessment 8—Digital portfolio rubric

Digital Portfolio Rubric

CATEGORY	Exemplary	Proficient	Developing	Unsatisfactory	RATING
Selection of Artifacts	All artifacts and work samples are clearly and directly related to the purpose of portfolio.	Most artifacts and work samples are related to the purpose of the digital portfolio.	Some of the artifacts and work samples are related to the purpose of the digital portfolio.	None of the artifacts and work samples is related to the purpose of portfolio.	
Reflections	All reflections clearly describe growth, achievement and accomplishments, and include goals for continued learning (long and short term).	Most reflections describe growth and include goals for continued learning. It is clear student put thought and consideration into writing.	A few of the reflections describe growth and include goals for continued learning. It is not clear student put thought into his/her writing.	None of the reflections describe growth and does not include goals for continued learning. It is clear student put little thought into these writings.	
Use of Multimedia	Photographs, graphics, audio and/or video files enhance concepts, ideas and relationships, create interest, and are appropriate for chosen purpose.	Most graphic elements and multimedia contribute to concepts, ideas and relationships, enhance the written material and create interest.	Some of the graphic elements and multimedia do not contribute to concepts, ideas and relationships.	Multimedia doesn't contribute to concepts, ideas and relationships. The inappropriate use of multimedia detracts from content.	
Documentation & Copyright	All images, media and text follow copyright guidelines with accurate citations. All content throughout portfolio displays appropriate copyright permissions.	Most images, media and text created by others are cited with accurate, properly formatted citations.	Some images, media or text created by others are not cited with accurate, properly formatted citations.	No images, media or text created by others are cited with accurate, properly formatted citations.	
Ease of Navigation	Navigation links are intuitive. The various parts of portfolio are labeled, clearly organized and allow reader to easily locate an artifact.	Navigation links generally function well, but it is not always clear how to locate an artifact or move to related pages or different section.	Navigation links are confusing and it is often unclear how to locate an artifact or move to related pages or section.	Navigation links are confusing, and it is difficult to locate artifacts and move to related pages or a different section.	
Layout and Text Elements	Digital portfolio is easy to read. Fonts and type size vary appropriately for headings, sub-headings and text. Use of font styles (italic, bold, underline) is consistent and improves readability.	Digital portfolio is generally easy to read. Fonts and type size vary appropriately for headings, sub-headings and text. Use of font styles (italic, bold, underline) is generally consistent.	Digital portfolio is often difficult to read due to inappropriate use of fonts and type size for headings, sub-headings and text or inconsistent use of font styles (italic, bold, underline).	Digital portfolio is difficult to read due to inappropriate use of fonts, type size for headings, subheadings and text, and font styles (italic, bold, underline).	
Captions	All artifacts are accompanied by a caption that clearly explains importance of item including title, author, and date.	Most artifacts are accompanied by a caption that clearly explains importance of item including title, author, and date.	Some artifacts are accompanied by caption that explains importance of item including title, author, and date.	No artifacts are accompanied by a caption that explains importance of item.	
Writing Mechanics	There are no errors in grammar, capitalization, punctuation, and spelling.	There are few errors in grammar and spelling. These require minor editing and revision.	There are four or more errors in grammar and spelling requiring editing and revision.	There are more than six errors in grammar and spelling requiring major editing and revision.	

Askatechteacher©

Which Class Internet Start Page is Best?

The Internet is unavoidable in education. Students go there to research, access homework, check grades, and a whole lot more. As a teacher, you do your best to make it a friendly, intuitive, and safe place to visit, but it's challenging. Students arrive there by iPads, smartphones, links from classroom teachers, suggestions from friends—the routes are endless. The best way to keep the Internet experience safe is to catch users right at the front door, on that first click.

How do you do that? By creating a **class Internet start page**. Clicking the Internet icon opens the World Wide Web to a default page. Never take your device's default because there's no guarantee it's G-rated enough for a typical classroom environment. Through the 'settings' function on your browser, enter the address of a page you've designed as a portal to all school Internet activity, called an 'Internet start page'. Sure, this takes some time to set-up and maintain, but it saves more than that in student frustration, lesson prep time, and the angst parents feel about their children entering the virtual world by themselves. They aren't. You're there, through this page. Parents can save the link to their home computer and let students access any resources on it, with the confidence of knowing you've curated everything.

In searching for the perfect Internet start page, I wanted one that:

- *quickly differentiates for different grades*
- *is intuitive for even the youngest to find their page*
- *is customizable across tabbed pages to satisfy changing needs*
- *presents a visual and playful interface to make students want to go there rather than find work-arounds (a favorite hobby of older students)*
- *includes an immediately visible calendar of events*
- *hosts videos of class events*
- *provides collaborative walls like Padlet*
- *includes other interactive widgets to excite students about technology*

Here are four I looked at:

Symbaloo

A logo-based website curation tool with surprising flexibility in how links are collected and displayed. It's hugely popular with educators because collections are highly-visual and easy to access and use. Plus, Symbaloo collections made by one teacher can be shared with the community, making link collections that much easier to curate.

The downside: Links are about all you can collect on Symbaloo.

Ustart

Offers a good collection of useful webtools for students including links, news, calendar, notes, even weather. It provides tabs for arranging themed collections (like classes) and is intuitive to set up and use. It even includes options for embeddable widgets like Padlet. This is the closest to what I needed of all three.

Overall: This is a good alternative to the one I selected.

Protopage

Protopage did everything on my list. It's flexible, customizable, intuitive, and quick to use with a scalable interface that can be adjusted to my needs (2-5 columns, resize boxes, drag widgets between tabs—that sort). I set up a separate tab for each grade (or you can set up tabs for subjects). The amount of tabs is limited only by space on the top toolbar. Resources included on each tab can be curated exactly as you need. Mine includes:

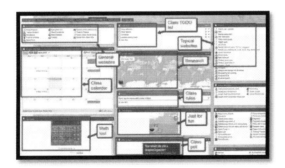

- *oft-used websites*
- *themed collections of websites*
- *a To Do list*
- *an interactive map*
- *a calculator*
- *a calendar of events*

- *edit-in-place sticky notes*
- *pictures of interest*
- *rss feeds of interest*
- *weather*
- *news*
- *widget for polling the class (Padlet)*

In addition, the Protopage folks are helpful. Whenever I have a problem (which is rare), they fix it quickly.

13 Ways Blogs Teach Common Core

If you aren't blogging with your students, you're missing one of the most effective tools available for improving student literacy and math. Blogs are easy to use, fun for students, encourage creativity and problem-solving, allow for reflection and feedback, enable publishing and sharing of work, and fulfill many of the Common Core Standards you might be struggling to complete. Aside from math and literacy, Common Core wants students to become accomplished in a variety of intangible skills that promote learning and college and career readiness. Look at these 13 benefits of blogging and how they align with Common Core:

1. **provide and get feedback**—building a community via comments is an integral part of blogging. If you didn't want feedback, you'd publish a white paper or submit work the old fashioned hard copy way. When students publish their ideas in blogs, other students, teachers, parents can provide feedback, join the conversation, and learn from the student.

2. **write-edit-review-rewrite**—teachers don't expect students to get it right the first time. Part of the writing process is revising, editing, rewriting. This is easy with blogs. Students publish a topic, collect comments, incorporate these ideas into their own thinking, and then edit their post.

3. **publish**—the idea that student work is created for a grade then stuffed away in a corner of their closet is disappearing. Current educators want students to publish their work in a way that allows everyone to benefit from the student's knowledge and work. There are many ways to do that—blogs are one of the easiest.

4. **share**—just like publishing, students no longer create for a grade; they share with others. Blogs allow for sharing of not only writing, but artwork, photography, music, multimedia projects, pretty much anything the student can create.

5. **collaborate**—blogs can easily be collaborative. Student groups can publish articles, comment on others, edit and rewrite. They can work together on one blog to cover a wider variety of topics and/or make its design attractive, appealing and enticing to readers.

6. **keyboarding**—blogs are small doses of typing—300-500 words, a few dozen for comments. This is an authentic opportunity to practice the keyboarding skills students will need for Common Core Standards in 4th grade and up.

7. **demonstrate independence**—blogs are about creativity. No two are alike. They offer lots of options for design and formatting so students can tweak it to their preference. Because they are open 24/7, students can do blog work when it suits them, not in the confines of a 50-minute class.

8. **build strong content knowledge**—blog posts can be drafted as the student collects information, posted when the student is ready. Links can be included to provide evidence of student statements, as well as linkbacks for reference and deeper reading for interested students.

9. **respond to the varying demands of audience, task, purpose, and discipline**—Students can create their work in whatever digital tool fits the audience, task, purpose they are focused on, and then embed it into their blog post. This is possible even in a simplified blogging platform like Kidblog. Most

online tools (such as Voki, Wordle, and Tagxedo) provide the html codes that can be easily placed in the blog post. Then, the student at their option can focus on presenting their ideas as music, art, photos, text, an infographic, a word cloud—whatever works for their purposes.

10. **comprehend as well as critique**—student bloggers are expected to critique the posts of others by thoroughly reading the post and commenting based on evidence. If the reader doesn't understand, they ask questions in the comments. This insures that when they evaluate the post, they have all the information required to reach a conclusion.

11. **value evidence**—blogs make it easy to provide all the necessary evidence to support a point of view. Students can link back to sources to provide credit and link to experts to provide credibility for statements. In fact, in the blogosphere, good bloggers are expected to do this as a means of building credibility for opinions they write

12. **use technology and digital media strategically and capably**—certainly blogs are great for writing, but they're also excellent as digital portfolios to display student work developed in a variety of places. Students pick the technology that fits what they're expected to accomplish in a class, then publish it to the blog. Have you seen the movies students put together on a topic? Some are amazing.

13. **understand other perspectives and cultures**—blogs are published to the Internet. Even private blogs are accessed by many more people than possible with a hand-written paper. Students write knowing that people of all cultures and perspectives will read their material, knowing they can add comments that share their beliefs. This encourages students to develop the habit of thinking about *perspective* as they write.

Don't try all of this at once. Spiral into it, starting in second or third grade. Let their blogging grow with their intellectual skills.

How to Integrate Web Tools into the Classroom

'**Web 2.0**' is a term familiar to all teachers. Stated in its simplest form, it's the set of interactive internet-based tools used by students to enrich educational opportunities—blogs, wikis, class internet homepages, class internet start pages, twitter, social bookmarks, podcasting, photo sharing, online docs, online calendars, even Second Life—tools that require thoughtful interaction between the student and the site. For teachers, it's a challenge to keep up with the plethora of options as the creative minds of our new adults stretch the boundaries of what we can do on the internet. Students, adults, teachers who use this worldwide wealth of information and tools are referred to as 'digital citizens'. They leave a vast digital footprint and it is incumbent upon them to make healthy and safe decisions, including:

- *Treat others and their property with respect (for example, plagiarism—even undiscovered—is immoral and illegal)*
- *Act in a responsible manner*
- *Look after their own security*

Here are some activities you can do in your classroom that will make your lessons and activities more student-centered and more relevant to this new generation of students:

1. Create a **classroom blog**. Blogging has become one of the most effective learning tools in education. It introduces students to new methods of communicating, improves their writing, and motivates them to find their voice. You ask students about it, they'll tell you—blogs make learning fun.

2. Create a **classroom internet start page.** When students log onto the internet, have them bring up a start page with information relevant to them—targeted links, a To Do list, RSS feeds, search tools, email. Ask them what should be on it. Maybe they'd like sponge websites to fill extra minutes. Make it exciting!

3. Each has a library of custom fields to individualize the start-up experience.

4. Build your own **classroom webpage**. Make it a learning portal open for business 24/7. Make sure it engages students while facilitating authentic real-world activities. You can make a free page through Google Sites.

5. Create **online calendars** for students. These replace the traditional planners students carry to classes (and lose who knows where which becomes a traumatic event in young lives). Create

your own on Google Calendars with viewing privileges for students and parents only, and then embed it into your class webpage, start page or wiki.

6. Create a **wiki**—a web page built by and for students. The most famous example is Wikipedia. Wikis can communicate school news, information on a research topic, terminology—whatever you want. For example, after teaching a lesson, have students go to the class wiki and summarize what they understood. Then, when test time arrives, students can study from everyone's notes.

7. Set up **social bookmarking** so students can save links to webpages they use for research, sports, music, and share them with others. Imagine the vast database you can compile by having students investigate a topic—say, the French Revolution—save the sites they visit to a group folder, and benefit from each other's research. What an amazing tool!

8. **Twitter** is a free social messaging utility that allows you to update parents and older students via short messages everyone will have time to read. In my case, I have one account for parents (it's private, so I won't share it here) and one for my PLN (personal learning network—I'd love to have you follow me). You can incorporate twitter widgets into webpages, add it to your Google desktop/ smartphone/ iPad, even your blog.

9. **Photo sharing** through Flikr or Photobucket (or others). Free online photo collections enable students/parents/teachers to share pictures from school events, sports and more. Students can search for photos to help with research (be sure to teach them correct annotations) and educators can upload photos for classes, school events, and more. At my school, students had to complete a photo journal after a field trip. Everyone uploaded their pictures, creating a huge pool to use for the follow-up project.

10. **Podcasting** is an efficient method of sharing lectures, instructions, and information. They appeal to those multi-intelligences that prefer visual and audio and can be replayed 24/7. With a nominal amount of equipment, anyone can create files and post them to the internet that can be accessed from a personal computer or handheld device. The most popular site is YouTube, but also try Vimeo.

11. Everyone should try **online docs.** Google Docs has become the standard for free, easy-to-use document sharing at schools and can be limited to the school community of registered users. Even if you don't use it in your school, share it with parents. You'll be surprised how many will appreciate the alternative to MS Office.

Which others do you use to enhance and enrich your school teaching?
Photo credit: Johns Hopkins School of Education

8 Things My Blog Taught Me

When I started blogging, I wasn't sure where to take it. I knew I wanted to connect with other tech teachers so I used that as the theme. Now, thanks to the 491,000+ people who have visited, I know much more about the 'why'. It's about getting to know kindred souls, but there is so much more I've gotten from blogging. Like these:

How to write

I've learned to be frugal with my words. I choose verbiage that conveys more than one-word's-worth of information and I leave tangential issues for another post. Because I realize readers are consuming on the run, I make sure to be clear—no misplaced pronouns or fuzzy concepts like 'thing' or 'something'.

Prove my point

This part of writing transcends what print journalists must do. Yes, they do it, but my readers expect me to support ideas with interactive links to sources. If I'm reviewing a tech ed concept, I link to other websites for deeper reading. That's something that can't happen in paper writing. Sure, they can provide the link, but to put the paper down, open the laptop, copy that link—I mean, who does that? In a blog, I get annoyed if someone cites research and doesn't provide the link.

Listen

When I write an article, I cross post to other parts of my PLN, sometimes to ezines I contribute to in other parts of the world. And then I listen. What are readers saying? What are their comments/suggestions to me? Often, I learn as much from readers as what I thought I knew when I wrote the article.

How to market my writing

I try lots of ideas to market my writing, but thanks to the blogosphere, I know what everyone else is doing. I can try as much or little of it as I want. For me, I found a comfortable baseline and add a few pieces every year (this year, it's Pinterest).

One point worth mentioning is headlines. Usually, all I get from a reader is seven seconds–long enough to read the title, maybe the first line. If my title doesn't seem personal and relevant, potential readers move on. There are over 450 million English language blogs. That's a lot of competition. I better hit a home run with the title.

There are lots of opinions out there

Often, I share my thoughts on the future or current status of tech ed. Sometimes, I'm surprised at comments I get. They might touch a corner of the idea I hadn't thought of or be 180 degrees from my conclusions. It forces me to think bigger as I write, consider how people who aren't me will read my words. That's both humbling and empowering. I think I'm much better at that than I used to be.

There are a lot of smart people in the world

In a previous lifetime when I built child care centers for a living, I read lots of data that said people thought the education system was broken–but not in their area. They considered themselves lucky because their schools worked. Well, as I meandered through life, I realized that applies to everything. People are happy with what they're comfortable with and frightened/suspicious of what they aren't used to. Through blogging, I get to delve into those ideas with them because we feel like friends. I've found that lots of people are smart, intuitive, engaged in life, looking to improve the world. I'm glad I learned that.

How to be responsible

Yes, blogging is demanding. I have to follow through on promises made in my blog profile and posts. When I say I'll offer tech tips weekly, I have to do that even if I'm tired or busy with other parts of my life. It's not as hard as it sounded when I first started. If you're a mom, you've got the mindset. Just apply it to blogging.

How to be a friend

My readers visit my posts and comment or poke me with a 'like'. Maybe, on my good days, they repost. Those are nice *attaboys*. I always return the favor by dropping by their blogs to see what they're up to, leave a comment on their latest article. It takes time, but like any relationship, is worth it. I have online friends I've never met who I feel closer to than half the people in my physical world. I've seen them struggle with cancer, new jobs, unemployment, kid problems. I've learned a lot about life from them.

12 Ways Twitter Improves Education

Twitter can easily be dismissed as a waste of time in the elementary school classroom. Students will get distracted. Students will see tweets they shouldn't at their age. How does one manage a room full of Tweeple without cell phones? Is it even appropriate for the lower grades?

Here's ammunition for what often turns into a pitched verbal brawl as well-intended teachers try to reach a compromise on Twitter (in fact, many of the new Web 2.0 tools—blogs, wikis, websites that require registrations and log-ins, discussion forums. You can probably add to this list) that works for all stakeholders:

You learn to be concise.

Twitter gives you only 280 characters to get the entire message across. *Letters, numbers, symbols, punctuation and spaces all count as characters on Twitter.* Wordiness doesn't work. Twitter counts every keystroke and won't publish anything with a minus in front of the word count.

At first blush, that seems impossible. It's not. True, you must know the right word for every situation. People with a big vocabulary are at an advantage because they don't use collections of little words to say what they mean, they jump right to it. All those hints your English teacher gave you–picture nouns and action verbs, get rid of adverbs and adjectives–take on new meaning to the Twitter aficionado.

Twitter isn't intimidating

A blank white page that holds hundreds of words, demanding you fill in each line margin to margin is intimidating. 280 characters aren't. Anyone can write 140 characters about any topic. Students write their 280 characters and more, learn to whittle back, leave out emotional words, adjectives and adverbs, pick better nouns and verbs because they need the room. Instead of worrying what they'll say on all those empty lines, they feel successful.

Students learn manners

Social networks are all about netiquette. People thank others for their assistance, ask politely for help, and encourage contributions from others. Use this framework to teach students how to engage in a community—be it physical or virtual. It's all about manners.

Students learn to be focused

With only 140 characters, you can't get off topic. You have to save those for a different tweet. Tweeple like that trait in writers. They like to hear what your main topic is and hear your thoughts on it, not your meanderings. When you force yourself to write this way, you find it really doesn't take a paragraph to make a point. Use the right words, people get it. Consider that the average reader gives a story seven seconds before moving on. OK, yes, that's more than 140 characters, but not much.

Here's an idea. If you feel you must get into those off-topic thoughts, write them in a separate tweet.

Students learn to share

Start a tweet stream where students share research websites on a topic. Maybe the class is studying Ancient Greece. Have each student share their favorite website (using a #hashtag — maybe #ancientgreece) and create a resource others can use. Expand on that wonderful skill they learned in kindergarten about sharing their toys with others. Encourage them to RT posts that they found particularly relevant or helpful.

Writing short messages perfects the art of "headlining".

Writers call this the title. Bloggers and journalists call it the headline. Whatever the label, it has to be cogent and pithy enough to pull the audience in and make them read the article. That's a tweet.

Tweets need to be written knowing that tweeple can @reply

Yes. This is the world of social networks where people will read what you say and comment. That's a good thing. It's feedback and builds an online community, be it for socializing or school. Students learn to construct their arguments expecting others to respond, question, and comment. Not only does this develop the skill of persuasive writing, students learn to have a thick skin, take comments with a grain of salt and two grains of aspirin.

#Hashmarks develop a community

Create #hashmarks to help students organize tweets: #help for a question, #homework for homework help. Establish class ones to deal with subjects that you as the teacher want students to address.

Students learn tolerance for all opinions

Why? Because Tweeple aren't afraid to voice their thoughts. They only have 140 characters—why not spit it right out. Because the Twitter stream is a public forum (in a classroom, the stream can be private, but still visible to all members of the class), students understand what they say is out there forever. That's daunting. Take the opportunity to teach students about their public profile. Represent themselves well with good grammar, good spelling, and well-chosen tolerant ideas. Don't be emotional or spiteful because it can't be taken back. Rather than shying away from exposing students to the world at large, use Twitter to teach students how to live in a world.

Students are engaged

Twitter is exciting, new, and hip. Students want to use it. It's not the boring worksheet. It's a way to engage students in ways that excite them.

Consider this: You're doing the lecture part of your teaching (we all have some of that), or you're walking the classroom helping where needed. Students can tweet questions that show up on the Smartboard. It's easy to see where everyone is getting stuck, which question is stumping them, and answer it in real time. The class barely slows down. Not only can you see where problems arise, students can provide instant feedback on material without disrupting the class. Three people can tweet at once while you talk/help.

Twitter, the Classroom Notepad

I tried this out after I read about it on Online Universities and turns out, it works as well for 8th graders as it does for higher education. Springboarding off student engagement, Twitter can act as your classroom notepad. Have students enter their thoughts, note, and reactions while you talk. By the time class is done, the entire class has an overview of the conversation with extensions and connections that help everyone get more out of the time spent together.

Twitter is always open

Inspiration doesn't always strike in that 50-minute class period. Sometimes it's after class, after school, after dinner, even 11 at night. Twitter doesn't care. Whatever schedule is best for students to discover the answer, Twitter is there. If you post a tweet question and ask students to join the conversation, they will respond in the time frame that works best for them. I love that. That's a new set of rules for classroom participation, and these are student-centered, uninhibited by a subjective time period. Twitter doesn't even care if a student missed the class. S/he can catch up via tweets and then join in.

Please take a moment to vote in this poll. Tell me how you think Twitter would best benefit your classroom if you were using it.

Lesson #3 Keyboarding

Vocabulary	Problem solving	Homework
<ul><li>Cumulative</li><li>F row</li><li>Home row</li><li>Hunt-and-peck</li><li>Keyboard shortcuts</li><li>Mulligan</li><li>QWERTY</li><li>Shortkey</li><li>Tilde</li><li>Touch typing</li><li>Wpm</li></ul>	<ul><li>I can't remember key placement (trust yourself to know)</li><li>Can't remember some keys on quiz (skip them)</li><li>I can't type with hands covered (Keep practicing)</li><li>Can't type faster (slow down, relax)</li><li>I keep losing home row (find bump on F and J with pointers)</li><li>I do fine with 2-4 fingers (but you won't get fast)</li></ul>	Practice keyboarding for 45 minutes, 15 minutes at a time Add quizzes to class calendar Bring questions to class
Academic Applications	**Required skills**	**Standards**
Writing, research, any topic requiring keyboarding	Familiarity with touch typing, tech problem solving, speaking/listening skills, PDF annotation	CCSS: W.7.6,7 NETS: 1d, 6a

Essential Question

How can I type three pages without stopping?

Big Idea

Work on essential keyboarding—technique, speed, accuracy

Teacher Preparation/Materials Required

- Curated touch typing and keyboard websites.
- Have lesson preview materials online.
- Have student workbooks (if using).
- Integrate domain-specific tech vocabulary into lesson.
- Ensure all required links are on student digital devices.
- Know which tasks weren't completed last week.
- Something happen you weren't prepared for? Show students how you fix the emergency without a meltdown and with a positive attitude.

Assessment Strategies

- Previewed required material; came to class prepared
- Annotated workbook (if using)
- Worked independently
- Used good keyboarding habits
- Completing required quizzes
- Completed warm-up
- Joined classroom conversations
- [tried to] solve own problems
- Decisions followed class rules
- Left room as s/he found it
- Higher order thinking: analysis, evaluation, synthesis
- Habits of mind observed

Steps

Time required: *Spread throughout the school year with time set aside for quizzes*
Class warm-up: *Keyboarding on the class typing program, paying attention to posture*

_____ Homework will be assigned the week before you start this lesson so students are prepared for the flipped classroom.
_____ Any questions from preparatory homework?

_____Using *Figure 31*, discuss why students should care about keyboarding:

Figure 31—Why learn to keyboard

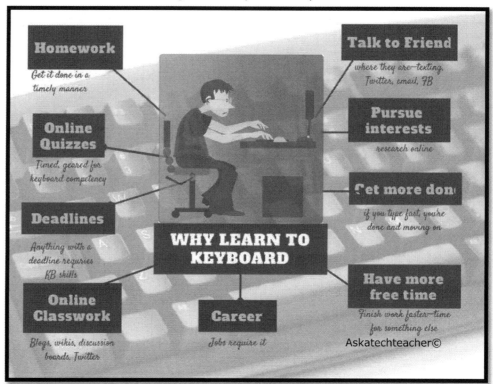

_____At this point in student keyboarding development, they should:

- *keep the copy to the side of the keyboard*
- *use correct posture—legs in front, body in front and one hand's width from table, elbows at sides, posture upright, feet flat on floor, hands curled over home row*
- *take proper care of tech equipment*
- *effectively use software and internet-based sites for keyboard practice*

_____Have students check the posture of a neighbor. If correct posture isn't already a habit, encourage students to sit this way when they use any digital device—home, school, the library, everywhere (*Figures 32a-b*):

Figure 32a—Keyboarding posture; 32b—position

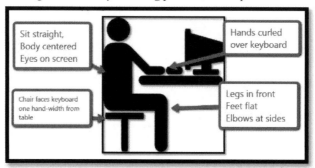

_____Review how student hands should look (*Figure 33*):

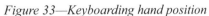

Figure 33—Keyboarding hand position

_____Keyboarding is cumulative. What can be learned depends heavily upon what was learned earlier. If hunt 'n peck becomes ingrained, it's difficult to develop competence later.

_____Review keyboarding best practices that you will observe as students work. *Figure 34* is a list (full-size assessment at end of Lesson):

Figure 34—Keyboarding technique checklist

Student _____					
Keyboarding Technique Checklist (3rd – Middle School Grades)					
Technique	Date	Date	Date	Date	Date
Feet placed for balance and sits up straight.					
Body centered to the middle of keyboard.					
Eyes on the screen.					
Types with correct fingering.					
Types with a steady, even rhythm.					
Keeps fingers on home row keys.					
Has a good attitude and strives for improvement.					
WPM (words per minute)					
Accuracy percent					

4 pts = Mastery level   2 pts = Partial Mastery level
3 pts = Near Mastery level   1 pt = Minimal Mastery level

- *Keep hands curved over home row.*
- *Use correct posture:*

  - *Sit straight, shoulders back, head up, body centered one hand's width from table, feet flat on ground.*
  - *Keep elbows close to sides.*
  - *Reach for keys—don't move hands (only fingers).*

- *Touch type with a steady, even pace.*
- *Keep copy to side of keyboard, eyes on copy or screen—NOT keyboard.*
- *Use keyboard shortcuts (i.e., Ctrl+B, Shift+Alt+D).*

_____If your students have just started to practice keyboarding, pick only a few of these criteria to assess. As the K-6th graders get more practice, they'll come to 7th grade with a greater facility and you can expect more out of them.

_____Add each keyboarding activity to class calendar.

_____By the end of 7th grade, students should:

> **The more you know about key placement, the faster and more accurately you type.**

- *type 40 wpm*
- *type three pages in a single sitting*
- *compose at the keyboard with ease*
- *keep eyes on copy*
- *know at least twenty shortkeys (i.e., Alt+F4, Esc, Ctrl+P, Ctrl+S, Ctrl+C, Ctrl+V, Ctrl+Alt+Del, Ctrl+B/I/U, double-click to enlarge window, Alt+Tab, Win key, Shift+tab, right mouse button key, Ctrl+, Ctrl-, ???)*
- *reach fingers from home row to other keys. When viewed, hands should appear still with fingers moving—no flying hands.*
- *touch type all keys*
- *write thoughts that represent student well—good formatting, minimal errors*
- *understand keyboard parts and functions*

Keep Keyboarding Fun

1. *In-class keyboarding*
2. *Varied quizzes*
3. *Monthly homework*
4. *Authentic practice*
5. *Shortkeys*
6. *Keyboard Challenge*

_____Let students know **Mulligan Rule** applies (poster in Appendix). What's that? Any golfers? A 'mulligan' is a do-over. Students can retake any quiz/project/test covered by Mulligan Rule without losing credit. I love the Mulligan Rule. It covers those times students complain they weren't ready, didn't know about a quiz, were sick, shouldn't be graded because [fill in the blank]. I don't argue. I smile and let them retake it. Few do. It requires little from me, yet I seem like the world's fairest teacher.

_____Practice one keyboard row at a time. Here's a schedule for the **first six weeks**:

- *Weeks 1-2: home row*
- *Weeks 3-4: QWERTY row*
- *Weeks 5-6: lower row*

_____Enter these into class calendar.

_____Students practice 10-15 minutes during class and 45 minutes per week as homework.

_____**Throughout year**, evaluate mistakes students make as they type. The cause may be more important than the mistake:

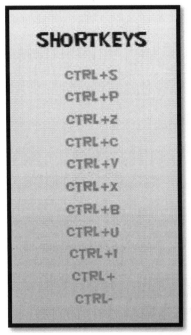

Figure 5--Shortkeys

- *tension, wandering attention, faulty reading, or the wrong mind set.*
- *Watch students for fatigue—moving heads, massaging, and tight facial expressions.*

_____For more, review the article at the end of the lesson, *"How to Prepare Students for Year-end Tests"*.

_____Here are nine activities included in this lesson:

- *blank keyboard quiz*
- *formative assessments*
- *important keys quiz*
- *keyboarding challenge*
- *keyboarding using inquiry-based projects*
- *shortkeys*
- *summative speed/accuracy quizzes*

_____For more activities, see *"5 Ways to Make Keyboarding Fun"* at end of lesson.

Authentic keyboarding using inquiry-based projects

_____Typing is best learned through class inquiry. As soon as possible, begin project-based typing. These can be short reports, magazines, trifolds, a story—what works for your students. *Figures 36a-e are projects included in the K-6 curriculum that reinforce authentic keyboarding:*

Figure 36a-e—Project-based learning and keyboarding

Shortkeys

_____Throughout the year, reinforce the use of shortkeys. For example:

- *when saving, Ctrl+S*
- *when printing, Ctrl+P*
- *when needing to undo an action, Ctrl+Z*

- *when copying, Ctrl+C; pasting, Ctrl+V (why not Ctrl+P?)*
- *when enlarging a window, double click title bar*
- *when unable to close a program, Alt+F4*
- *when toggling between two windows (say, for research), Alt+Tab*
- *when indenting in a list, use Tab and Shift+tab*

_____If using student workbooks, have students take a screenshot of *Figure 35*, print, and tape to their digital device or notebook.

_____See *Figures 37a-d* for platform-specific shortkeys (full-size posters in Appendix):

Figure 37a—iPad shortkeys; 37b—Chromebook shortkeys; 37c—PC shortkeys; 37d—Internet shortkeys

Formative assessments

_____Once a month, practice on a site like TypingTest.com to see how fast/accurately students are typing. More than five errors? Slow down. Less than five—speed up.

Summative speed/accuracy quizzes

_____**Each grading period,** students test speed and accuracy to track improvement.

_____The first quiz is a benchmark—to evaluate skills. The rest are graded based on improvement. If students do their homework and use good habits at the computer, they'll do fine.

• *20% improvement* *10/10*	• *No improvement* *7/10*
• *10-20% improvement* *9/10*	• *Slowed down* *6/10*
• *1-10% improvement* *8/10*	

_____Grade level standard: **40 wpm.** If students haven't practiced keyboarding for several years (or used this curriculum as long), you can adjust this to a speed more suited to their skillset.

_____The speed quiz can be delivered several ways:

- *a page from a book being read placed on the class screen. Students copy it for the quiz. This method forces their heads up rather than on their hands*
- *a page from a book being read in class placed to the side of keyboard*
- *an online typing test*

_____Students type for three-five minutes, then save/share/print.

_____Load a digital copy of *Assessment 9* at end of lesson onto your iPad and anecdotally complete it for each student with an annotation tool like Notability or Adobe Reader.

Important Keys Quiz

_____Discuss why it's important that students memorize keys.

_____**Each grading period**, students take a blank _Important Keys_ quiz (see _Figure 38_ and _Assessment_ at end of Lesson—adapt to your digital device) to test key placement knowledge. They can work in pairs or alone for ten minutes. Success here translates to speed and accuracy.

_____If you give this quiz once a grading period, use this first one as a baseline. Next time, score it like the keyboard speed quiz.

Figure 38—Important keys on keyboard

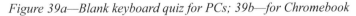

Blank keyboard quiz

_____**Each grading period**, students take a blank keyboard quiz (_Figures 39a-b_ are blank keyboards for PC and Chromebooks. Adapt for your digital device. Find _Assessments_ at lesson's end) to test knowledge of key placement. They can work in pairs and must retake until they pass. Success here translates to speed, accuracy, and facility with touch typing.

_____Discuss why it's important to memorize keys.

_____Students get ten minutes to complete. The first quiz is a baseline. Next quizzes are graded like keyboard speed quiz—on improvement.

_____Common mistakes are forgetting _Esc_ at the left side of the F row, forgetting the tilde at the left side of the number row, and getting the QWERTY row wrong.

Figure 39a—Blank keyboard quiz for PCs; 39b—for Chromebook

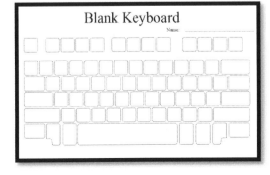

Keyboarding Challenge

_____Divide students into teams. Select a captain—the only person who can answer questions. Responses must be quick—show team knows the right key. See *Assessment* at end of this lesson.

_____Ask Team #1 a question, i.e., *"Which finger types f?"* Give them 3 seconds to answer (may be visual). If they can't, go to Team #2 but don't repeat question. If they can't answer, move to Team #3 and then Team #4.

_____Next question goes to Team #2—even if they were the ones who answered Team #1's question. This is how teams get ahead. Pose question to Team #2 and repeat step above.

_____Sound dull? I thought so, but kids love it. Every time we play, it's a hit and they want more.

Class exit ticket: None.

Differentiation

- Assign a student to enter keyboarding assignment dates.
- Put Keyboard Challenge into a Jeopardy template.
- K-8 Keyboard Curriculum available from Structured Learning LLC.

Assessment 9—Keyboarding quiz

Student _____

Keyboarding Technique Checklist
Rate 1-4

Technique	Date	Date	Date	Date	Date
Feet placed for balance and sits up straight					
Body centered to the middle of keyboard					
Eyes on the screen					
Types with correct fingering					
Types with a steady, even rhythm					
Keeps fingers on home row keys					
Has a good attitude and strives for improvement					
WPM (words per minute)					
Accuracy percent					

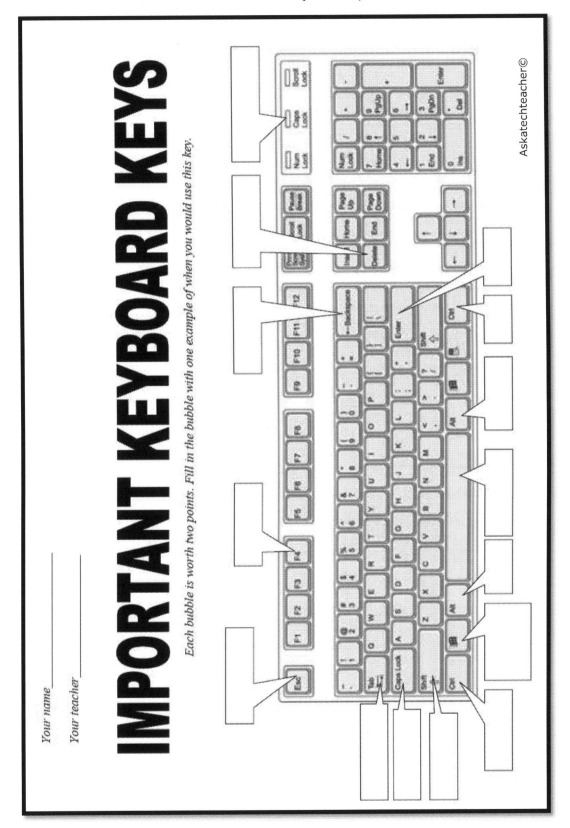

IMPORTANT KEYBOARD KEYS

Each bubble is worth two points. Fill in the bubble with one example of when you would use this key.

Your name _____

Your teacher _____

Askatechteacher©

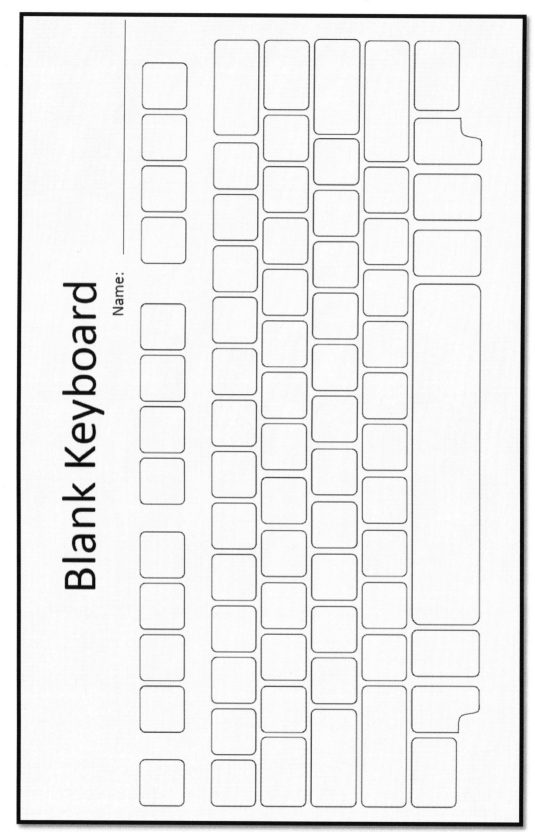

Blank Keyboard

Name:

Assessment 12—Chromebook blank keyboard quiz

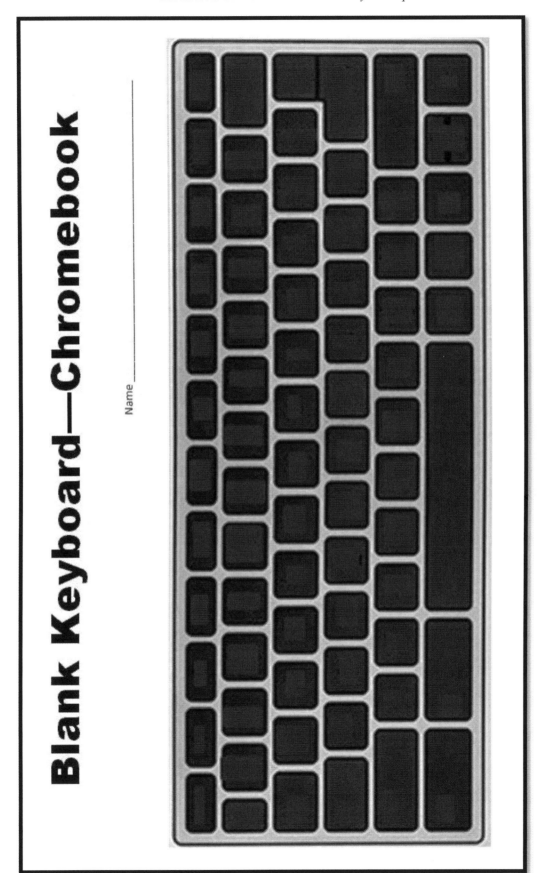

Blank Keyboard—Chromebook

Name

KEYBOARDING TEAM CHALLENGE

Review the following concepts. These are similar to questions that will be asked during the upcoming Team Challenge to find the year's most tech-savvy student!

1. Name computer login
2. Name computer password
3. Name TTL4 password
4. What row do fingers rest on
5. What row's above home
6. What row's below home
7. How do you find the f and j key without looking
8. Name three keys you use your pinkie to push
9. 3 keys pushed with pinkie
10. 3 keys pushed with middle finger
11. 3 keys pushed with pointer
12. 1 key right thumb pushes
13. Finger to push backspace
14. Finger to push shift key
15. Finger to push enter
16. Finger to push escape
17. 3 rules for sitting at keyboard
18. Do you have cat's paws or dog paws at the computer
19. Why? (answer above)
20. What part of chair do you sit on to keyboard

21. Where are your elbows when keyboarding
22. Where do you rest your right thumb to keyboard
23. What do you call typing without looking at keys
24. Finger that pushes A
25. Finger that pushes B
26. Finger that pushes C
27. Finger that pushes D
28. Finger that pushes E
29. Finger that pushes F
30. Finger that pushes G
31. Finger that pushes H
32. Finger that pushes I
33. Finger that pushes J
34. Finger that pushes K
35. Shortkey for exit program
36. As a general rule, which finger pushes a key
37. How do you capitalize
38. Generally, do fingers or hands move to find keys
39. Name a shortkey
40. What is a desktop

Article 10—5 Ways to make classroom keyboarding fun

5 Ways to Make Classroom Keyboarding Fun

The goal of typing isn't **speed and accuracy**.

The goal of keyboarding is students type well enough that it doesn't disrupt their thinking.

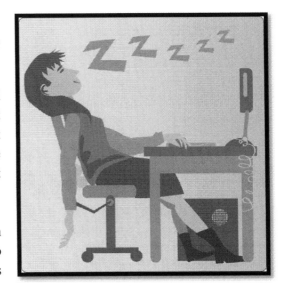

Much like breathing takes no thought, fingers should automatically move to the keys. Searching for key placement shouldn't interfere with how they develop a sentence. Sure, it does when students are just starting, but by third grade students should be comfortable enough with key placement to be working on speed.

To type as fast as the speed of thought isn't difficult. When referring to students in school, 'speed of thought' refers to how fast they develop ideas that will be recorded. 30 wpm is the low end. 45 wpm is good.

Students used to learn typing in high school, as a skill. Now, it's a tool for learning. So much of what we ask students to do on the way to authentic learning requires typing. Consider the academic need to:

- *write reports*
- *research online (type addresses into a search bar)*
- *take digital notes (using Evernote, OneNote and similar)*
- *collaborate on Google Apps like Docs, Sheets, Presentations*
- *take online quizzes (like PARCC, SB)*

If you're a Common Core state, keyboarding shows up often in the Standards:

- *Starting in 4th grade, students must be able to type *** pages in a single sitting.*
- *By 3rd grade, keyboarding is used to **produce** work.'*
- *Keyboarding is required to take **Common Core Standards assessments** in the spring.*

The myth is that students will teach themselves when they need it. That's half right. They will teach themselves, but it won't necessarily be in time for their needs. If you're in a tech-infused school, it's your obligation to teach them the right way to type so they can organically develop the tools to support learning.

Most teachers roll out typing with a graduated program. In September of the new school year, students start Lesson 1. Sometime around May, they are through all the lessons and considered trained. Everything is on auto-pilot with little intervention from the teacher. That works for about ten percent of students. Those are the ones who are intrinsically motivated to learn and nothing gets in their way.

The other 90% need a little more help. Here are six ideas to make your typing lessons fun and effective:

Drill

Drill is part of every granular typing program. Students must learn key placement, finger usage, posture, and all those other details.

There are a lot of options for this—both free like Typing Web and fee-based like QwertyTown. Students usually start enthusiastically, which wanes within a few months as it becomes more of the same rote practice.

Games

When your organic typing program shows signs of wearing on students, throw in a sprinkling of games that teach key placement, speed and accuracy. Big Brown Bear is great for youngers; NitroTyping for olders, and Popcorn Typer for the in-between grades of 2nd-5th.

Offer games sporadically, not on a schedule. Make it a reward for keyboarding benchmarks.

Team Challenge

Students work in teams to answer keyboard-related questions in a game show format. You can use a Jeopardy template that includes not only keyboard questions, but shortkeys that students use often.

Integrate into Class Inquiry

Within a month of starting a keyboarding program, have students use their growing skills authentically in class projects. This can be book reports, research, a brochure for history class, or a collaborative document through Google Apps. The keyboarding is a tool to communicate knowledge in a subject, much like a pencil, an artist brush or a violin. The better their keyboarding skills, the easier it is to complete the meat of the project, like a blog response, trading cards on characters in a book, or a family tree.

Remind students to use their keyboarding skills to make this real-life experience easier—hands on their own side of the keyboard, use all fingers, good posture, elbows at their sides. Let their team of grade level teachers know what traits to look for as students research in class or the library. Get parents to reinforce it at home.

ASCII Art

ASCII Art uses keyboarding skills to create artistic representations of class learning. This is a fun way to use keyboarding in other classes. All students do is find a picture that represents the class inquiry topic being addressed, put it as a watermark into the word processing program, type over the washed out image with a variety of keys, then delete the watermark. This takes about thirty minutes usually and always excites students with the uniqueness of their work.

How to Prepare Students for Year-end Tests

As part of my online tech teacher persona, I get lots of questions from readers about how to make technology work in an educational environment. This one from Terry is probably on the minds of thousands of teachers:

Any help for identifying and re-enforcing tech skills needed to take the online PARCC tests (coming in 2014-15)? Even a list of computer terms would help; copy, cut, paste, highlight, select; use of keys like tab, delete, insert; alt, ctrl and shift. There does not seem to be any guidelines as to prepping students on the "how to's" of taking an online test and reading and understanding the directions. It would be great to take advantage of the time we have before the PARCC's become a reality. Thanks!

Every spring, more than 4 million students in 36 states and the District of Columbia will take near-final versions of the PARCC and Smarter Balanced efforts to test Common Core State Standards learning in the areas of mathematics and English/language arts. Tests will be administered via digital devices (though there are options for paper-and-pencil). The tests won't produce detailed scores of student performance (that starts next year), but this field-testing is crucial to finding out what works and doesn't in this comprehensive assessment tool, including the human factors like techphobia and sweaty palms (from both students and teachers).

After I got Terry's email, I polled my PLN to find specific tech areas students needed help with in preparing for the Assessments. It boils down to five tech areas:

Keyboarding

Students need to have enough familiarity with the keyboard that they know where keys are, where the number pad is, where the F row is, how keys are laid out. They don't need to be touch typists or even facilely use all fingers. Just have them comfortable enough they have a good understanding of where all the pieces are. Starting next school year, have them type fifteen minutes a week in a class setting and 45 minutes a week using keyboarding for class activities (homework, projects—that sort). That'll do it.

Basic computer skills

These skills—drag-and-drop, keyboarding with speed and accuracy, highlighting, playing videos—are not easy for a student if they haven't had an instructive course in using computers. It won't surprise any adult when I say using and iPad isn't the same as using a computer. The former has a bunch more buttons and tools and the latter more intuitive. And typing on an iPad virtual keyboard is not the same as the reassuring clackity-clack of a traditional set-up. Will students get used to that? Yes, but not this month.

Make sure students are technologically proficient in their use of a variety of digital devices, including computers and iPads. This means students have an understanding of what defines a digital device, how it operates, what type of programs are used on various types (for example, apps are for iPads and software for laptops) and how do they operate, and what's the best way to scaffold them for learning? Being comfortable with technology takes time and practice. Make digital devices and tech solutions available at every opportunity—for note-taking, backchannel communications, quick assessments, online collaboration, even timing an activity. Make it part of a student's educational landscape.

One area Terry asks about is vocabulary. The words she mentioned—*copy, paste, cut, highlight*—these are domain-specific. Use the correct terminology as you teaching, but observe students. If they don't understand what you're saying, help them decode it with context, affixes, or an online dictionary for geek words. Keep a list of those words. Soon, you'll have a vocabulary list for technology that's authentic and specific to your needs.

Stamina

Expect students to type for extended periods without complaint. Common Core requires this. That's what 'one page in a sitting in 4th grade, 2 pages in a sitting in 5th grade, 3 pages in a sitting in 6th grade' means. The Assessments expect students have that sort of stamina. They're long tests with lots of keyboarding and other tech skills. Make sure your students have practiced working at computers for extended periods.

A good idea is to have students take some online assessments prior to this summative one. These can be created by the teacher using any number of online tools like Google Forms or use already-created tests like those that follow BrainPop videos.

Problem Solving

Make sure students know what to do when a tech problem arises. They should be able to handle simple problems like 'headphones don't work' or 'caps lock won't turn on' or 'my document froze'. This is easily accomplished by having students take responsibility for solving tech problems, with the teacher acting as a resource. They will soon be able to differentiate between what they have the ability to handle and what requires assistance.

A great starting point when teaching problem solving are Common Core Standards for Mathematical Practice. These are aligned with the Math Standards but apply to all facets of learning.

Teacher Training

Make sure teachers administering the online tests are familiar with them and comfortable in that world. They should know how to solve basic tech issues that arise without calling for outside help. This is effectively accomplished by having teachers use technology in their classroom on a regular basis for class activities, as a useful tool in their educational goals. Helps teachers make this happen.

Lesson #4 Problem Solving

Vocabulary	Problem solving	Homework
• Cerebral • Context • Delineate • Evidence • Fail • Sequence • Shortkeys • Strategic • Task	• I can't solve problem (what strategies have you tried?) • I don't like method I picked. (why?) • Sign-up website doesn't work (use your problem-solving strategies) • I didn't finish homework (why?) • Did poorly on ** (Mulligan Rule) • I know how to solve all problems listed (that's OK—you'll be teaching)	Review word processing, quotes, problem-solving strategies Select problem/date for Problem-solving Board Keyboard for 45minutes, 15 minutes at a time
Academic Applications Critical thinking, math, other academic topics	**Required Skills** Familiarity with speaking and listening standards, problem solving, keyboarding, digital citizenship	**Standards** CCSS: Stds for Math.Practice NETS: 4a, 5c

Essential Question

How does technology help problem solving?

Big Idea

Problem solving is challenging and cerebrally-stimulating.

Teacher Preparation/Materials Required

- Have backchannel available.
- Have lesson materials online to preview.
- Update class calendar with class activities.
- Integrate domain-specific tech vocabulary into lesson.
- Ensure all required links are on student digital devices.
- Ask what tech problems students had difficulty with.
- Have Problem-solving Board sign-up available.
- Something happen you weren't prepared for? Show how you react.
- Know which tasks weren't completed last week and whether they are necessary to move forward.

Assessment Strategies

- Previewed required material; came to class prepared
- Annotated workbook (if using)
- Signed up for Board
- Worked well in a group
- Completed warm-up, exit ticket
- Joined classroom conversations
- [tried to] solve own problems
- Decisions followed class rules
- Left room as s/he found it
- Higher order thinking: analysis, evaluation, synthesis
- Habits of mind observed

Steps

Time required: *90-270 minutes, spread throughout the class grading period*
Class warm-up: *Keyboard on class typing program, paying attention to posture*

_____Homework is assigned the week before you start this lesson.
_____Any questions from homework? Expect students to come to class with questions.
_____Review *"How to Teach Students to Problem Solve"* and *"Let Students Learn From Failure"* at the end of the lesson.

_____Discuss what it means to be a 'problem solver'. Who do students go to when they need a problem solved? Parents? Do students believe that person gets it right more often than others? Would they believe most people are wrong half the time?

_____Problem solving is closely aligned with logical thinking, critical thinking, reasoning, and thought habits. Discuss why students should become problem solvers (hint: refer to prior point—most people students go to for assistance are wrong half the time). Discuss characteristics of a 'problem solver' (from Common Core):

- *attend to precision*
- *value evidence*
- *comprehend and critique*
- *demonstrate independence*

- *make sense of problems and persevere in solving them*
- *use appropriate tools strategically*
- *understand other perspectives*

_____Discuss 'Big Idea': How/why is problem solving 'cerebrally-stimulating? Is it fun? Why or why not? Discuss great quotes about problem solving in *Figure 40*.

Figure 40—Problem-solving quotes

Great Quotes About Problem Solving

"In times like these it is good to remember that there have always been times like these."
— Paul Harvey *Broadcaster*

"Never try to solve all the problems at once — make them line up for you one-by-one.
— Richard Sloma

"Some problems are so complex that you have to be highly intelligent and well-informed just to be undecided about them."
— Laurence J. Peter

"Life is a crisis - so what!"
— Malcolm Bradbury

"You don't drown by falling in the water; you drown by staying there."
— Edwin Louis Cole

"The significant problems we face cannot be solved at the same level of thinking we were at when we created them."
— Albert Einstein

"It is not stress that kills us. It is effective adaptation to stress that allows us to live."
— George Vaillant

"The most serious mistakes are not being made as a result of wrong answers. The truly dangerous thing is asking the wrong questions."
— Peter Drucker *Men, Ideas & Politics*

"The problem is not that there are problems. The problem is expecting otherwise and thinking that having problems is a problem."
— Theodore Rubin

It's not that I'm so smart, it's just that I stay with problems longer.
—Albert Einstein

No problem can stand the assault of sustained thinking.
—Voltaire

The problem is not that there are problems. The problem is expecting otherwise and thinking that having problems is a problem.
—Theodore Rubin

Problems are only opportunities with thorns on them.
—Hugh Miller

_____Discuss shortkeys. How are they problem solving? Demonstrate this by asking students to tell you how to perform a skill. Is it easier to share the shortkey?

_____Discuss problem-solving strategies:

- o *Act out a problem*
- o *Break a problem into parts*
- o *Distinguish between relevant and irrelevant information*
- o *Draw a diagram*
- o *Guess and check*
- o *Observe and collect data*
- o *See patterns*

- o *Think logically*
- o *Try to solve before asking for help*
- o *Try, fail, try again*
- o *Use Help files*
- o *Use tools available*
- o *Use what has worked in past*
- o *Work backwards*

_____See *Figure 41* for list of '***How to Solve a Problem***' (full size in appendix):

Figure 41—How to solve a problem

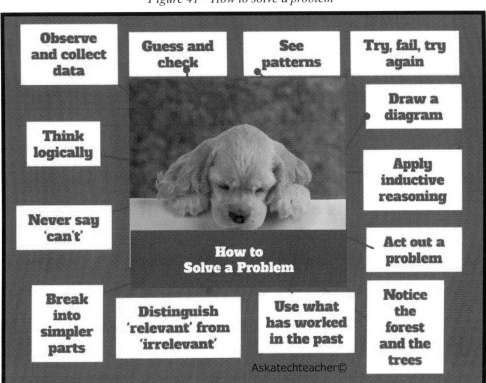

_____When students face a problem, use *Figure 41* strategies to solve it before asking for assistance.
_____Here are two projects to reinforce problem solving in everyday life:

- *Problem-solving Board*
- *Analysis of authentic problem-solving skills*

Problem-solving Board

_____Students sign up to teach classmates common problems faced with technology. Ideally, you have collected these throughout the year from students, other teachers, and parents—the types of problems that stopped students as they tried to use tech. This list might include (*Figure 42*):

Figure 42—Common tech problems

Problem	
My browser is too small	I can't find a tool
Browser toolbar missing	My screen is frozen
Can't exit a program	My menu command is grey
What's today's date	Can't find Bold, Italic
Double click doesn't work	Can't find the program
Start button disappeared	Internet toolbar's gone
Program disappeared	My computer doesn't work
Erased my document	My programs are gone

_____See a longer list at end of lesson. By the end of 7th grade, students should know all of these.

_____Students sign up via a Padlet wall embedded into the class start page (*Figure 43a*), SignUp Genius, a shared spreadsheet (*Figure 43b*) or another method that works for you.

Figure 43a-b—Problem-solving Board sign-ups

_____Note: As you move through the year, keep a list of problems for next year's Board.

_____Here's how it works. Students:

- *Select presentation date and problem to teach classmates by signing up as required.*
- *Get solution from online resources, family, friends, help files--teacher is last resort.*
- *Teach classmates how to solve problem.*
- *Present findings, emphasizing points in a focused, coherent manner with pertinent descriptions, facts, details, examples.*
- *Use appropriate eye contact, adequate volume, and clear pronunciation.*
- *Adapt speech to the context and task.*
- *Take questions. Audience is responsible for making sure speaker makes sense.*

_____Students can get answers through any of the strategies mentioned earlier in this lesson.

_____Review digital rights and responsibilities before using the internet search functions.

_____Entire presentation takes about three minutes. *Figure 44 (Assessment* at end of lesson*)* is a sample of the rubric you can fill out from your iPad.

_____Students should own these tech problems by end of 7th grade.

Figure 44—Problem-solving Board rubric

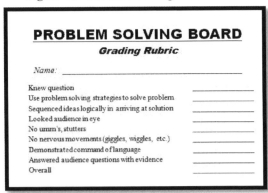

Analysis of authentic problem-solving skills

_____During the grading period, student must identify five-ten problems faced in any part of their life—home, school, or personal—and what problem-solving strategy they used to solve it. They'll record them in a collaborative spreadsheet that is shared with classmates. They'll include (see sample—*Assessment 14a-b*):

- *what tech problem they faced*
- *how they solved it*
- *what strategy they used from the list*
- *any additional comments*

_____At the end of class, it will be a resource students can draw on for future problems.

_____Here's how this works:

- *Student records 5-10 problems faced during the grading period in a Google Spreadsheet created by you and shared with students.*
- *Student answers a Google Forms poll (like* Assessment 14a*) that you create and share.*
- *They must have 5-10 of these during grading period.*

Assessment 14a-b—Problem solving authentic data

_____At the end of the class, share collected data with students.

Class exit ticket:　　*Enter one problem into Google Form.*

Differentiation

- *Have one student create Google Form for Problem Solving to be used to track class results.*
- *Add 'other' to the poll and let students share their own unique strategy with classmates.*
- *Students may present with video or a podcast (done appropriately).*
- *Students may use visual props during their presentation.*
- *If student can't attend class, they can present virtually (with parent permission).*
- *Student has a problem they'd like to share that isn't from the list. Consider allowing it.*

Assessment 15—Problem-solving Board

PROBLEM-SOLVING BOARD
Grading Rubric

Name: _____

Problem solved: _____

Knew question　　　　　　　　　　　_____

Knew answer　　　　　　　　　　　_____

Asked audience for help if didn't know answer _____

No umm's, stutters　　　　　　　　　_____

No nervous movements (giggles, wiggles, etc.) _____

No slang　　　　　　　　　　　　　_____

Overall　　　　　　　　　　　　　_____

Assessment 16—Problem-solving Presentation Assessment

Problem Solving Presentation Assessment

	Project: Problem Solving		Student/Team:			
Pts	**Investigate**	**Design**	**Plan**	**Create**	**Evaluate**	**Group**
0	Team does not complete investigation to standard discussed in class	Team does not complete design to standard discussed in class	Team does not complete plan to standard discussed in class	Team does not complete work to standard discussed in class	Team does not complete evaluation to standard discussed in class	Team does not work together to standard discussed in class
1-2	Team states problem but not clearly, vaguely, understanding skills required. Students have difficulty verbalizing steps required to complete	Team addresses some detail about how project will be presented with selected tool, but leaves critical elements out	Team project plan contains some goals for completing project; timeline is not sustainable	Team creates at least part of storyboard, timeline, product/solution	Team evaluates product/solution as they work, but does not adapt plan or project to problems that arise	Team occasionally works well as a group, but has difficulty allocating work and arriving at consensus
3-4	Team states problem clearly with a strong understanding of skills required. Team shows evidence of researching and describes solution in detail	Team addresses all specifics required to create a how-to and present to class	Team produces a plan that contains a clear and achievable goal for using time wisely during class	Team uses appropriate techniques and equipment, storyboard is effective. Team follows plan, and modifies when required, resulting in good quality project	Team evaluates how-to project and their performance; suggests ways to improve, and tests solution before presenting to class	Team frequently incorporates group member input into project, showing respect for the value of all members
Sub tot al						
Tot al						/20

Figure 45—Common tech problems

Common problems students face with computers

Problem	Solution
1. **My browser is too small**	*Double click blue bar*
2. **Browser toolbar missing**	*Push F11*
3. **Can't exit a program**	*Alt+F4*
4. **What's today's date**	*Hover over clock* *Shift+Alt+D in Word*
5. **Double click doesn't work**	*Push enter*
7. **Start button disappeared**	*Use Windows button*
8. **Program disappeared**	*Check taskbar*
9. **Erased my document**	*Ctrl+Z*
10. **I can't find a tool**	*Right click on screen; it'll show most common tools*
11. **My screen is frozen**	*Clear a dialogue box* *Press Escape four times*
12. **My menu command is grey**	*Press escape 4 times and try again*
13. **Can't find Bold, Italic, Underline**	*Use Ctrl+B, Ctrl+I, Ctrl+U*
14. **Can't find the program**	*Push Start, use 'Search' field*
15. **Internet toolbar's gone**	*Push F11*
16. **My computer doesn't work**	*Check monitor/tower power, plugs*
17. **My programs are gone**	*Are you logged in correctly?*

Article 12—How to Teach Students to Solve Problems

How to Teach Students to Solve Problems

Of all the skills students learn in school, **problem solving** arguably is the most valuable and the hardest to learn. It's fraught with uncertainty—what if the student looks stupid as he tries? What if everyone's watching and he can't do it—isn't it better not to try? What if it works, but not the way Everyone wants it to? When you're a student, it's understandable when they decide to let someone tell them what to do.

But this isn't the type of learner we want to build. We want risk-takers, those willing to be the load-bearing pillar of the class. And truthfully, by a certain age, kids want to make up their own mind. Our job as teachers is to provide the skills necessary for them to make wise, effective decisions.

It's not a stand-alone subject. It starts with a habit of inquiry in all classes—math, LA, history, science, any of them. I constantly ask students questions, get them to think and evaluate, provide evidence that supports process as well as product. Whether they're writing, reading, or creating an art project, I want them thinking what they're doing and why.

Common Core puts problem solving front and center. It comes up in ELA ("*Students will be challenged and asked questions that push them to refer back to what they've read. This stresses critical-thinking, problem-solving, and analytical skills that are required for success in college, career, and life.*"), but is inescapable in Math. In fact, students cannot fully meet the Math Standards without understanding how to effectively approach the unknown. Consider the Standards for Mathematical Practice that overlay all grade levels K-12:

- *Make sense of problems and persevere in solving them*
- *Reason abstractly and quantitatively*
- *Construct viable arguments and critique the reasoning of others*
- *Model*
- *Use appropriate tools strategically*
- *Attend to precision*
- *Look for and make use of structure*
- *Look for and express regularity in repeated reasoning*

Do these sound like great strategies for more than math? How about deciding what classes to take? Or whether to make a soccer or basketball game on the weekend? Or which college to attend? Using these eight tools strategically, with precision, and tenaciously is a great first step.

The question becomes: How do students **learn to use them**? Certainly, as they accomplish their grade-level math curriculum, you as teacher remind them they aren't doing a multiplication problem (or an Algebra one); rather they're reasoning abstractly or using appropriate tools strategically, or expressing regularity in repeated reasoning. But for deep learning, hands-on authentic experience is required. Let's say, for example, the class is investigating the purchase of an MP3 player. Should they purchase an iPod, a smartphone, a dedicated use MP3 player, or a different option? How do students arrive at a decision—solve that problem? Ask students to work through the steps below as they address a decision. Ask them to note where they accomplish one or more of the Standards for Mathematical Practice above:

1. What do you want in an MP3 player? Should it play music, show videos, pictures, communicate with others, be a phone also? Make that list so you know how to evaluate information as you collect it (**compare/contrast).**

2. What do you know about the topic (**evidence**)? Have you seen some you liked or didn't like? What have you heard about those on your list? You are a good resource to yourself. Don't discount that. You'll be surprised how much you know on a variety of topics. This step is important to college and career. Future employers and schools want you to think, to use your intelligence and your knowledge to evaluate and solve problems.

3. What advice do knowledgeable friends have (**perspective taking, collaboration**)? You want the input of MP3 users. Your friends will think whatever they own is the best, because they're vested in that choice, but listen to their evidence and the conclusions they draw based on that. This is important to a team-oriented environment. Listen to all sides, even if you don't agree.

4. **Dig deeper (close reading).** Check other resources (**uncover knowledge**). This includes:
   o *people who don't like the product*
   o *online sources. Yep, you might as well get used to online research if you aren't yet. Statistics show more people get their news from blogs than traditional media (newspapers, TV) and you know where blogs are.*
   o *your parents who will bring up topics friends didn't, like cost, longevity, reliability*

5. **Evaluate your resources (integration of knowledge).** How much money do you have? Eliminate the choices that don't fit your constraints (money, time, use, etc.) If there are several choices that seem to work, this will help you make the decision. You might have to save money or get a job so you can afford the one you've chosen. Or, you might decide to settle for a cheaper version. Just make sure you are aware of how you made the choice and are satisfied with it.

6. What are the **risks involved** in making the decision (**reflection**)? Maybe buying an MP3 player means you can't do something else you wanted. Are you comfortable with that choice?

7. **Make a decision (transfer learning).** That's right. Make a decision and live with it knowing you've considered all available information and evaluated it logically and objectively.

Optionally, you might have students evaluate problem solving in their favorite game, say, Minecraft. All it requires is that as they play, think about what they're doing:

- *What is the goal of Minecraft? How is it best achieved*
- *What does the student know about playing the game that can be used in achieving the goal?*
- *Does working with friends and gaining feedback make life easier in Minecraft?*
- *How does experience in the game affect progress?*
- *And so on...*

This is how students become the problem solvers required of their Future. When the day comes that how they solve a problem affects the direction their life takes (college, career, marriage, children, a tattoo), they'll be happy to have strategies that make it easier.

5 Must-have Skills for New Tech Teachers

If you teach technology, it's likely you were thrown into it by your Admin. You used to be a first grade teacher or the science expert or maybe even the librarian and suddenly, you walked into school one day and found out you'd become that tech person down the hall you were always in awe of, the one responsible for classroom computers, programs, curriculum, and everything in between. Now that's you—the go-to person for tech problems, computer quirks, crashes and freezes, and tech tie-ins for classroom inquiry.

You have no idea where to begin.

Here's a peek into your future: On that first propitious day, everything will change. Your colleagues will assume you received a data upload of the answers to every techie question. It doesn't matter that yesterday, you were one of them. Now, you will be on a pedestal, colleague's necks craned upward as they ask, *"How do I get the class screen to work?" "We need microphones for a lesson I'm starting in three minutes. Can you please-please-please fix them?"* You will nod your head, smile woodenly, and race to your classroom for the digital manuals (if you're lucky) or Google for online help.

Let me start by saying: Don't worry. Really. You'll learn by doing, just as we teach students. Take a deep breath, engage your brain, and let your brilliance shine.

That's the number one skill—confidence—but there are a five other practical strategies that have worked for those who came before you. Consider:

Be a communicator

Talk to grade-level teachers weekly. Scaffold your lessons with what they teach. Ask them to stay during tech class and offer on-the-spot tie-ins between what you teach and they say in class. Yes, they might want/need the time for planning or meetings, but the benefit to students of this team-teaching approach is tremendous. And it benefits the teachers, also. Many of them are not yet sold on integrating tech into their classrooms. They know they must if they're in one of the 46 Common Core adoptive states, but they don't like it, don't know how to do it, and don't see why it's so important. When they see you do it, they will be more willing to weave it into their lessons. For example, when they hear how you reinforce good keyboarding skills, they will be more likely to insist on those traits in their classroom.

Be a risk-taker

Flaunt your cheeky geekiness. Start a Twitter feed. Use your iPhone as a timer or the iPad to scan in an art project for a digital portfolio. At any opportunity, share your geek glee. Let them see that tech is part of life, not a subject taught in school. It's a habit, a time-saver, a facilitator, a joy. It won't take long to convert them. A couple of admiring glances from friends or appreciative thanks from parents and they'll be sold.

Be an explorer

Go to the grade-level classrooms and demonstrate how technology is part of learning. This can be via iPads, the class pod of computers, the netbooks, or whatever is available. Ask students what they are doing in class and offer tech methods to make it easier. For example, are they submitting homework in a pile on the teacher's desk? Try a dropbox—or email. Could they type reports instead of handwrite them (I know—this gets philosophic, so be prepared for that discussion)? Instead of hand-drawn posters where success leans toward the artistically-talented, could they use Glogster? Encourage students to plug in during class.

Be a negotiator

You need parental buy-in on tech ed, but it is a topic typically outside their comfort zone. I often hear from 2nd grade parents that their children know more than they do (I'm talking MS Office, internet use, and some online tools). Understand that this frightens them and part of your job is to mitigate their fears. Here are some ideas:

- Have your door always open. Be ready and willing to talk with them about how to complete their child's projects—not so they can do for them, but so they feel it is within their child's grasp. Take as long as needed and welcome them to return.
- Answer parent tech questions, even if it's about a home computer. My experience is these are often simple, but intimidating. If you mitigate fear, you maximize support for tech ed.
- Offer a parent class to teach skills students are learning. Listen to your group. What makes these intelligent adults nervous about tech? Solve it for them. I often start with an agenda and end with a free-for-all, where I answer questions or help parents create fliers for soccer teams or solve home-based tech problems. It's all good. They leave feeling I'm a partner.

Don't take life too seriously

Have a sense of humor about everything. You're going to have computer meltdowns. It's why robots can't replace teachers, so embrace chaos. One of the true joys of tech is the puzzling. Why doesn't the mouse work? Why does a website work on one computer and not another? Where'd the taskbar go? Let students see how much fun it is to engage the brain.

Article 14—Let Students Learn From Failure

Let Students Learn From Failure

Too often, students—and teachers—believe learning comes from success when in truth, it's as likely to be the product of failure. Knowing what doesn't work is a powerful weapon as we struggle to think critically about the myriad issues along our path to college and/or career. As teachers, it's important we reinforce the concept that learning has many faces. Here are ten ways to teach through failure:

Use the Mulligan Rule

What's the Mulligan Rule? Any golfers? A mulligan in golf is a do-over. Blend that concept into your classroom. Common Core expects students to write-edit-resubmit. Make that part of every lesson. After submittal, give students a set amount of time to redo and resubmit their work. Some won't, but those who do will learn much more by the process.

Don't define success as perfection

When you're discussing a project or a lesson, don't define it in terms of checkboxes or line items or 100% accuracy. Think about your favorite book. Is it the same as your best friend's? How about the vacation you're planning—would your sister pick that dream location? Education is no different. Many celebrated 'successful' people failed at school because they were unusual thinkers. Most famously: Bill Gates, who dropped out of college because he believed he could learn more from life than professors.

Education pedagogists categorize these sorts of ideas as ***higher-order thinking*** and ***Habits of Mind***—traits that contribute to critical thinking, problem solving, and thriving. These are difficult to quantify on a report card, but critical to life-long success. Observe students as they work. Notice their risk-taking curiosity, how they color outside the lines. Anecdotally assess their daily efforts and let that count as much as a summative exam that judges a point in time.

Let students see you fail

One reason lots of teachers keep the same lesson plans year-to-year is they are vetted. The teacher won't be surprised by a failure or a question they can't answer. Honestly, this is a big reason why many eschew technology: Too often, it fails at just that critical moment.

Revise your mindset. Don't hide your failures from students. Don't apologize. Don't be embarrassed or defeated. Show them how you recover from failure. Model the steps you take to move to Plan B, C, even X. Show your teaching grit and students will understand that, too, is what they're learning: How to recover from failure.

Share strategies for problem solving

Problems are inevitable. Everyone has them. What many people DON'T have is a strategy to address them. Share these with students. Post these on the classroom wall. When students have problems, suggest they try a strategy from this list, and then another, and another. Eventually, the problem will resolve, the result of a tenacious, gritty attack by an individual who refuses to give up.

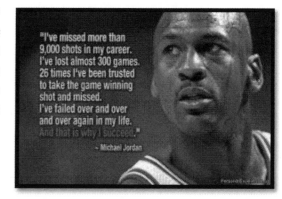

Exult in problems

If you're geeky, you love problems, puzzles, and the maze that leads from question to answer. It doesn't intimidate or frighten you, it energizes you. Share that enthusiasm with students. They are as likely to meet failure as success in their lives; show them your authentic, granular approach to addressing that eventuality.

Assess grit

Success isn't about right and wrong. More often, it's about grit—tenacity, working through a process, and not giving up when failure seems imminent. Statistically, over half of people say they 'succeeded' (in whatever venture they tried) not by being the best in the field but because they were the last man standing.

Integrate that into your lessons. Assess student effort, their attention to detail, their ability to transfer knowledge from earlier lessons to this one, their enthusiasm for learning, how often they tried-failed-retried, and that they completed the project. Let students know they will be evaluated on those criteria more than the perfection of their work.

Let students teach each other

There are many paths to success. Often, what works for one person is based on their perspective, personal history, and goals. This is at the core of differentiation: that we communicate in multiple ways—visually, orally, tactally—in an effort to reach all learning styles.

Even so, students may not understand. Our failure to speak in a language they understand will become their failure to learn the material. Don't let that happen. Let students be the teachers. They often pick a relationship or comparison you wouldn't think of. Let students know that in your classroom, brainstorming and freedom of speech are problem-solving strategies.

Don't be afraid to move the goal posts

Even if it's in the middle of a lesson. That happens all the time in life and no one apologizes, feels guilty, or accommodates your anger. When you teach a lesson, you constantly reassess based on student progress. Do the same with assessment.

But make it fair. Let students know the changes are rooted in your desire that they succeed. If you can't make that argument, you probably shouldn't make the change.

Success is as much serendipity as planning

Think of Velcro and post-it notes—life-changing products resulting from errors. They surprised their creators and excited the world. Keep those possibilities available to students.

Don't reward speed

Often, students who finish first are assigned the task of helping neighbors or playing time-filler games. Finishing early should not be rewarded. Or punished. Sometimes it means the student thoroughly understood the material. Sometimes it means they glossed over it. Students are too often taught finishing early is a badge of honor, a mark of their expertise. Remove that judgment and let it be what it is.

Lesson #5 Digital Citizenship

Vocabulary	Problem solving	Homework
• Avatar • Cyberbullying • Cyberstalking • Digital citizen • Digital commerce • Fair use • Flaming • GPS • Netiquette • Plagiarism • Public domain	• Can't find answer to problem (did you try problem-solving strategies?) • Internet toolbar disappeared (click 'full screen mode' on CB) • Parents can't know where I am (why?) • Online's anonymous! Why follow rules? (do the right thing even when no one's watching—see poster) • My parents let me spend money online (have you discussed it with them?) • My parents let me have a FB account	Draw a picture using a graphic program Review notes to prepare for project Watch all videos; prepare reflections Practice keyboarding for 45minutes, 15 minutes at a time
Academic Applications	**Required Skills**	**Standards**
research, collaboration, sharing, online safety	Familiarity with social media, speaking/listening skills, problem solving, keyboarding, digital citizenship	CCSS: CCRA.L.6 NETS: 2a-d

Essential Question

How should I act in the virtual neighborhood?

Big Idea

The digital world bestows rights and requires responsibilities.

Teacher Preparation/Materials Required

- Integrate domain-specific tech vocabulary into lesson.
- Have lesson materials online to preview lesson.
- Know whether you need extra time to complete lesson.
- Make available digital citizenship links.
- Have student workbooks available (if using).
- Ask what tech problems students had difficulty with.
- Talk with grade-level team to tie into conversations about using the internet.
- Know which tasks weren't completed last week and whether they are necessary to move forward.
- Something happen you weren't prepared for? Show students how you fix the emergency without a meltdown and with a positive attitude.

Assessment Strategies

- Previewed required material; came to class prepared
- Worked independently
- Used good keyboarding habits
- Completed warm-up, exit ticket
- Joined classroom conversations
- [tried to] solve own problems
- Decisions followed class rules
- Left room as s/he found it
- Higher order thinking: analysis, evaluation, synthesis
- Habits of mind observed

Steps

Time required: *90 minutes or more, spread throughout the school year*
Class warm-up: *Keyboarding on the class typing program*

_____**Homework is assigned the week before this unit so students are prepared.**

_____Any questions from homework? Expect students to review unit and come to class prepared.

_____Goals for this unit include:

- *students understand human, cultural, societal issues related to technology and practice legal/ethical behavior*
- *students exhibit a positive attitude toward technology, a mindset that supports collaboration, learning and productivity*
- *students advocate and practice safe, legal, and responsible use of information*
- *students understand 'digital footprint'*
- *students demonstrate personal responsibility for lifelong learning*
- *students understand part they play in preventing cyberbullying*
- *students use internet legally to gather information*
- *students use technology and digital media strategically and capably*

_____Discuss what it means to be a good digital citizen? Why is this important if no one knows who you are? Must you be honest if you're anonymous? Who does it hurt? What does the quote in *Figure 46* mean—by legendary football coach, John Wooden?

Figure 46—Personal responsibility quote

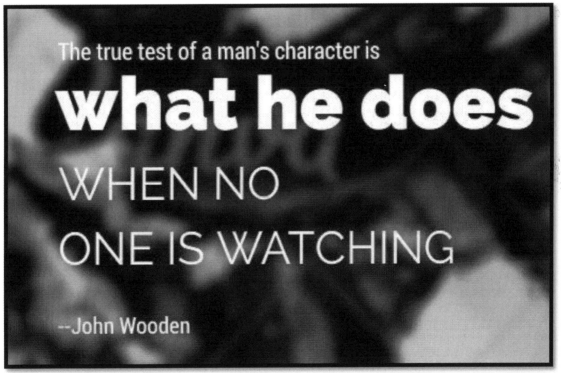

_____Throughout the school year when relevant, discuss the topics listed in *Figure 47* under '7th grade'. If you haven't covered K-6 topics, discuss those before moving into 7th-grade material. They scaffold learning, making lessons more authentic and relevant. Where possible, let students lead the discussion, set the pace, and ask questions that are native to them. Be prepared to spend extra time and adapt to student interests as needed. There is no rush. It's more important that students understand than get through all topics.

Figure 47—Digital Citizenship topics

Digital Citizenship Topics	K	1	2	3	4	5	6	7	8
Cyberbullying	x	x	x	x	x	x	x	x	x
Digital commerce					x		x	x	x
Digital communications				x		x	x	x	x
Digital footprint and Online presence			x	x	x	x	x	x	x
Digital law				x			x	x	x
Digital privacy			x	x	x	x	x	x	
Digital rights and responsibilities	x	x	x	x	x	x	x	x	x
Digital search and research				x	x	x	x	x	x
Fair use, Public domain			x	x	x	x	x	x	x
Image copyright			x		x	x	x	x	x
Internet safety	x	x	x	x	x	x	x	x	x
Netiquette		x	x	x	x	x	x	x	x
Online Plagiarism			x	x	x	x	x	x	x
Passwords	x	x	x		x	x		x	x
Social media						x	x	x	x
Stranger Danger	x	x	x						

_____Preview the topics to be sure they're appropriate for your unique student group.

_____Before beginning, put backchannel device onto class screen (Socrative, Padlet, class Twitter account, Google Forms). Show students how to access it on their devices.

Cyberbullying

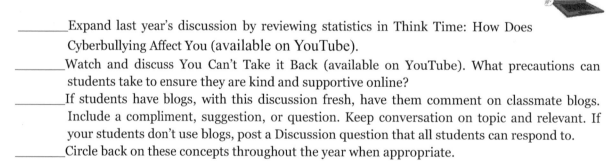

_____Expand last year's discussion by reviewing statistics in Think Time: How Does Cyberbullying Affect You (available on YouTube).

_____Watch and discuss You Can't Take it Back (available on YouTube). What precautions can students take to ensure they are kind and supportive online?

_____If students have blogs, with this discussion fresh, have them comment on classmate blogs. Include a compliment, suggestion, or question. Keep conversation on topic and relevant. If your students don't use blogs, post a Discussion question that all students can respond to.

_____Circle back on these concepts throughout the year when appropriate.

Digital Commerce

_____What is 'digital commerce' (the buying and selling of goods online)?

_____How many students have bought something online? If so, did they:

- *check with parents first?*
- *verify website was legitimate and secure?*
- *feel safe because friends were shopping there?*

_____Demonstrate what to look for by using a legitimate site like Amazon.com. Go through process of buying something online:

- *Students must have the money (even with a credit card).*
- *They must provide sensitive information (i.e., credit card number).*
- *Website keeps information and might sell it.*

_____What are the pros and cons of digital commerce? Include:

- *It's easy.*
- *It's private.*
- *Products from other countries are available, even those in conflict with host nation laws and morals, i.e., pornography, illegal music, other illegal downloads.*
- *Website keeps your private information—or worse, sells it.*
- *Website could be hacked and your financial and personal information stolen.*
- *Website could take your money and provide no product.*
- *Website could steal not only your credit card but your identity. Discuss that.*

_____Consider this scenario: 'Josie' sees a Wii online for $20. She knows that is too cheap. What should she do?

_____What is the best way to be good digital citizens and effective consumers?

_____Circle back on these concepts throughout the year when appropriate.

Digital Communications

_____Digital communications includes:

- *email*
- *IMs*
- *texting*
- *cell phones*
- *chat rooms*

_____Review email etiquette:

- *use proper formatting, spelling, grammar*
- *CC anyone you mention*
- *make 'Subject line' topic of email*
- *answer swiftly*
- *re-read before sending*
- *don't use all caps—THIS IS SHOUTING*
- *don't attach unnecessary files*
- *don't overuse high priority*
- *don't email confidential information*
- *don't email offensive remarks*
- *don't forward chain letters or spam*
- *don't open attachments from strangers*

_____Why is correct grammar/spelling important in email and not so much with texting? Hint:

Consider CCSS.W.7.4: *Produce clear and coherent writing in which development, organization, and style are appropriate to* **task and audience**.

_____Email is often required for online tools. Do students have one? Do they use parents?

_____Discuss 'spam'. What is it? Why is it sent? Cover these reasons:

- *It's a free way to find people interested in a product.*
- *Sender earns money on 'click-through' (what's a 'click through'?).*
- *It gathers personal information.*
- *It wears the receiver down until they finally order the product.*
- *It spreads viruses that hurt computers (why do that?).*

_____What should students do when spam shows up in their email?

_____When students get an email, follow this simple checklist:

- *Do you know sender?*
- *Is it legitimate? For example, does the 'voice' sound like the sender?*
- *Is sender asking for personal information? Legitimate sources never do.*
- *Is there an attachment? If so, don't open it.*

_____Have students send a well-built email to a classmate (if students have email accounts) and reply to one they receive appropriately.

_____Is it rude to text around others? Watch and discuss Digital Passport Communication (available on SchoolTube)

_____Does school allow cell phones? What are reasons teens should have one:

- *stay in touch with parents*
- *for emergencies*
- *so parents know where they are (via GPS)*
- *to collaborate and share*

_____What are reasons they shouldn't?

_____How many parents try to control cell phone use by:

- *limiting student time on it*
- *limiting the plan*
- *having them share in the cost*
- *set up text-free zones, like dinner*

_____Does this work? What would students suggest instead?

_____Discuss responsible use of cell phones, including:

- *Don't let them interfere with classwork.*
- *Don't use them for academic dishonesty or cyberbullying.*
- *Don't use them to share inappropriate information.*

_____What about chat rooms? Here are rules for chatting online:

- *parents approve; student shares nothing private, never meets an online 'friend'*

> • *student agrees to leave the site and tell an adult if it becomes uncomfortable*
> • *student screen name includes nothing linkable to student*

_____Discuss **texting** (**article at end of lesson**).
_____Is it rude to **text** around people?
_____Circle back on these concepts throughout the year when appropriate.

Digital footprint

_____Last year, students Googled their names to discover their digital footprint. Do this again. Has it changed?
_____Watch and discuss digital footprints (all available on YouTube):

- *Digital Footprint*
- *Digital Life 101*
- *What's a digital dossier (footprint)*

_____Circle back on these concepts throughout the year when appropriate.

Digital Law and Plagiarism

_____More on this in the lesson on *Image Legalities*.
_____Some people want to share their work. Watch and discuss *Wanna Work Together* (available from Creative Commons) about licensing.
_____Circle back on these concepts throughout the year when appropriate.

Digital privacy

_____Watch and discuss *6 Degrees of Information* (available on YouTube). How easy it is to find about anyone through crumbs left online.
_____Watch and discuss the online life of a photo (available on YouTube).
_____Watch *Two Kinds of Stupid* (available on YouTube).
_____Discuss using avatars to protect online privacy. For more, see lesson on *Digital Tools*.
_____Expand discussion into *Online Reputations* (video through Carnegie Cyber Academy).
_____Wrap up with a discussion on hacking. Talk about how kids 'hack' game codes. Should they? Is it a victimless crime? What other issues should they consider? What is the difference between 'hacking' and 'cracking'? Black Hat and White Hat?
_____Circle back on these concepts throughout the year when appropriate.

Digital rights and responsibilities

_____Watch *Digital Rights and Responsibilities* (available on YouTube).
_____What are 'they? Most students come up with 'rights'—access to internet, use of information, creation of documents to be published and shared, freedom of expression—but what are 'responsibilities' of a digital citizen? Help students come up with:

- *Don't share personal information. Don't ask others for theirs.*
- *Be aware of your cyberspace surroundings. Act accordingly.*
- *As in real life, be kind to others. Anonymity doesn't protect you.*
- *If someone is 'flaming' another, help stop it within your abilities.*

_____Circle back on these concepts throughout the year when appropriate.

Digital search and research

_____*Discussed in "Internet Search and Research" lesson.*

Fair use, Public domain, Image Copyright

_____*Discussed in "Online Image Legalities" lesson.*

Internet safety

_____Discuss password guidelines and rules. Remind students they never share passwords.

_____Watch and discuss *Broken Friendship* (available on YouTube).

_____Watch video on passwords (available on YouTube).

_____Ask students how they protect their passwords and online safety when using the Internet.

_____What's the difference between 'http' and 'https'? How important is this level of security?

Social Media

_____What is 'social media'? What should be included on a social media profile?

_____What is responsible social media use? Think about digital rights and responsibilities.

_____What are long-term consequences of using/abusing social media? What about cyberbullying,

_____Watch *Teens Talk Back* (available on YouTube). Discuss.

_____Circle back on these concepts throughout the year when appropriate.

_____Watch and discuss *Hashtag, You're It* (available on YouTube).

_____In groups, discuss social media. What are challenges of so much openness? Then discuss as a class and share thoughts via a blog post or class Twitter feed. Thoughts should be objective with domain-specific language appropriate to the task, audience, and purpose.

_____Post the pyramid in *Figure 48b* on the wall in your classroom (full-size poster in appendix). Every time you've discussed a topic, check it off.

_____Circle back on these concepts throughout the year when appropriate.

Netiquette

_____What is '**netiquette**' to a seventh grader?

_____Discuss the list of criteria in *Figure 48a* (full-size poster in appendix)?

Figure 48a—Netiquette Rules; 48b—Digital pyramid

Class exit ticket: **Tweet on the class Twitter account (or comment on the class blog) about how to stay safe online.**

Differentiation

- Assign a student to enter classwork and homework due date into class calendar.
- Full digital citizenship curriculum for K-8 available from Structured Learning.
- Create a Glogster poster on what it means to be a good digital citizen with links to resources.
- Blog about a video watched during unit. Why is it important to be good digital citizens?
- Create a map showing where student goes digitally daily/weekly. Connect locations with 'footprints'. At the end of the path, add a Tagxedo with all words and locations in map.
- Create poll on one of the topics above and embed into student blog or wiki. For example, for cell phone use, student might ask classmates to select all that apply:

  - I can use my cell any time I want.
  - I often use my cell at meals.
  - I often use my cell in the car.
  - I have a limit on how much time I can spend on phone.

- Track and post where students found sources for class research project by placemarking on a world map. This will show how diverse we are in collecting information.
- Draw a picture of a digital customer. Make pieces interactive, linked back to products they use and where to find them. Give proper credit. Include IPads, iPhones, clothing bought at an online store.
- Debate social media pros and cons. Tape and upload to class website or blog.
- Follow Common Sense's Digital Passport units on cyberbullying, internet search, digital world.

11 Ways Twitter Improves Education

A teacher must communicate with students in a way they will hear. Twitter might be perfect for your class.

Twitter can easily be dismissed as a waste of time in the elementary school classroom. Students get distracted. They might see inappropriate tweets. How does a teacher manage a room full of Tweeple?

But, you've read a lot about Twitters usefulness in writing skills and sharing information so you—of the Open Minded Attitude—want to try it. Here's ammunition for what often turns into a pitched, take-sides verbal brawl as well-intended educators try to reach a compromise on using Twitter (in fact, many Web 2.0 tools—blogs, wikis, discussion forums, and websites that require registrations and log-ins—can be added to the list) that works for all stakeholders:

You learn to be concise

Twitter gives you only 140 characters to get the entire message across. *Letters, numbers, symbols, punctuation and spaces all count as characters on Twitter.* Wordiness doesn't work. Twitter counts every keystroke and won't publish anything with a minus in front of the word count.

At first blush, that seems impossible. It's not. It challenges students to know the right word for every situation. People with a big vocabulary are at an advantage because they don't use collections of little words to say what they mean. All those hints from English teachers about picture nouns and action verbs and getting rid of adverbs and adjectives take on new importance to the Twitter aficionado.

Twitter isn't intimidating

A blank white page holds hundreds of words, demanding you fill in each line margin to margin is intimidating. 140 characters aren't. Anyone can write 140 characters about a topic. Students write their 140 characters and more, learn to whittle back, leave out emotional words, adjectives and adverbs, pick better nouns and verbs because they need the room. Instead of worrying what to say on all those empty lines, they feel successful.

Students learn manners

Social networks are all about netiquette. People thank others for their assistance, ask politely for help, and encourage contributions from others. Use this framework to teach students how to engage in a community— be it physical or virtual. It's all about manners.

Students learn to focus

With only 140 characters, you can't get off topic or cover tangential ideas. You have to save those for a different tweet. Tweeple like that trait in writers. They like to hear the writer's thoughts on the main topic, not meanderings. When forced to write this way, students will find it doesn't take a paragraph to make a point. Use the right words, people get it. Consider that the average reader gives a story seven seconds before moving on. OK, yes, that's more than 140 characters, but not much.

Here's an idea: If you must get into those off-topic thoughts, write them in a separate tweet.

Students learn to share

Start a tweet stream where students share research on a topic. Maybe it's Ancient Greece. Have each student share their favorite website (using a #hashtag — maybe #ancientgreece) and you've created a resource others can use. Expand on that wonderful skill learned in kindergarten about sharing personal toys. Encourage students to RT (retweet) posts they found particularly relevant or helpful.

Writing short messages perfects the art of "headlining"

Writers call this the title. Bloggers and journalists call it the headline. Whatever the label, it has to be cogent and pithy enough to pull the audience in and make them read the article. That's a tweet.

Tweets need to be written knowing that tweeple can @reply

This is a world of social networks where people comment on what you say. That's a good thing. It's feedback and builds an online community, be it for socializing or school. Students learn to construct their arguments expecting others to respond, question, and comment. Not only does this develop the skill of persuasive writing, students learn to have a thick skin, take comments with a grain of salt and two grains of aspirin.

#Hashtags develop a community

Create #hashtags that will help students organize their tweets—#help if they have a question, #homework for homework help. Establish class hashtags to deal with subjects you want students to address.

Students learn tolerance for all opinions

Why? Because Tweeple aren't afraid to voice their thoughts. They only have 140 characters—so they spit it right out. Because the Twitter stream is a public forum (in a classroom, the stream can be private, visible to only class members), students understand what they say is out there forever. That's daunting. Take the opportunity to teach students about their public profile. Represent themselves well with good grammar, good spelling, and well-chosen tolerant ideas. Don't be emotional or spiteful because it can't be taken back. Rather than shying away from exposing students to the world, use Twitter to teach students how to live in it.

Twitter, the Classroom Notepad

I tried this out after I read about it through my PLN. Springboarding off student engagement, Twitter can act as your classroom notepad. Have students enter their thoughts, note, and reactions while you talk. By the time class is done, the entire class has an overview of the conversation with extensions and connections that help everyone get more out of the inquiry.

Twitter is always open

Inspiration doesn't always strike in that 50-minute class period. Sometimes it's after class, after school, after dinner, even 11 at night. Twitter doesn't care. Whatever schedule is best for students to discover the answer, Twitter is there. If you post a tweet question and ask students to join the conversation, they will respond in the time frame that works best for them. That's a new set of rules for classroom participation, and these are student-centered, uninhibited by a subjective time period. Twitter doesn't even care if a student missed class. S/he can catch up via tweets and then join in.

Article 16—Will texting destroy writing skills?

Will Texting Destroy Writing Skills?

Across the education landscape, student text messaging is a bone of contention among teachers. It's not an issue in the lower grades because most K-5 schools successfully ban cell phones during school hours. Where it's a problem are grades 6-12, when teachers realize it's a losing battle to separate students from their phones for eight hours.

The overarching discussion among educators is texting's utility in providing authentic experiences that transfer learning from the class to real life. Today, I'll focus on a piece of that: Does text messaging contribute to 1) shortening student attention span, or 2) destroying their nascent writing ability

Let's start with attention span. TV, music, over-busy daily schedules, and frenetic family life are likely causes of a student's short attention span. To fault text messaging is like blaming the weather for sinking the Titanic. Texting has less to do with the inability to spit out a full sentence than a student's 1) need for quickness of communication, 2) love for secrecy, and 3) joy of knowing a language adults don't.

What about writing? In the thirty years I've been teaching everyone from kindergarteners to college, I can tell you with my hand on a Bible that children are flexible, masters at adjusting actions to circumstances (like the clothes they wear for varying events and the conversations they have with varying groups of people). There is no evidence to support that these elastic, malleable creatures are suddenly rigid in their writing style, unable to toggle between casual texting shorthand with friends and a professional writing structure in class.

In general, I'm a fan of anything that encourages student writing, and there are real benefits to giving students the gift of textual brevity rather than the stomach-churning fear of a five-paragraph structured essay. I've done quite a few articles on the benefits of Twitter's 140-character approach to writing and my teacher's gut says the same applies to text messaging. Truth, studies are inconclusive. Some suggest that because young students do not yet have a full grasp of basic writing skills, they have difficulty shifting between texting's abbreviated spelling-doesn't-matter language and Standard English. But a British study suggested students classify 'texting' as 'word play', separate from the serious writing done for class so it results in no deterioration of writing skills. Yet another study found that perception of danger from texting is greater than reality: 70% of the professionals at one college believed texting had harmful effects on student writing skills. However, when analyzed, the opposite was true: Texting was actually beneficial.

It's interesting to note that texting can be a boon to children who struggle with face-to-face situations. These 'special needs' students flourish in an environment where they can write rather than speak, think through an answer before communicating it, and provide pithy conversational gambits in lieu of extended intercourse. In the texting world, socially-challenged children are like every other child, hidden by the anonymity of a faceless piece of metal and circuits.

To blame texting for student academic failures is a cop-out by the parents and teachers entrusted with a child's education. Treated as an authentic scaffold to academic goals, teachers will quickly incorporate it into their best-practices pedagogy of essential tools for learning.

How to Thrive as a Digital Citizen

Thanks to the pervasiveness of easy-to-use technology and the accessibility of the internet, teachers longer lecture from a dais as the purveyor of knowledge. Now, students expect to take ownership of their education, participate actively in the learning process, and transfer knowledge learned in the classroom to their lives.

In days past, technology was used to find information (via the internet) and display it (often via PowerPoint). No longer. Now, if you ask a fifth-grade student to write a report on space exploration, here's how s/he will proceed:

Understand 'Digital Citizenship'

Before the engines of research can start, every student must understand what it means to be a citizen of the World Wide Web. Why? Most inquiry includes a foray into the unknown vastness of the www. Students learn early (I start kindergartners with an age-appropriate introduction) how to thrive in that virtual world. It is a pleasant surprise that digital citizenship has much the same rules as their home town:

Don't talk to bad guys, look both ways before crossing the (virtual) street, don't go places you know nothing about, play fair, pick carefully who you trust, don't get distracted by bling, and sometimes stop everything and take a nap.

In internet-speak, students learn to follow good netiquette, not to plagiarize the work of others, avoid scams, stay on the website they choose, not to be a cyber-bully, and avoid the virtual 'bad guys'. Current best practices are not to hide students from any of these, but to teach them how to manage these experiences.

That's harder than it sounds. Children, as new digital citizens, feel anonymous in the vastness provided by the www. They think they can say/do anything and no one will know. But they don't yet know about something called a 'digital footprint' that tracks every step an individual takes across the internet landscape and—to many people's horror—forgets nothing. Comments made in high school, pictures posted in college, are available for a future employer to view.

Yes, this isn't learned in kindergarten. In fact, it takes me six years, a little bit at a time, before students accept these truths as their own.

Research smart

Today's students are expected to understand how to find information despite the billions (literally) of places to look. For example, if you Google 'space', you get over 4 billion hits. That much information is worthless. Students must learn how to whittle this list down to what their specific need is.

Collaborate with others

Where students used to have to find a common time that everyone was free, arrange to meet at someone's house or the library, and then share notes by copying them and passing out hard copies, now students can sit in their own bedrooms, or on their own laptop or iPad. They collect information, post it to a common document, and edit it collectively in one of many ways:

- via Google Apps—an Education account that allows for real-time editing of documents and enables teachers to see who's doing what
- through a Wiki—students collect all the information on a required subject in one spot and go from there
- for larger docs, a Cloud-based storage site like DropBox—invite group members to view
- with the teacher via email or the transparency offered by Google Docs (now, Google Drive)
- with subject experts via Skype

Share the wealth

Sharing used to be via PowerPoint slideshows, a written report, a student-driven play, maybe a poster. Technology has opened the floodgates of student creativity. Some Web 2.0 options for publishing are:

- blogs—post the article of all classmates and comment on each other's work. Then, edit the article to incorporate changes
- website—via Google Sites. If students have Google Apps for Education, this is included and requires no additional set-ups or log-ins.
- wikis—again, a great way to share information, videos, music, widgets of all kinds in a creative manner where presentation is as powerful as the content
- web-based tools (see below)

One of the most gratifying changes in my view as a teacher is the equity afforded by web-based tools. These online programs have flipped the classroom, turning student into teacher, making learning inquiry-driven, encouraging risk-taking rather than memorization. No longer does a family have to shell out hundreds of dollars for software because their children must have it for school. Now, there are a plethora of web-based, mostly FREE tools that record movies, sounds, turn pages into magazines, take polls, brainstorm, and test knowledge.

It's not your mother's classroom—or even yours. With the advent of interactive textbooks and Siri-type voice input devices, who knows where we'll be in another decade.

Lesson #6 Word Processing Options

Vocabulary	Problem solving	Homework
• Alignment • Footer • Format • Hyperlinks • Outlining • Right click • Serialized • Word processing • Word wrap	• I want to indent outline (tab) • I want to exdent (Shift+tab) • I want a new page (Ctrl+Enter) • I want a hyperlink (Ctrl+K) • Got out of outline (backspace to the last point. Push enter) • Why do I use word processing? • I wanted to do a different activity (ask teacher if you can)	Bring book to outline (if doing this) Complete compare-contrast table Writing for activity Keyboard 45minutes, 15 minutes at a time
Academic Applications	**Required Skills**	**Standards**
Writing, research, note-taking	Familiarity with word processing, outlining, problem solving, keyboarding, note-taking	CCSS: CCRA.L.6 NETS: 1d, 3d, 4b, 6a

Essential Question

How do I use technology to organize ideas?

Big Idea

There are many ways word processing can organize ideas

Teacher Preparation/Materials Required

- Have backchannel device available.
- Have homework posted well before start of class.
- Have student workbooks available (if using).
- Have word processing summative digital or hard copies.
- Integrate domain-specific tech vocabulary into lesson.
- Ensure all required links are on student digital devices.
- Ask what tech problems students had difficulty with.
- Have a book or chapter for students to outline (if doing this activity).
- Something happen you weren't prepared for? Show students how you fix the emergency without a meltdown and with a positive attitude.

Assessment Strategies

- Previewed required material; came to class prepared
- Completed writing activity
- Worked well in a group or independently
- Used good keyboarding habits
- Completed warm-up, exit ticket
- [tried to] solve own problems
- Decisions followed class rules
- Left room as s/he found it
- Higher order thinking: analysis, evaluation, synthesis
- Habits of mind observed

Steps

Time required: **45-90 minutes for each activity**
Class warm-up: **Keyboarding on the class typing program, paying attention to posture**

Some of these activities must be spread over several weeks (such as the serialized novel).

_____**Homework listed on this lesson will be assigned before you start unit so students are prepared for the flipped classroom.**

_____Any questions from homework? Expect students to come to class prepared.

_____Before beginning, put backchannel device onto class screen (Socrative, Padlet, class Twitter account, Google Forms page, or another) Show students how to access it on their devices. During class, pay attention to student concerns.

_____What is 'word processing'? Students will want to use this to:

- *communicate ideas effectively to multiple audiences with a variety of media*
- *understand how email/forums/blogs communicate (why are these word processing?)*
- *know what tasks are best suited to word processing instead of presentation programs or spreadsheets*
- *produce/publish writing and present relationships between ideas (from Common Core)*
- *integrate information from different media to understand a topic (from Common Core)*
- *write routinely for a range of tasks, purposes, and audiences (from Common Core)*

_____What are examples of word processing programs students have used?

- *Blogs*
- *Evernote*
- *Twitter*
- *KidPix/TuxPaint*

- *Discussion Boards*
- *Google Docs/Word/Open Office*
- *Text program*
- *Digital storytelling*

_____What projects have they completed (1st grade: *Figure 49a*; 2nd grade: *Figure 49b*; 3rd grade: *Figure 49c*; 5th grade: *Figure 49d*):

Figure 49a-c—Word processing examples 1st-5th grade

  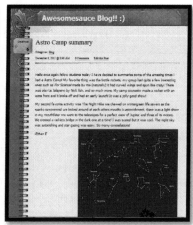

_____Maybe students don't think of 'Evernote' or 'Twitter' as word processing. Discuss.

_____Compare word processing to other communication methods students use (*Figure 50*). Put the table on class screen, but not filled in (as in *Assessment 17*). Prompt students to discuss each category as it relates to a productivity tool. For example: When discussing the 'purpose' of a word processing program, how does that help student select it as the appropriate tool for a particular task, rather than, say, a spreadsheet or a slideshow? How does 'Presentation' inform which tool would be best for the student needs?

Figure 50—Compare-contrast: Productivity tools

Element	Presentation	Word processing	Spread-- sheets	DTP
Purpose	Share a presentation	Share words	Turn numbers into information	Share information using a variety of media
Basics	Graphics-based Design is important to content Layout communicates Few words, lots of images	Text-based Design is secondary to content Layout may detract from words Primarily words communicate	Number-based Focus on tables, graphs Little text; lots of statistics and date Almost no words	Mix of media—equal emphasis on text, images, layout, color
Sentences	Bulleted, phrases	Full sentences with proper conventions	None	Full sentences, bullets,
Content	Slides cover basics, to remind presenter what to say	Thorough discussion of a topic. Meant to be complete document	Statistics, data, charts, graphs	To draw an audience in;
Use	As a back-up to presentation	As complete resource	To support other presentation methods	Good way to group information for easy consumption
Presentation	Speaker presents with their back to the slideshow	Speaker reads from document	Speakers uses it in a presentation or 1:1	Speaker passes out as a handout or take-way
What else				

_____If using workbooks, ask students to complete the table in it, with a partner, before starting the class discussion:

Assessment 17—Compare-contrast productivity tools

Element	Presen-tation	Word Processing	Spread-sheets	DTP
Purpose				
Basics				
Sentences				
Content				
Use				
Presentation				
What else				

_____Open a document in class word processing program. Go to 'save as' and click drop down box with 'save as type'. What's available? What do those 'types' mean? What's 'plain text'? RTF? Open Source? Why save in a different format than what they created the document in?

_____Review **program menu bar, ribbons, toolbars**:

- *Alignment*
- *Bullets*
- *Icons/Ruler*
- *Drop down menus*
- *Font options*
- *Indent*

_____Discuss **tools**. Remind students how similar they are to other software like Excel, PowerPoint, Publisher, Google Sheets, or Numbers (*Figure 51*):

Figure 51—Tools on toolbars

_____Discuss right click menu options—what are those? What do they bring up?
_____Pick one or more of the projects included in this lesson:

- *Comics/cartoons*
- *Outlining*
- *Round Robin—Summative*
- *Serialized novel—multiple authors*
- *Serialized novel—one author*
- *Twitter novel*
- *Word processing—summative*

- *Writing with art*
- *Writing with audio*
- *Writing with desktop publishing*
- *Writing with music*
- *Writing with slideshows*
- *Writing with spreadsheets*
- *Writing with videos*

Outlining

_____As a class, **review outlining**. What is its purpose? What do they remember about outlining from earlier grades (if you used this tech curriculum before)?
_____Today, they will independently create an outline using a textbook or chapter they brought from a different class (*Figure 52a in MS Word, 52b in Google Docs, and 52c in Workflowy*).

Figure 52a-c—Examples of outlines in word processing programs

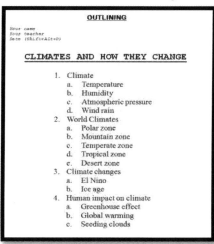
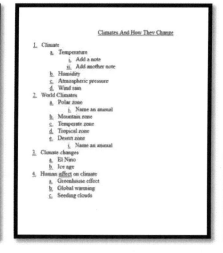

_____If you don't use MS Word or Google Docs on your digital devices, try:

- *OneNote—software, a web app, or an iPad app*
- *Workflowy – online outliner (Figure 52c—search online for website)*

_____If you're an iPad school, try:

- *Google Docs or MS Word app*
- *Quicklyst – quick notes and list on iPads (search for website)*
- *OmniOutliner –for iPads and online (search for website)*

_____Any time students go online, remind them how to do so safely.

_____When done, add information learned during class, independent research, and discussions by adding points and subpoints. See how easy it is to adjust outline to reflect changes.

_____Save (Ctrl+S) every ten minutes.

Word processing summative

_____Give students the word processing skills *Assessment 19* (at the end of lesson). *Figure 53a* is MS Word and *Figure 53b* Google Docs. Adapt as needed for Chromebooks and iPads:

_____Adjust the assessment to include only skills students learned by 7th grade, such as:

- *heading right-aligned at top of page*
- *title centered underneath in Comic Sans, 14 font size, bold*
- *story written in 12 font size, Times New Roman*
- *2nd paragraph written in 16 font size, Papyrus*
- *bulleted list*
- *'The End' in Word Art or another title font and appearance*
- *footer with student name*

Figure 53a—MS Word; 53b—Google Docs

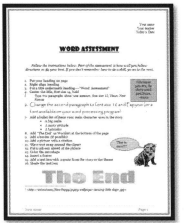
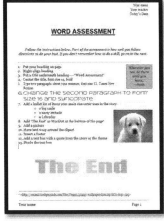

_____If students are using workbooks, they can access assessment there.

_____Allow 30-45 minutes to complete—enough to share what students know without struggling. You're assessing knowledge, not experimentation.

_____Evaluate assessments before next class to evaluate word processing knowledge.

_____Spend next class reviewing problems identified. If most students remembered most skills, add new tools such as how to adjust margins, add hyperlinks (Ctrl+K), move text within a document, force a new page with Ctrl+Enter, insert images from file/internet, create/use embedded links, and find synonyms.

_____Remind students: Every time they use digital devices, practice good keyboarding.

Twitter Novel

_____There's a lot Twitter brings to education:

- *It's non-intimidating. Anyone can write 140 characters.*
- *It forces writing to be pithy.*
- *It's fun. Students want the 'forbidden fruit'.*

_____In this activity, students write a novel in Twitter. Just to be clear: That means squeeze all those fiction parts—

- *plot/pacing*
- *character development*
- *story arc/scene*

_____...into 280 characters. Here are examples (find more by searching *#twitternovel*):

'He said he was leaving her. "But I love you," she said. "I know," he said. "Thanks. It's what gave me the strength to love somebody else." **James Meek**

I opened the door to our flat and you were standing there, cleaver raised. Somehow you'd found out about the photos. My jaw hit the floor. **Ian Rankin**

Rose went to Eve's house but she wasn't there. But Eve's father was. Alone. One thing led to another. He got 10 years. **Rachel Johnson**

Clyde stole a lychee and ate it in the shower. Then his brother took a bottle of pills believing character is just a luxury. God. The twins. **Andrew O'Hagan**

"It's a miracle he survived," said the doctor. "It was God's will," said Mrs. Schicklgruber. "What will you call him?" "Adolf," she replied. **Jeffrey Archer**

Figure 6--Twitter novel sample

_____You can also write the novel in a series of 280-character tweets. *Figure 54* is **David Mitchell's** Twitter novel (search Twitter for the complete novel if interested).

_____Here are tips on writing Twitter novels:

- **Think token action,** dialogue and description. Not: *He sat and looked at the computer for ten minutes before he....* Rather: *Laptop in hand, he wrote.*
- **Think installments.** If writing a series of 140-character tweets, releasing the novel over time increases suspense. **Douglas Sovern** wrote his as 1600 tweets.
- **Think multimedia** and add links, images, video, articles or anything that adds meaning to the story. A Twitter novel can combine text with other media.
- **Think movement.** Every tweet should advance the plot. You don't want your readers ignoring tweets out of boredom.

Serialized novel—one author

_____Discuss serialized novels—a normal length novel published by chapter--smaller bites for reading. Many early writers were published this way including Leo Tolstoy, Joseph Conrad, and Charles Dickens.
_____Show examples of serialized novels from authors students are reading.
_____Why are serialized novels making a resurgence? Consider:

Figure 7--Serialized

- *The average person's attention span is 8.8 seconds.*
- *The average goldfish attention span is 9 seconds.*

_____This can be a stand-alone activity or an optional approach to the lessons on *Writing and Publishing an Ebook.*
_____Here's how this works:

- *Write an outline of the planned story.*
- *Write a character study of each character.*
- *Develop a plot line of what is happening when.*
- *Research any setting characters will visit.*
- *Every class, students publish one installment of a serialized novel to their blog. They can use a word processing tool, a comic creator, or even an audio tool, but it must be embeddable into their blog (there are many tools in each category that will work). Let students select the best tool for their communication style.*

_____When done, students visit and comment on three of the stories written by classmates.

Serialized novel—multiple authors

_____Discuss 'vignettes', that they are a verbal sketch, brief essay, or short work of fiction or nonfiction. Well-known authors include *Dickens' Sketches by Boz* and *Cisneros' The House on Mango Street*
_____In this option, students work in groups to write vignettes around a cast of characters and a central atmosphere. Discuss what *atmosphere* means. Why is this important to a vignette—so important that it sets it apart from other forms of writing?
_____Here are basic rules to follow when writing vignettes:

- *Each fits the collection atmosphere.*
- *Each is 800 words. They can be shorter, but not usually longer.*
- *The vignette must evoke emotion--shares a moment rather than a plot line.*
- *The collection is tied together by a common mood.*

_____There are more rules which vary depending upon your curriculum. Share what fits your students.
_____Here's how this works:

- *Students work in groups organized by the media they'll use to write their vignette. For example, those who wish to use a comic creator would join the same group. Those who will use art will work together.*
- *As a group, write a character study of each character. Work together to agree on what defines each character.*
- *As a group, decide on setting and atmosphere. Work together to agree on what defines the overarching setting and atmosphere of the story.*
- *Develop a schedule of who will publish their vignette when. Alternatively, students have three-five weeks to write their vignette, and then use the balance of the time to meld all the pieces into one book.*
- *These will be published in a collaborative student blog or another location you have selected to curate these stories.*

_____When done, students visit and comment on three of the stories written by classmates.

Comics/Cartoons

_____Discuss how comics relay a story differently from other storytelling methods. Why focus on drawings? Do they make a serious theme light-hearted? What do students like about comics?

_____Before starting, chat with students about the topic they'll be covering in their comic strip. How does it fit into class discussions?

_____Writing with comics includes the same elements students include in a story:

- *Each panel includes detail to support the plot, characters, and setting.*
- *Each panel flows into the next, just as story paragraphs and scenes flow.*
- *Images, text, bubbles, and captions communicate ideas, story, and empathy.*

_____Students have used comics to explore a topic in the past. *Figures 56a-c are examples students created 1st -5th grade (if you've been using this curriculum). It is a robust medium for developing a story and/or sharing empathy and perspective. Comics are appropriate for fiction and nonfiction.*

Figure 56a-c—Comic samples

_____Comics include these parts:

- *3-4 panels—as fits your group (#6 in Figure 57)*
- *dialogue—delivered via speech bubbles (#1 in Figure 57)*
- *thoughts—delivered via thought bubbles (#2 in Figure 57)*
- *captions—to summarize the action in the panel (#4 in Figure 57)*

- *sound effects—delivered via bubbles like 'Blam!' or 'And then' (#3 in Figure 57)*
- *student avatar—a character that represents the student. Fold this into a discussion of digital citizenship (#5 in Figure 57)*

_____Have students open an online comic creator like (search internet for websites):

- *Powtoons Figure 57*
- *Storyboard That Figure 56c*

_____If you're an iPad school, try *Pixton – Figure 56a*.
_____Note: Any time you use the internet in class, remind students how to do that safely and privately.

Figure 57—Decoding a comic strip

_____Students can work in pairs, small groups, or as a large group to write narratives that recount a sequenced event. Include opening, plot, details, temporal words to signal event order, and a sense of closure.

_____If you have workbooks, students can use included panels to sketch out their comic.
_____Done? Open the comic tool and select the desired number of panels. Create:

- *background*
- *captions*
- *characters*
- *props*

- *sound effects*
- *speech bubbles*
- *text*
- *thought bubbles*

_____Follow class writing conventions. An exception may be in speech bubbles. Explain why.
_____When done, students read their comic with a partner. Revise and edit as needed, save as a PDF, print/publish/share as is the custom in your classroom. Students may find it easier to save it as a screenshot using the appropriate tool in your digital device.

Writing with Art

_____A picture is worth a thousand words—what better way for a writer to understand their characters and setting than to draw these pieces. Daniel Tammet is famous for seeing the answers to math problems as a colorful video across the landscape of his brain. This can be a stand-alone picture or a comic about the history of Greek civilization.
_____Students have used art to communicate often in the SL curriculum (see *Figures 58a-d*):

Figure 58a-d—Writing with Art K-6

_____Here are excellent drawing tools such as (search internet for websites):

- *Lunapic*
- *Paint Studio*
- *Pixlr (software download, web app, or mobile)*
- *Paint (comes free with Windows)*
- *Google Draw (comes free with Google Apps)*
- *Photoshop (ultimate drawing tool; if this isn't in your budget, try Photoshop Elements)*
- *GIMP (free software download—similar to Photoshop)*

_____Before selecting this option, students should evaluate it using *Assessment 18*. Does it fulfill what they require? Content? Use? Presentation? Other categories?

Writing with Audio

_____Presentation methods such as podcasting have exploded in popularity. In 2020, 144 million people listened to podcasts.

_____Before selecting this option, students should evaluate it using the table in *Assessment 18*:

Assessment 18—Evaluate writing options

Element	Art	Audio	DTP	Music	Slide-show	Spread sheet	Video
Purpose							
Basics							
Sentences							
Content							
Use							
Presentation							
What else							

_____Here are options for producing audio writing:

- *Audacity – free software*
- *VoiceThread*
- *SonicPics*

Writing with Desktop Publishing

_____If students have used this curriculum since 2nd grade, they have created a wide variety of projects using desktop publishing including cards and timelines in 2nd grade (*Figure 59a*), a magazine in 3rd grade (*Figure 59b*), and stories/trifolds/newsletters/posters in 4th grade (*Figure 59c-f*).

_____Desktop publishing is a communication tool that focuses as much on design and layout as on the selection of the perfect word. What do students use it for—meaning, when is this artistic balance (i.e., when a balance of all communication elements is required—text, images, color, layout)? How does it differ from word processing? Slideshows? Spreadsheets?

Figure 59a-f—DTP project from 2nd-6th

_____Compare/contrast DTP to sharing information with a word processing program, a presentation tool, or a spreadsheet using the table provided earlier in this lesson.

_____Discuss how *Figure 60a* is better/worse as a communication tool than *Figure 60b*:

Figure 60a-b—Compare-contrast report covers

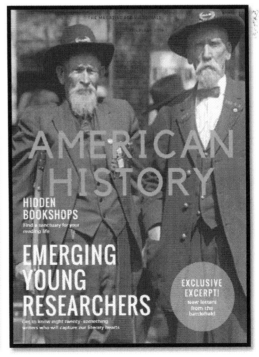

American History

Emerging Young Researchers

By Student

Writing with Music

_____For some students, it's all about music. Country music is famous for the story that's part of every song, the plot that's unveiled quickly in two-three stanzas. By the time the song is completed, listeners identify emotionally with the main character (the singer). But it doesn't have to require lyrics. *Chariots of Fire* had millions of listeners and the *Rocky* theme motivated thousands more to reach their goals.

_____That's what writing with music is about: Putting the plot, characters, scene into the song in a way that listeners identify with.

_____Here are three popular choices for composing music that communicates thoughts:

- *GarageBand (find the app in the App store)*
- *Notepad (free version of fully-featured Finale)*
- *ProMetronome—set a musical pace while writing*

_____Before selecting this option, students should evaluate it using the table in *Assessment 18*. Does it fulfill what student requires for purpose? Content? Use? Presentation? Other categories?

Writing with Slideshows

_____Slideshows are a story told not just with words, but color, movement, dazzling layout and sound. They encourage differentiation of instruction.

_____Students have completed several slideshows in 3rd-6th grade throughout the Structured Learning tech curriculum, such as *Figure 61a-d*:

Figure 61a-d—Writing with slideshows

_____Why did students choose the slideshow presentation method for these rather than word processing? Or desktop publishing? Compare-contrast these using the tables earlier in this lesson.

_____Here are several traditional tools and others you will want to try out (search internet for websites or visit Ask a Tech Teacher resource pages for *Presentations*):

- *PowerPoint, Google slides, Zoho (most available as online tool, software, or iOS app)*
- *Adobe Voice_– Figure 61a*
- *Haiku Deck_— web-based or as an app (Figure 61c)*
- *Adobe Slate_– Figure 61d*
- *PhotoPeach*
- *Kizoa*

_____Before selecting this option, ask students to evaluate the use of *Presentations* or *Slideshows* using the table provided at the beginning of lesson. Does it fulfill what student requires? Content? Use? Presentation? Other categories?

Writing with Spreadsheets

_____Explaining numbers with words is usually less convincing than providing a colorful chart or graph. That requires a spreadsheet program like Excel, Numbers, or Google Sheets. Both are available as software, webtools, and mobile apps, but the tools available in each platform vary so be sure to preview yours before using in your classroom.

_____Here are examples students may have created if you've used this curricula in earlier grades. See if they remember them:

Figure 62a-b—Writing with spreadsheets

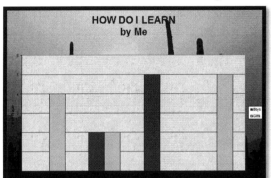

Which way do you like to save electricity?		
Your Name		
	Adults	Children
Turn off your lights	25	21
Unplug things	5	10
Use solar or wind energy	3	7
Pay attention to electricity use	33	21
None	1	5

_____It's also a great option for drawing, using what's called 'pixel art' that makes use of the graph provided in a spreadsheet (*Figures 63a-b*):

Figure 63a-b—Drawing with spreadsheets

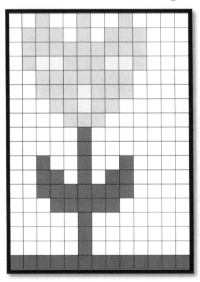

	Y	Y	Y						Y	Y	Y	
Y	Y	P	Y	Y				Y	Y		Y	Y
Y	Y	Y	Y	Y	Y	B	Y	Y	Y	Y	Y	Y
Y	Y	Y	Y	P	Y	B	Y	P	Y	Y	Y	Y
	Y	Y	P	Y	Y	B	Y	Y	P	Y	Y	
	Y	Y	Y	Y	B	Y	Y	Y	Y			
		O	O	O	B	O	O	O				
		O	O	G	O	B	O	G	O	O		
O	O	O	O	O	B	O	O	O	O	O		
O	Y	Y	O	O	B	O	O	Y	Y	O		
O	Y	Y	O	O		O	O	Y	Y	O		
	O	O	O			O	O	O				

_____Finally, students can use spreadsheets for a variety of precision projects, like *Figures 64a-f* done in the past with this curriculum:

_____Before selecting this option to present ideas, students should evaluate it using the table provided at the beginning of this lesson. Does it fulfill what student requires for purpose? Content? Use? Presentation? Other categories?

Figure 64a-f—Projects with spreadsheets

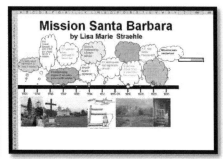
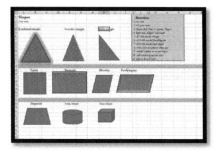
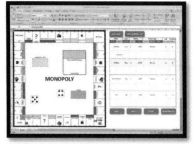

Writing with Video

_____For students who have difficulty presenting to a group, writing with video is perfect. Here are three options:

- *Animoto – mobile platforms, plug-ins, web-based*
- *Vine videos – iOS, Android, Windows*
- *WeVideo – mobile platforms*

_____Before selecting this option, students should evaluate it using the table earlier in this lesson. Does it fulfill what student requires for purpose? Content? Use? Presentation? Other categories?

Round Robin Story—Summative

_____A fun writing project is a Round Robin story where a group of students collaborate to write a story. By the end, each student realizes that s/he offers a unique perspective that reshapes and redefines the story.

_____Here's how it works: Form students into groups of five. Give them ten minutes to roughly plot out the story including five categories: 1) characters, 2) setting, 3-4) two plot points, 5) climax and ending. Now the fun starts.

_____Each student goes to their computer and writes Part 1—an introduction to the characters based on the outline created by the group. After five-ten minutes, a bell rings and students move to the next group member's computer. Here they read what has been written and add

Part 2—the setting—making sure the two parts blend together. After another five-ten minutes, they again move to the next computer in their group, review the two parts already written and add Part 3—the first of two plot points. This continues for five switches. When the story is completed, each student reviews the final story at their own seat for spelling, grammar, flow, and consistency—or other writing elements discussed in class. Read several for the class.

This also works well for non-fiction. In this case, segments include 1) introduction, 2-4) three points to be discussed, 5) conclusion. This follows the well-accepted five-paragraph essay used in many elementary classrooms.

Class exit ticket: ***Have neighbor make sure student saved to digital portfolio.***

Differentiation

- *Practice word processing skills with a journal.*
- *Have students blog (if available) on difficulties/ease of these options. If no student blogs, set up a Discussion Board.*
- *Have students prepare for and take the MS Word certification. Google for an address.*
- *After submitting Summative Assessment, student highlights words that indicate effective technique, descriptive details, and clear event sequences.*

Assessment 19—Word processing summative

Your name
Today's Date

WORD PROCESSING ASSESSMENT

Follow the instructions below. Part of the assessment is how well you read and complete directions.
Do your best. If you don't remember how to do a skill, go on to the next.

- Put your heading on page
- Right-align heading
- Put a title underneath heading——"Word Processing Assessment"
- Center the title, font Comic Sans, font size 14, bold
  - Type two paragraphs about yourself, font size 12, Times New Roman
- Change the second paragraph to font size 16 and Papyrus
- Add bullets with
  1. Your daily activities
  2. What you like to read
  3. Who you play with
- Add "The End" as WordArt at the bottom of the page
- Add a border

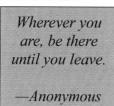

Wherever you
are, be there
until you leave.

—Anonymous

- Add a picture
- Have text wrap around the clipart
- Put a call-out aimed at the picture
- Add an autoshape
- Color the autoshape pink or red

This is easy!!!

- Insert a footer
- Add a text box with what your mom said the most this summer
- Shade the text box
- Add a table with seven columns and three times during the day
- Add information for each day and each time of day
- Add footer with student name and class

Sunday	Monday	Tuesday	Wednesday	Thursday	Friday	Saturday
Ate breakfast						
Ate lunch						
Ate dinner						

The End

Lesson #7 Spreadsheets

Vocabulary	Problem solving	Homework
• Algorithm • Autosum • Axis • Formula • Legend • Model • Spreadsheet • Symbols • Workbook • Worksheet	• Formula doesn't work (add =) • Still doesn't work (text in cell?) • Graph is empty (is data highlighted) • Can't format plot area (click plot area –not chart) • Chart doesn't look right (highlight ONLY data, headings) • Why use spreadsheet program? • Spreadsheet answer is different from mine (use standard algorithm)	Review spreadsheets, formulas, charts, graphs, and other skills required for summative. Bring questions to class Keyboard for 45minutes, 15 minutes at a time
Academic Applications Math, problem solving, compare-contrast	**Required Skills** Familiarity with problem solving, keyboarding, spreadsheet formulas, graphs and charts	**Standards** CCSS: Math.Practice.MP1-8 NETS: 5a-d, 6a

Essential Question

How do I make data interesting and allow viewers to draw their own conclusions?

Big Idea

Students turn data into information

Teacher Preparation/Materials Required

- Have backchannel available.
- Have lesson materials online upcoming unit.
- Have screenshot program available.
- Have student workbooks available (if using).
- Ensure links are on student digital devices.
- Have data for sample spreadsheet.
- Integrate domain-specific tech vocabulary into lesson.
- Ask what tech problems students had difficulty with.
- Have the skills assessment (for class screen or download) if using.
- Know which tasks weren't completed last week and whether they are necessary to move forward.
- Know whether you need extra time to complete this lesson with your student group.

Assessment Strategies

- Previewed required material; came to class prepared
- Worked independently
- Used good keyboarding habits
- Completed project
- Completed warm-up, exit ticket
- Joined classroom conversations
- [tried to] solve own problems
- Decisions followed class rules
- Left room as s/he found it
- Higher order thinking: analysis, evaluation, synthesis
- Habits of mind observed

Steps

Time required: **180 minutes**
Class warm-up: **Keyboarding on the class typing program, paying attention to posture**

_____Homework listed on this lesson will be assigned the week before you start.

_____Any questions from homework? Expect students to review upcoming unit and come to class with questions.

_____Discuss the following Common Core goals and how a spreadsheet is uniquely qualified to assist in attaining them:

- *Make sense of problems and persevere in solving them (with charts and graphs)*
- *Reason abstractly and quantitatively (numbers is what spreadsheets do best)*
- *Construct viable arguments and critique reasoning of others*
- *Model with mathematics (demonstrate a scenario in a spreadsheet)*
- *Use appropriate tools strategically (When is a spreadsheet exactly the tool to sort data)*
- *Attend to precision (with the spreadsheet's mathematical properties)*
- *Look for and make use of structure (formulas, charts, graphs)*

_____What tasks are best suited to spreadsheets instead of word processing? Slideshows? What spreadsheet programs have students used? Compare-contrast these two approaches using the table provided in earlier lessons.

_____This lesson has two activities:

- *Formulas*
- *Summative*

Formulas

_____Students typically use add, subtract, multiply, divide, average, and alphabetize, but spreadsheets offer many more. How do these compare to formulas discussed in class?

Figure 65a-b—Two formulas

_____Using class spreadsheet program, explore the formula bar. If you don't have Excel, Numbers, or Google Spreadsheets, or require an online program, try *Zoho Docs.*

_____Discuss the most popular formulas, i.e., standard deviation, Sin/Cos (Trigonometry), if-then arguments, PMT (to calculate the payment for a particular loan), depreciation of an asset, concatenations. Demonstrate a few.

_____Let's look at how several spreadsheet formulas students are familiar with (i.e., subtracting, multiplying, and dividing) are constructed.

_____Formulas are a tool, like a calculator, strategically used to analyze data, and draw conclusions that would be difficult to comprehend without the assistance of automaticity. They do not supplant student responsibility for learning the process.

_____Formulas are composed of four parts:

- = *(introduce formula)*
- **Function** *(add, subtract, multiply, divide)*
- **Location** *(cells function applies to)*
- **( )** *(group numbers)*

_____Resulting formula will look like either *Figures 66a* or *66b*. Students should reproduce the formula independently or with nominal assistance. Let them work in groups if you prefer:

Figure 66a-b—Formula unpacked

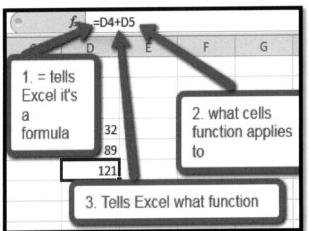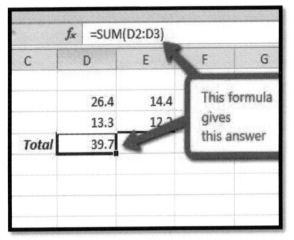

_____Discuss where students might find spreadsheets. In fact, they're all over the internet. Demonstrate how these five locations (or others of your choice) can be downloaded and used:

- *NASA Wavelength (available online)*
- *From NASA--Wind speed data*
- *Batch Geo--text data can be converted to visual data (available online for free)*

_____Reflect on what students have learned about spreadsheets. Prod them toward answers aligned with Common Core ideas:

- *Spreadsheets facilitate reasoning abstractly and quantitatively.*
- *Spreadsheets facilitate construction of viable arguments.*
- *Spreadsheets aid in making sense of problems and identifying a solution.*
- *Spreadsheets allow for modeling problems.*
- *Spreadsheets use repeated reasoning to solve problems.*

Summative Spreadsheet Skills

_____Students assess their 1) general knowledge of spreadsheets culled from what they learned prior years (especially if you've been using the SL curricula), and 2) skills they are most likely to use in Middle School/High School. *Assessment 20* is a sample; collect skills relevant to your students. The rubric is at the end of this lesson.

Assessment 20—Spreadsheet summative

	A	B	C	D	E	F	G	H
1		**SUMMATIVE SPREADSHEET QUIZ**						
2	1	Read all directions first	4	Watch spelling--errors count against you				
3	2	Enter information in the correction location (see Column A)	5	If you're stuck, you may use the 'help' files				
4	3	If you get stuck, move on to the next step	6	When you're finished, try the Extra Credit				
5	**Cell**	**Skill**						
6	A1	Enter title 'Fifth Grade Skills'--font size 26; Merge-center over A1-F1		*Extra Credit*				
7		rename the worksheet tab 'quiz'		Step 8: format chart (change bars, colors,				
8		recolor the 'quiz' tab		background)				
9	A2	Your name--font size 10, font color red		Enter time using keyboard shortcut				
10	A3	Your teacher's name; font comic sans		Turn picture into a hyperlink to your file folder				
11	A4	The date, using keyboard shortcut		Add text 'Click Here for Falcon.net'; make it a				
12	G1-J6	Insert any picture		hyperlink to falcon.net				
13		resize Row 3 and Column D						
14	A6-C10	Enter the data and labels to the right		Subject	boys	girls		
15		Include shading and border		Arts	5	3		
16				LA	0	0		
17		Make a chart from data (step 9); add a title and the X and Y labels		Math	5	8		
18		FAVORITE SUBJECTS--MS. MURRAY		Science	1	0		
19								
20								
21				Sample only --yours will be on a separate worksheet				
22								
23								
24								
25								
26		Color row 5 and row 11 blue (on the 'quiz' worksheet)						
27	A12-E21	Type the table below, including all data; use Excel formulas to find						
28		the answers						
29		Average		Addition	Subtract	Multiply	Divide	
30		22		44	123	33	144	
31		33		32	33	55	12	
32		44						
33		55						
34		66						
35		77						
36		77						
37		88						

_____Give students one class to complete assessment. Do not answer questions. All skills have been covered between 2nd and 7th grade. Adjust assessment as needed to satisfy particular circumstances. You may choose to make this a collaborative exercise or individual.

_____Display assessment on class screen or make it available for download in read-only format.

_____Test-taking strategies:

- *Answer questions you know first—go back for others.*
- *Don't know entire answer? Answer what you know.*
- *Check work when done.*

_____There are two extra credit items. Use these, or add different ones suited to your students.

_____When finished, students upload quiz to dropbox and save/share to digital portfolio. Or both.

_____During second weekly class, review challenging skills.

_____Remind students to 'save early save often'—about every ten minutes—if not in Google Sheets.

_____Throughout class, check for understanding.

Class exit ticket: ***Using Twitter, a class forum or Discussion Board, or a student blog, write 3-5 sentences about spreadsheets.***

Differentiation

- *Assign a student to enter homework and classwork due dates. This can change monthly.*
- *Early finishers: visit class internet start page for websites that tie into classwork.*
- *Play Lemonade Stand or Coffee Shop in small groups (find it online and free). Collect data in spreadsheet and evaluate for both games.*
- *Pick three-four formulas. Walk students through the creation of one (i.e., turning all cells of a certain value red). Have them figure out the rest by using help files, Google search, and other problem-solving strategies.*
- *Discuss sorting data with Filter tool. Apply it to data students are using in class.*
- *Blog on spreadsheet activity. If students don't have blogs, set up a Discussion Board with spreadsheet-related question.*

Problem solving: If screen freezes:

- *Smash forehead on keyboard to continue...*
- *Enter any 11-digit prime number to continue...*

Assessment 21—Spreadsheet summative

Spreadsheet Grading Rubric

*Name*_____ *Teacher*_____

1. Worksheet title added, font size 26_____ in A1 _____
2. Title merge-centered A1-F1 _____
3. Worksheet tab renamed 'quiz' _____ recolored _____
4. Name filled in, font size 10 _____ font color red_____ in A2 _____
5. Teacher's name filled in, font comic sans_____ in A3 _____
6. Date filled in (using keyboard shortcut)_____ in A4 _____
7. Picture added (any picture) _____ in G1-J6 _____
8. Row 3 resized _____ Column D resized _____
9. Data table entered (labels, data) _____ in A6-C10 _____
10. Data table heading row shaded _____ with border _____
11. Chart created from data ____ Titles added (chart name, x/y axis labeled) _____
12. Row 5 colored blue _____ Row 11 colored blue _____
13. Data entered from 2ⁿᵈ table _____
14. Average calculated with formula _____
15. Addition calculated with formula _____
16. Subtraction calculated with formula _____
17. Multiplication calculated with formula _____
18. Division calculated with formula _____
19. No spelling errors _____
20. Overall _____

EXTRA CREDIT

1. Format chart (change bars, colors, background) _____

2. Turn the picture into a hyperlink _____
3. Add text 'Click here for Falcon.net' _____
4. Enter time using keyboard shortcut _____

Askatechteacher©

14 Factors to Consider for Tech Report Cards

It used to be simple to post grades. Add up test scores and see what the student earned. Very defensible. Everyone understood.

It's not that way anymore. Here are the factors I consider when I'm posting grades:

- Does s/he remember skills from prior lessons as they complete current lessons?
- Does s/he show evidence of learning by using tech class knowledge in classroom or home?
- Does s/he participate in class discussions?
- Does s/he complete daily goals (a project, visit a website, watch a tutorial, etc.)?
- Does s/he save to their digital portfolio?
- Does s/he try to solve tech problems themselves before asking for teacher help?
- Does s/he use core classroom knowledge (i.e., writing conventions) in tech projects?
- Does s/he work well in groups?
- Does s/he use the internet safely?
- Does s/he [whichever Common Core Standard is being pursued by the use of technology. It may be 'able to identify shapes' in first grade or 'able to use technology to add audio' in fourth grade]?
- Does s/he display creativity and critical thinking in the achievement of goals?
- Has student progressed at keyboarding skills?
- Anecdotal observation of student learning (this is subjective and enables me to grade students based on effort)
- Grades on tests, quizzes, projects

I'm tempted to put everything in a spreadsheet, award a value, calculate a total and find an average. Then–Magic! I have a grade! It's risk-averse, explainable to parents and Admin, a comfort zone of checklists and right-and-wrong answers. But, I know I can't do that. In an inquiry-based classroom, too much is a subjective analysis, a personal evaluation of the student's uniqueness. I can't–and don't want to–get away from that approach.

What do you use that I haven't mentioned? I'm already thinking ahead to the next grading period.

Lesson #8-9 Google Earth

Vocabulary	Problem solving	Homework
• Custom pin • Dialogue box • Embedded link • Fly-to • Lats and longs • Layers • Overlay • Placemark • Screenshot • Temp file • Tour • Voiceover	• My writing disappeared (Ctrl+Z) • Google Earth can't find what I'm searching for (is it misspelled?) • Tour doesn't play correctly (are locations in order?) • I don't have enough time for all the placemarks (reduce number) • I don't remember how I did something (check Help/Google Earth Communities) • I can't find my placemark (is it in temp file?)	Review Google Earth; install on home computer if possible Complete storyboard (if using) Have 3-5 Civil War battles and info on each (if using) Keyboard 45minutes, 15 minutes at a time

Academic Applications	Required Skills	Standards
Geography, history, map-making	Familiarity with problem solving, keyboarding, Google Earth	CCSS: RH.6-8.7 NETS: 3a, 4a

Essential Question

How can I use technology to understand history?

Big Idea

Geography affects a country's history

Teacher Preparation/Materials Required

- Have Google Earth installed or have a work-around.
- Have class keyboarding tool available.
- Have Civil War websites (or similar).
- Have project rubric available (if not using workbooks).
- Be familiar with Google Earth skills covered today.
- Have lesson materials online to preview upcoming unit.
- Talk with grade-level team so you tie into inquiry.
- Integrate domain-specific tech vocabulary into lesson.
- Ask what tech problems students had difficulty with.
- Know which tasks weren't completed last week and whether they are necessary to move forward.
- Know whether you need extra time to complete lesson.

Assessment Strategies

- Previewed required material; came to class prepared
- Used good keyboarding habits
- Included all elements in tour
- Transferred knowledge from prior projects
- Worked well in a group
- Backed up personal Places to personal folder
- Took advantage of GE's collaborative tools
- Took advantage of GE layers
- Completed project and rubric
- Completed warm-up, exit ticket
- [tried to] solve own problems
- Decisions followed class rules
- Left room as s/he found it
- Higher order thinking: analysis, evaluation, synthesis
- Habits of mind observed

Steps

Time required: **180 minutes**
Class warm-up: **Keyboarding on the class typing program**

_____Homework is assigned the week before you start unit—so students can prepare.

_____Any questions from homework? Expect students to have reviewed Google Earth unit.

_____Students will explore Google Earth for the next two weeks and use it to tie into class inquiry (i.e., Civil War, immigration, or another topic).

_____What is Google Earth? If you've been using the SL technology curriculum, students have already done these projects (*Figures 67a-e*):

Figure 67a-e—Prior Google Earth projects

_____How did Google Earth extend learning? Here are ideas:

- *modeled/explored issues (i.e., which geographic features impacted history?)*
- *identified trends and forecast possibilities (Time Slider)*
- *supplemented research (tours and layers on Google Earth, Google Sky, Google Mars, Google Moon)*
- *contributed to cultural understanding and global awareness (photos attached to locations)*

_____Open Google Earth. Review what students know about program:

- *What is included on menu bar—file, edit, view, etc.?*
- *What is included on top toolbar—placemark, polygon, ruler? Demonstrate how to switch to Sky, Moon, and Mars. Show how to measure distances.*
- *What is included on sidebar—fly to, directions, layers, places?*
- *What are right-hand tools—compass rose, move, zoom, and Street View guy?*
- *What is included on bottom toolbar—latitude/longitude, 'eye view'?*
- *How do students drill down into 'My Places' to find file folders?*
- *How do students run tours?*
- *How do students activate lats and longs?*
- *Where can students find help—Google Earth Help, Google Earth Communities?*
- *How can students save an image and share?*
- *How can students add/edit/format a placemark?*

_____Students have done most of these in prior lessons. You are reminding—not teaching.

_____On class screen, play a Google Earth tour created by students last year (or one created as a sample). Notice 1) tour locations are in the same file folder, 2) tour goes in order of selections, and 3) tour can be activated, paused, and continued.

_____Pick a topic students will explore with Google Earth. We'll use the American Civil War as an example. Students will create a tour of Civil War battlefields that 1) integrates charts, graphs, photographs, videos, maps with other information, and 2) highlights the importance of geography in history (or focus that works for your unique student group). Two more examples: Immigrant journey to America and Wonders of the World.

_____Discuss what students know about the Civil War—battles, individuals, causes, repercussions. As students mention information, demonstrate how it is brought to life in Google Earth (find the location of battles, show geography of historic event).

_____To show how Google Earth can contribute to Civil War research, have a student ask a question about battles and then demonstrate how it is brought to life in Google Earth. For example: the Siege of Vicksburg (see *Figure 68*):

Figure 68—Google Earth: Siege of Vicksburg

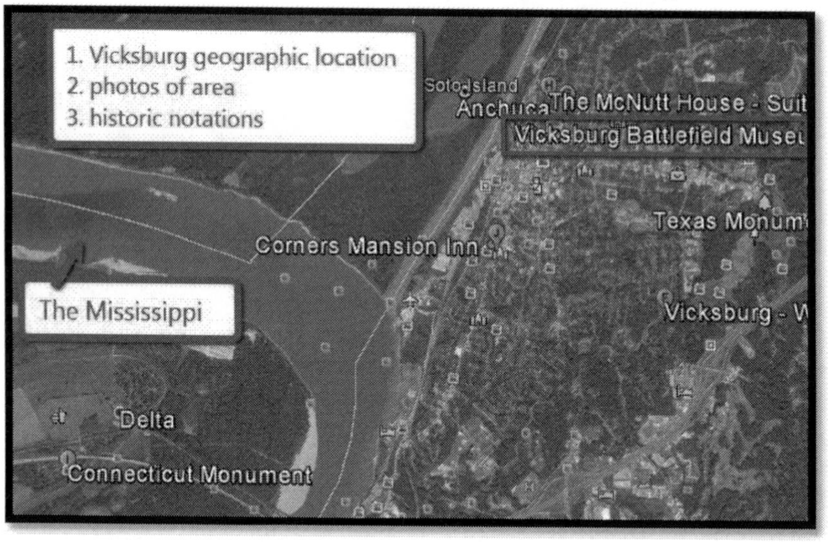

_____Students work in groups to provide at least three (or more, or less) locations that must be included, such as:

- o *Location of Emancipation Proclamation*
- o *Sherman's march*
- o *Surrender at Appomattox*

_____The tour will look something like *Figure 69a* and *Figure 69b*:

Figure 69a—Mini tour placemark; 69b—tour list

_____Demonstrate how to mark a location and customize placemark. Title is name of battle/event.

_____Tour will open with a placemark where Civil War began. Dialogue box will:

- o *introduce team*
- o *explain tour*
- o *explain importance of Civil War (or similar event)*

_____Students will not research for this project. Instead, they will use knowledge from class inquiry though they can verify facts and information with the Google Earth Community. For example, *History Illustrated* under *Help>Google Earth Community* reports: *"The battle, also known as the Siege of Vicksburg, consisted of a long siege brought about by the fact that the **city is located on a high bluff** overlooking the Mississippi River and **thus was largely impregnable** to invaders."*

_____Create a personal folder under 'My Places'. This is where students collect tour locations. All locations placemarked must be under this folder. If you can't find a placemark, check the Temp file (at the bottom of the left sidebar).

_____Open tour with a placemark where Civil War began. This initial dialogue box will:

- o *introduce team*
- o *explain tour*
- o *explain importance of Civil War (or similar event)*

_____Placemark subsequent geographic spots with a customized pin. Label it with the name of the battle (or person). Add a few sentences that summarize:

- o *date of battle*
- o *historic significance*
- o *how geography impacted battle*

Figure 70a—Placemark dialogue box in GE; 70b—in Google Maps

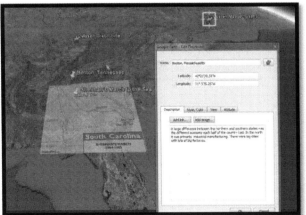

_____At least three placemarks include resource links for readers interested in digging deeper.

_____At least three placemarks must include image overlays of historic figures (*Figures 71a-b*).

_____Where significant (at least once), measure distance between locations (i.e., distance traveled between battles) and explain relevance in placemark dialogue.

_____End with a placemark noting the conclusion of the Civil War.

_____Each class period, back-up folder to student digital portfolio (or email to themselves). This is critical because most school computers are used by multiple students.

_____Once tour is completed, record using GE 'Record a Tour': Click on each location, wait for about three seconds, and click on next location in sequence. You can also add a voice-over. Save to digital portfolio with a reflection.

_____When done, run tour to be sure it works.

_____Spelling and grammar will be graded.

_____Continually check for understanding. Expect students to solve problems and make decisions.

Figure 71a—Overlay in ScribbleMaps; 71b in GE

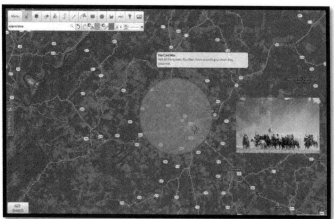 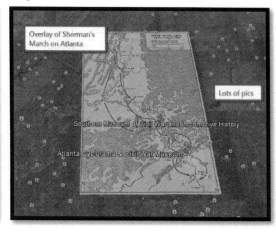

_____Student groups share their tour with classmates on class screen, narrated to show understanding of events. They take two-three questions.

_____When done, discuss conclusions they can draw about the effect of geography on history?

_____If you can't use Google Earth (for whatever reason):

- *adapt lesson to Google Maps (which works fine in Chromebooks)*
- *use Scribble Maps to annotate a map of Civil War geography (Figure 71a)*

Classroom Exit Ticket: ***Play someone else's tour.***

Differentiation

- *Set up a wiki page where students embed and share GE tours.*
- *Create Google Earth tour that previews a field trip students are taking (i.e., Washington DC). Include one fact about each location and a picture. Edit after field trip to include reflections.*
- *See lesson plan at end of this unit to track immigrant's arrival in the Colonies. Annotate worksheet in student workbook (if using).*
- *Love Google Earth? Here are more ideas for lesson plans:*

  o *Google Earth Lesson Plans*
  o *Planet in Action—Google Earth*
  o *Pompeii—via Google Earth*
  o *General resources on Google Earth*

Civil War Google Earth Assessment

	Beginning 1	Developing 2	Accomplished 3	Exemplary 4	Score
Relevant Pieces included	Project includes some of required elements, but not all categories or all information	Project includes all categories, but not all required elements in each.	Project includes many required elements. Those skipped were 'forgotten', not that creators lacked knowledge to complete	includes 4 battles, 3 events, title/ description, placemarks, 3 images, 3 links, 3 overlays, 1 distance, tour, embed	/4
Grammar and Spelling	Numerous grammar and spelling errors, most of which could be caught with a simple edit process	Substantive grammar and spelling errors, indicating that the creators did not do a final once-over before submitting	Few errors, most minor. Grammar errors are limited to those that creators may not know	There are minimal grammar and spelling errors, none which could have been caught by an edit program.	/4
Knowledge of Events Evident	Many errors in names and chronology; all should have been known through discussion or research	Creators made errors in names and chronologic time, some should have been known through classroom discussion or research	Creators made few errors in names and chronologic time, most attributed to lack of in-depth research on the topic	No errors in events, people, chronology. Facts, figures, images are right demonstrating respect for themselves and the story.	/4
Technical Knowledge Evident	There is insufficient knowledge of the technology required to complete the required elements.	Creators seemed to struggle with the technology, but showed an effort to figure out how to deliver the required elements.	Creators showed an understanding of all required elements involved in creating this Google Earth tour, even those requiring self-teaching.	Creators demonstrated a deep and thorough understanding of all technology required to create a masterful and professional tour.	/4
Summative	Google Earth tour lightly touches on project theme (effect of geography on history), but does not effectively use the program's tech tools to emphasize important points	Google Earth tour points out importance of geography on history, but misses opportunities to use the program's tech tools to emphasize essential points	Google Earth tour sporadically explores effect of geography on history. Creators identify occasionally but effectively use Google Earth tools to emphasize salient points	Google Earth tour nicely explores the question (effect of geography on history). Creators identify relevant trends and use Google Earth tools to effectively emphasize salient points	/4

Google Earth Tour—England to the Colonies

Tour locations—include these spots and this information:

1. Your home in England
   a. Introduce yourself; tell us why you're leaving England
   b. Share your hopes and dreams
   c. Include distance from your home in England to the Colonies_____
2. Jamestown
   a. Tell me what would draw colonists to settle here
   b. Tell me about the jobs
   c. Tell me about the geography and climate
   d. Tell me about the organization of Jamestown
3. The Hudson Bay
   a. What is its impact on colonization and life in this area?
   b. Include width of Hudson Bay_____
4. The Appalachian Mountains
   a. What is its impact on colonization and life in this area?
5. Plymouth Rock
   a. What is its impact on colonization and life in this area?
6. Chesapeake River/Bay
   a. What is its impact on colonization and life in this area?
   b. Include length of Chesapeake River_____
7. The Potomac River
   a. What is its impact on colonization and life in this area?
   b. Include length of Potomac River_____
8. One colony from each region (northern, middle, southern)
   a. Tell me what would draw colonists to settle in each of these areas
   b. Tell me about the jobs
   c. Tell me about the geography and climate
   d. Tell me about the colonial organization of each area

Setup:

1. Set up a file folder in My Places, with your name
2. Customize placemark with your picture
3. Copy-paste each placemark for each location into your file folder
4. To edit a placemark, right click and go to **Properties**
5. Back up this folder to your digital portfolio

Lesson #10-11 Online Image Legalities

Vocabulary	Problem solving	Homework
• Attribution • Citation • Copyright • Creative Commons • Crop • Fair use • Image • Layer • Macro • Plagiarism • Public domain • Watermark	• Project disappeared (use search) • There's a watermark on picture I picked (Use one not copyrighted) • Someone stole my artwork (options?) • It takes a while to find the copyright information on an image (it's not a race) • I want to merge two pictures (be a problem solver) • Why can't I always use Fair Use—I'm always a student (only for educational purposes) • Who will know I 'borrowed' an image?	Review material Watch videos to prepare for class Draw an original piece of artwork Practice keyboarding for 45 minutes, 15 minutes at a time
Academic Applications Writing, research, reading, art	**Required Skills** Problem solving, keyboarding, digital citizenship, online images	**Standards** CCSS: WHST.6-8.6 NETS: 2b-c

Essential Question

Why should I learn to create my own unique images rather than use those of others? I'm not creative.

Big Idea

The internet has a wealth of images that must be accessed carefully and judiciously

Teacher Preparation

- Have backchannel device available.
- Have links to plagiarism materials.
- Have lesson materials online for upcoming unit.
- Talk with grade-level team so you tie into inquiry.
- Have personal stories about using online images.
- Cover tech problems students have difficulty with.
- Ensure required links are on student digital devices.
- Integrate domain-specific tech vocabulary into lesson.
- Know whether you need extra time to complete this lesson with your student group.

Assessment Strategies

- Previewed required material; came to class prepared
- Annotated workbook (if using)
- Worked independently
- Completed project
- Used good keyboarding habits
- Completed warm-up, exit ticket
- Joined classroom conversations
- [tried to] solve own problems
- Decisions followed class rules
- Left room as s/he found it
- Higher order thinking: analysis, evaluation, synthesis
- Habits of mind observed

Steps

Time required: **90 minutes**
Class warm-up: **Keyboarding on the class typing program, paying attention to posture**

_____**Homework is assigned a week early so students can prepare for a flipped class.**

_____Any questions from preparatory homework? Expect students to review upcoming unit and come to class with questions.

_____Before beginning, put backchannel device onto class screen (Socrative, class Twitter account, or Google App). Show how to access if necessary.

_____This lesson includes three activities:

- *Copyrights*
- *Hoaxes*
- *Summative Project*

Copyrights

_____What do students remember from last year's discussion on image copyrights? Some are licensed under Creative Commons (what is this?), but many have more restrictive licenses. What does that mean? What is the legal way to use an online image?

_____Watch and discuss *A Fair(y) Use Tale* (available on YouTube).

_____Review copyright law (*Figure 72* is a rephrasing).

Figure 72—Digital law—rephrased

The law states that works of art created in the U.S. after January 1, 1978, are automatically protected by copyright once they are fixed in a tangible medium (like the internet) BUT a single copy may be used for scholarly research (even if that's a 2nd grade life cycle report) or in teaching or preparation to teach a class.

_____Copyrights range from public domain—creative work can be used without permission or notification—to intensely private— available only to view, on the host website.

_____When searching for images, adjust the search engine to provide only those that are in the public domain. *Figure 73* shows how to find this option in Google:

Figure 73—Copyright protections on browsers

_____Find several images online. Show students how to track them back to their source and then find the copyright protections that are invariably listed on the pages. This is often time-intensive, but necessary: Never assume an image is available freely to use. If students can't find the copyright notice, pick a different image.

_____Here are two examples (*Figure 74—zoom in to view better*):

Figure 74—Two copyrighted images

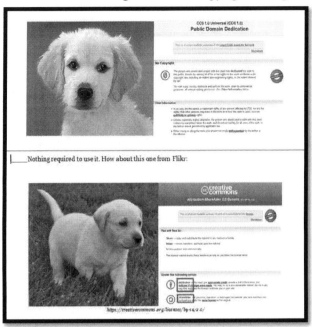

_____It requires attribution—a linkback or credit, which I've provided.

_____Some want to share work and collaborate with others. Watch and discuss *Wanna Work Together* (available on YouTube). about Creative Commons licensing.

_____Show students how to decode the copyright protections normally included with online images. Use the Creative Commons online licensing as an example—*Figures 75a-b*:

Figure 75a-b—Creative Commons licensing

_____Discuss how artists share material online. What do these terms mean?

- *Attribution*
- *Non derivative works*
- *Share alike*
- *Non-commercial*

_____*Figure 76a* was drawn by a student and posted to her/his public website to share with family and friends. Without her/his knowledge, it was used forty-seven times (*Figure 76b*), not always in places s/he or her/his parents would approve.

_____What could s/he do in the future? How about add a copyright notice to her/his website, announcing that all media contained on the website are protected by copyright laws and cannot be used without permission.

_____Discuss how students can find out if an image they've created is being used online. If they drag-drop it into TinEye or Google Images, it shows all the online sites were it appears:

Figure 76a-b—Student drawing used without permission

_____How would students feel if someone stole their drawing? What if thief posted it online? What if they made ugly comments about it? What if they made money off of it and didn't share it with creator. What if artist really needed that money to support a family or go to college?

_____Define '**plagiarism**'. Discuss how to cite a website. Visit EasyBib or Citation Machine.

_____When must you credit material found online? In general terms:

- *facts not commonly known or accepted; opinions that support research*
- *exact words and/or unique phrase*
- *reprint of diagrams, illustrations, charts, pictures, or other visual materials*
- *electronically-available media are copy-pasted, including images, audio, video*

Hoaxes

_____Discuss how easy it is to fake a picture with programs like Photoshop.

_____Look at *Figure 77*. Did President Roosevelt really ride a moose across a river?

Figure 77—Real or a hoax?

_____In *Figures 78a-b:* Was the tree added to or erased from the original photo?

Figure 78a-b: Add or remove pieces from a photo

_____Discuss as a class whether *Figures 79a-c* are accurate—and how do students know? It's no surprise photos are not accepted as proof in court.

Figure 79a-c—Real or hoax pictures?

_____Visit the Zapatopi website about tree octopuses. Is it real? How do you know?

_____Show 'War of the Worlds'—a famous video hoax (Google for address). Discuss how it confused fiction with reality if listeners missed the first ten minutes. Play it for students from that point.

Summative Project

_____Conclusion: It's a lot easier to create your own graphics than use someone else's.

_____Open school's graphic program. Have students draw a picture that collaborates with a class discussion (literature, history, or another).

_____When done, take a screen shot and share on blog/website.

Class exit ticket: ***Using Twitter, class Discussion Board, or student blog, share thoughts about copyrights and how they protect creative genius.***

Differentiation

- *Do Webquest Hoax or Not and discuss.*
- *Have students find five copyright-free images to support a project from another class, one each from a public domain website, Google images, created in a drawing program,*
- *Create a blog post that includes images from classmates. Provide proper credit.*
- *Students who finish early go to class internet start page for websites tied to inquiry.*

Lesson #12 Internet Search and Research

Vocabulary	Problem solving	Homework
• Alt+Tab • Copyright • Creative commons • Domain • Extension • Hits • Limiters • Plagiarism • Refine search • Search bar • Spoof • Toggle	• Browser toolbar gone (F11) • Browser too small (double click title bar) • Browser text small (Ctrl+) • Internet address doesn't work (spelling) • How do I switch between internet and notes (Alt+Tab) • How do I know if a website is reliable (evaluate, analyze) • It's on Google—it must be free • Doesn't 'fair use' cover me? • This website looks professional (looks can be deceiving)	Keyboard 45 minutes, 15 minutes at a time Review preparatory material; watch all videos Practice a search using included hints
Academic Applications	**Skills Required**	**Standards**
Research, varied academic subjects	Familiarity with problem solving, keyboarding, digital citizenship, Internet searches	CCSS: WHST.6-8.8 NETS: 2b-c, 3a-d

Essential Question

How do I gather information from digital sources, assess credibility, and integrate it while avoiding plagiarism?

Big Idea

Gather information using effective search terms; assess credibility; quote or paraphrase while avoiding plagiarism.

Teacher Preparation/Materials Required

- Have backchannel available.
- Have lesson materials online to preview.
- Have website evaluation sheets (if doing activity).
- Ensure required links are on student digital devices.
- Ask what tech problems students had difficulty with.
- Talk with grade-level team so you tie into inquiry.
- Integrate domain-specific tech vocabulary into lesson.
- Know whether you need extra time to complete lesson.

Assessment Strategies

- Previewed required material; came to class prepared
- Annotated workbook (if using)
- Worked well in a group
- Completed research projects
- Used a wide variety of sources
- Understood the importance of website selection
- Used good keyboarding habits
- Completed warm-up, exit ticket
- Joined class conversations
- [tried to] solve own problems
- Decisions followed class rules
- Left room as s/he found it
- Higher order thinking: analysis, evaluation, synthesis
- Habits of mind observed

Steps

Time required: **90 minutes, or 50 minutes per Google class**
Class warm-up: **Keyboarding on the class typing program**

_____Homework assigned week prior to unit—so students ready for flipped classroom.

_____Any questions from preparatory homework? Expect students to review upcoming unit and come to class with questions.

_____Before beginning, put backchannel device onto class screen (Socrative, Padlet, class Twitter account, Google Forms, or another).

_____Discuss essential question: *How do I gather information from digital sources, assess credibility, and integrate it while avoiding plagiarism?*

_____Ask: Why research? Encourage students to dig deeper than 'for classwork' or 'to find out something I don't know'. Overarching reasons include building and presenting **knowledge**.

_____In this Lesson, students will cover three activities:

- *internet safety*
- *internet search and research*
- *identify reliable websites*

Internet Safety

_____Review safe internet use. This is covered in detail in the *Digital Citizenship* lesson.

Internet Search and Research

_____Kick off research with BrainPOP's Internet Search video. Take ending quiz as a group. If your school doesn't have a BrainPOP account, visit Ask a Tech Teacher's resource pages for Digital Citizenship>Internet Search and pick another website on internet searches.

_____If you use Common Sense's Digital Passport (available for free online), have students play Search Shark.

_____Watch *How Search Works by Matt Cutts* (available on YouTube) and discuss.

_____Try Google's series of 50-minute classes called Power Search:

- *how to search*
- *how to interpret results*
- *how to find facts faster*
- *how to check facts*
- *how to put it all together*

_____Have students independently work through them (or cover in class if there's time).

_____After reviewing, discuss what students learned:

- *use key words to generate qualified hits*
- *have a general understanding of topic through class discussions, textbooks, or individual interest, as a method of focusing hits*
- *use site extensions to categorize results*
- *pay attention to sidebars, headings, hyperlinks to locate relevant information*
- *access article links to dig deeper*
- *use pictures, insets, maps for more information*

_____See *Figure 80* for Internet search tips (full size poster in Appendix):

Figure 80—Internet research

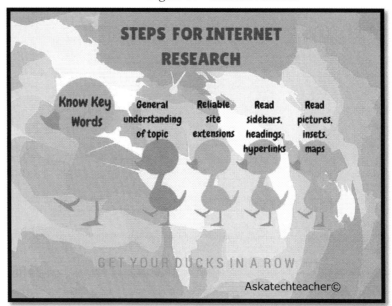

_____Practice with a topic students are discussing in class. For example, type *Winston Churchill*—no quotes—into search bar. Notice number of hits.

_____Type "Winston Churchill" (with quotes)—less hits.

_____Now type "Winston Churchill" "British Prime Minister"—adding words to refine hits.

_____Type "Winston Churchill" –"World War II"—minus skips sites with words "world war II".

_____Focusing on same topic, try search skills listed at end of unit, i.e., *what time is it in London, can students find a PowerPoint (.pptx) on WWII?*

_____How is research different in Word and Google Docs? What about other tools?

_____Discuss how to use online material safely and legally if you haven't delved into this topic before (see lesson on *Digital Citizenship*). Cover 1) citations, 2) copyrights, 3) plagiarism, and 4) digital rights and responsibilities.

_____Circle back on these concepts during year.

Identify Reliable Websites

_____Why is website credibility important? Consider:

- *How can you use websites to locate an answer to a question quickly or to solve a problem efficiently if you don't know website is reliable?*
- *How can you explain an author's reasons and evidence if you aren't convinced they're accurate?*
- *How can you integrate information from several texts knowledgeably if you don't know websites are knowledgeable?*

_____Ask students how they recognize a reliable website when they get that long list of hits on a search page. Disabuse them of the belief that reliability is related to ranking. Focus on two methods to identify reliable websites: 1) extension, and 2) the website itself.

_____Discuss the parts of a website address (see *Figure 81*).

Figure 81—What are the parts of a website?

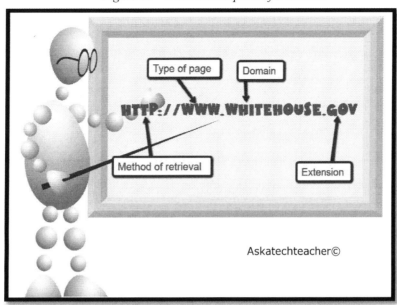

_____What's the difference between extensions like .gov, .edu, .net, .org, .com? What can be inferred about reliability from an extension? Does it matter if you're looking for a place to buy backpacks? How about if you're researching hiking?

_____Which popular extension is most reliable?

- *.gov—limited to US governmental entities*
- *.edu—limited to educational institutions*
- *.org—used to be non-profit groups.*
- *.net—used to be Internet service providers.*
- *.com—most common extension*

_____Watch and discuss two videos as a group from the Ask a Tech Teacher resource pages on Digital Citizenship, under 'Digital General' or 'Internet Safety'.

_____Demonstrate on class screen how you make decisions about these questions:

- *Is author(s) knowledgeable on subject?*
- *Is website publisher credible?*
- *Is content accurate based on what students know?*
- *Does content include depth in topic?*
- *Is information up to date?*
- *Is website unbiased?*
- *Is website age-appropriate? Can students understand verbiage?*

_____There are a variety of checklists to measure website reliability:

- *Common Sense Media (use search bar)*
- *Cornell University*

_____Using a website that ties into classroom discussion, demonstrate how to evaluate it and then have students work in groups to do the same.

Summative Search and Research Project

_____Students work in groups to research a topic that ties into class inquiry. Source selection will demonstrate that data is well-rounded, supports hypotheses with credible sources, that students understand topic, and enable students to fully answer question.

_____Use Assessment at the end of lesson (*Figure 82*) to track search terms.

Figure 82—Research skills

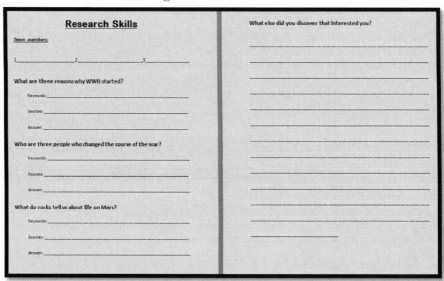

_____During class, check for understanding.

Class exit ticket: ***Tweet (or comment on class blog) about how student stays safe online.***

Differentiation

- *Try search skills—definitions, phone numbers, functions, convert currencies, area codes, specific file types, similar sites, time around world, * as general term--at the end of the lesson*
- *Have students play 'Search Shark' in Digital Passport.*
- *For more information on digital citizenship, follow K-8 Digital Citizenship Curriculum (from Structured Learning).*
- *Early finishers: visit class internet start page for websites that tie into classwork.*

"The difference between 'involvement' and 'commitment' is like an eggs-and-ham breakfast: the chicken was 'involved' - the pig was 'committed'."

- Unknown

Assessment 24--Research skills

Research Skills

Team members:

1_____ 2_____ 3_____

What are three reasons why WWII started?

Keywords:_____

Sources:_____

Answer:_____

_____

Who are three people who changed the course of the war?

Keywords:_____

Sources:_____

Answer:_____

_____

What are three quotations that became famous during WWII?

Keywords:_____

Sources:_____

Answer:_____

_____

What else did you discover that interested you?

_____

_____

_____

_____

_____

_____

_____

_____

HOW TO SEARCH ON GOOGLE

Definitions	Define:computer definitions of the word **computer** from Web.
Phonebook	'phonebook:Murray Irvine' Phonebook for people named 'murray' in Irvine
Calculator	33 + 33 provides the answer to any function
File type finder	filetype:ppt "civil war" finds PowerPoints on Civil War
Site type finder	Site:edu Lincoln finds .edu websites about Lincoln
Similar sites	related:www.google.com (or the website you want related)
License plate finder	Type plate number into search bar
Time finder	'time in New York' tells you current time in New York

What Matters in a Query

1	Every word matters. Try searching for [who], [the who], and [a who]
2	Order matters. Try searching for [blue sky] and [sky blue]
3	Capitalization does not matter. Try searching for [barack obama] and [Barack Obama]
4	Punctuation does not matter. Try searching for [red, delicious% apple&] and [red delicious apple]
*	There are some exceptions! Can you think of any? $ C# C++ Google+ but not ¶ £ € © ® ÷ § % () or @

Lesson #13-16 Robotics

Vocabulary	Problem solving	Homework
• Angle beams • Block • Bot • Debug • Forever loops • Fun • Loops • NXT • Rigid construction • Pegs • Qualitative • Quantitative • Sensor • Sentient • Ultrasonic sensor	• Website address won't link (push spacebar after address) Still won't work (does it start with 'http://'?) • What does 'Save early-save often' mean? (Ctrl+S often to save data) • I don't know how to *** (try different strategies) • Robotics doesn't work. (debug) • I like building robots, but not other stuff (this lesson's more about 'other stuff' than 'building') • My teammates aren't working as hard as I am • I run back-and-forth to computer and robot for instructions (use iPad)	Keyboard 45minutes, 15 minutes at a time Review robotics construction and programming mat'l Post 1st blog article about robotics Optional introductory robotics training at Carnegie Mellon's NXT Video Trainer

Academic Applications	Skills Required	Standards
Problem solving, critical thinking, math	Familiarity with keyboarding	CCSS: Math.Practice.MP NETS: 4a-b, 5c-d

Essential Question

How can technology make life better (and what is 'better'?)

Big Idea

Tech makes life easier, better, and more productive

Teacher Preparation/Materials Required

- Have lesson materials online to preview.
- Have robotics equipment.
- Have required programming tools for robots.
- Have pieces required for simulations.
- Ensure required links are on student digital devices.
- Integrate domain-specific tech vocabulary into lesson.
- Ask what tech problems students had difficulty with.

Assessment Strategies

- Previewed required material; came to class prepared
- Annotated workbook (if using)
- Completed warm-up, exit ticket
- Completed robot tasks
- Debugged program
- Participated in Bot Battles
- Joined classroom conversations
- [tried to] solve own problems
- Decisions followed class rules
- Left room as s/he found it
- Higher order thinking: analysis, evaluation, synthesis
- Habits of mind observed

Steps

Time required: **360 minutes**
Class warm-up: **Keyboarding on the class typing program, paying attention to posture**

_____Homework assigned the week before lesson.

_____Any questions from preparatory homework? Expect students to review upcoming unit and come to class with questions.

_____Any tech problems students would like to share?

_____Why learn robotics? If students have used robots in the past, what have they learned from them? Take time on this question. Transfer is at the core of why we teach topics like robotics. Prod students to come up with:

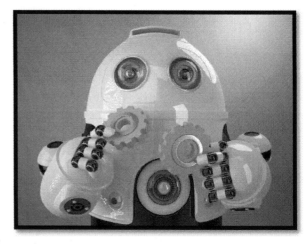

- *thinking skills*
- *problem-solving skills*
- *critical thinking*
- *application of learned math*

_____Common Core Standards for Mathematical Practice list traits necessary to succeed in math, but these are fundamental to life's daily decisions—*to evaluate new circumstances and determine a direction, to consider possible paths to an end and select the most likely to succeed, and to mull over new ideas and fit them into accepted constructs.* These are difficult to teach unless part of a larger process.

_____Discuss the meaning of:

- **Make sense of problems and persevere in solving them**—*robot does what it is told. Students must identify problem, find programming error, and fix it.*
- **Reason abstractly and quantitatively**—*robot program is based on symbols. This requires ability to visualize results and an abstract understanding of what is occurring.*
- **Construct viable arguments and critique reasoning of others**—*'Garbage in garbage out' remains the motto of programming. If a script fails to achieve desired results, work as a team to critique process. And, help neighbors if they are stuck.*
- **Model with mathematics**—*debugging scripts is like decoding a math formula.*
- **Use appropriate tools strategically**—*NXT program offers a plethora of scripts, blocks, tools. Adapt them strategically to unique needs.*
- **Attend to precision**—*again, 'garbage in garbage out'. For the program to accomplish what students want requires patience and precision.*
- **Look for and make use of structure**—*look at available tools, scripts, blocks, options, and select those that facilitate student needs*
- **Look for and express regularity in repeated reasoning**—*when a formula/program/script repeats itself, this provides shortcuts to goals.*

_____Specific goals of this unit include:

- *How do we create a robot?*
- *How do we program it to do what is needed?*
- *How do we problem-solve if/when it doesn't work correctly?*
- *How do we work collaboratively in accomplishing a common goal?*

_____Why are robots so appealing? Discuss popular robots like:

- *7 of 9 (in Star Trek)*

- *Bomb Disposal robots*
- *C-3PO and R2-D2*
- *Daleks (from Dr. Who)*
- *Data (from Star Trek)*
- *Consumer robots*
- *I, Robot (Asimov)*
- *Industrial robots*
- *Lost in Space robot*
- *Mars Curiosity*
- *Marvin the Paranoid Android (Hitchhiker's Guide to the Galaxy)*
- *Mining robots*
- *Tin Man (Oz)*
- *Transformers*

_____Show a sample of robot students will build with these main parts:

- *movable physical structure*
- *sensor system*
- *power supply*
- *"brain" to control parts*

_____Pass out box of parts and review. Working in groups, students play without mixing them up.

Figure 83a-b—Robotic pieces

_____Review user guide for the robotics system you're using. If students have iPads, load guide into iBooks or Kindle (or similar reading app).

_____Demonstrate how to build a basic robot by reading directions and identifying required parts. This is what you'll expect them to do. Students with the engineering gene will love this part!

_____Discuss how robot knows what to do. How do humans know what to do? Animals? The TV at home? The computer? What's the difference between a 'sentient' being and 'non-sentient'? Anyone see Matrix?

_____This robot isn't sentient, so will only do what it's told. Students do so via programming tool.

_____With students, review programming tool, test, try things, and see what happens. This is fun if they're more geek than engineer. Create a program with student help. Compare it to Algebraic expressions students use in math. See *Figures 84a-b* for examples.

_____Depending upon student group, they can either observe or work with you.

Figure 84a-b—Programming robot

 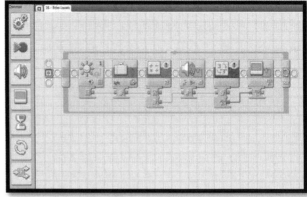

_____Demonstrate how to upload program to robot. If students have difficulty finding the program on the robot, share a diagram similar to *Figure 85b (Image Credit: NxtPrograms.com)*:

Figure 85a-b—Finding robot program

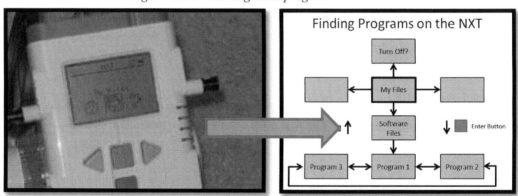

_____Students now build their robot and program it.

_____Each group must complete five tasks. Here's a sample list—add what works for your students:

- ○ *go in reverse*
- ○ *accelerate*
- ○ *turn*
- ○ *detect sound*
- ○ *detect touch*

_____This is a student-directed unit, student-paced. You guide, provide an overview, but students are expected to use available resources to figure out tasks independent of teacher direction. Why? This will be expected in high school, college, future jobs. This is problem solving.

_____Besides core robot, students must learn to attach and use parts such as:

- ○ *forklift arm*
- ○ *karate arm and chopping block*
- ○ *kicker and long arm*
- ○ *pusher*

_____When a group thinks they have completed a task, teacher observes. The group has three tries to correctly complete task.

_____Don't be surprised if students come up with questions you don't know the answer to. The joy of tech is exploration—finding answers to new questions. Remind students this is fun, and they should not be surprised if they must:

- *improvise*
- *change the rules*
- *try things they don't know the answer to*

In fact, you want this to happen.

Figure 86a-b—Completed robots

_____Throughout this unit, expect students to blog about their efforts. What works? What problems do they encounter? Get help from school blogger community. Take pictures and videos of what they're doing and share. Comment on posts of others. Answer questions. Applaud successes. Follow class discussion rules.

Figure 87a-b—Blogs about robotics

_____Culmination of lesson is *Bot Battles* (available on YouTube). Create a ring on carpet. Place two robots in ring (programmed to push opponent out of ring). Start programs and see what happens.

_____What strategies are required to battle another bot? For example:

- *Success is highly dependent upon construction. Discuss what elements might make a robot more/less successful. When a bot loses, evaluate why.*
- *Using a light sensor to detect ring border is a typical starting point, but more sophisticated robots might use touch or ultrasonic sensor to detect a robot. Try these.*

Figure 88a-b—Bot Battles

_____Use Tournament Elimination poster (similar to *Figure 89*) to track Challenges if desired. It's created in a spreadsheet (column/row designations are included in *Figure 89*).

Figure 89—Bot tournament

_____If desired, award certificates (sample at end of lesson) for participation and accomplishment.

Class exit ticket: ***Using Twitter, class Discussion Board, or student blog, post about student progress with robotics. Use #hashtags such as #myrobottoday and #botbattles.***

Differentiation

- *Pick one of 14 options on NASA's Mars Education website (search internet for address) to engage students. A few favorites: 1) create a Mars community, and 2) Rover Races.*
- *Try this NASA lesson plan on Mars (search internet for address). Students build Curiosity and explore the Red Planet*
- *Enter a robotics competition as a school team.*
- *Ask students to analyze how robots know what to do? How do they know where they are? How do they know where to go? How do they control their 'bodies'? How might they see the world? (from Carnegie Mellon grad student David S. Touretzky's paper, "Seven Big Ideas in Robotics, and How To Teach Them" (search internet for address).).*
- *Find hints and tricks at NxtPrograms.com (search internet for address).*

Assessment 25—Awesome Robotics Award

Lesson #17-20 Coding/Programming

Vocabulary	Problem solving	Homework
• Background • Blocks • Broadcast • Control • Debug • Hotkeys • Operators • Remix • Script • Sequence • Sprite • Stage • Variables • Widget • Wolfram-Alpha	• I can't understand how to *** (Check resources, Help files, neighbors before asking teacher) • I don't understand how to use a tool (right click and select 'help') • How do I know where scripts are (experiment) • How do I do basic skills (try Scratch Task Cards) • Is Scratch a drawing program or a presentation tool? • Can I use someone's script (that's 'remixing'—Scratch encourages it) • I just don't get it (see if you can try another lesson option)	Keyboard 45minutes, 15 minutes at a time Preview programming tool students will use in this lesson Add a blog post about the coding activity student would like to try. Include evidence. Review preparatory material
Academic Applications	**Skills Required**	**Standards**
Math, critical thinking, problem solving	Familiarity with problem solving, digital citizenship, keyboarding, programming	CCSS: Math.Practice.MP NETS: 4a-b, 5c-d

Essential Question

How can math be creative and collaborative?

Big Idea

I can learn mathematical ideas while thinking creatively

Teacher Preparation/Materials Required

- Have backchannel available.
- Have Scratch program on digital devices.
- Have lesson materials online to preview.
- Have Scratch resource links on internet start page
- Ensure required links are on student digital devices.
- Ask what tech problems students had difficulty with.
- Integrate domain-specific vocabulary into lesson.
- Go to ScratchEd for tutorials, rubrics, assessments and more.
- Talk with subject teachers about inquiry Scratch can support.

Assessment Strategies

- Created sprite
- Completed project
- Posted blog article about Scratch (with screenshot) and commented on classmate's
- Completed warm-up, exit ticket
- Joined classroom conversations
- [tried to] solve own problems
- Decisions followed class rules
- Left room as s/he found it
- Higher order thinking: analysis, evaluation, synthesis
- Habits of mind observed

Steps

Time required: **360 minutes**
Class warm-up: **Keyboarding on the class typing program, paying attention to posture**

_____Homework listed on this lesson will be assigned the week before you start this unit—so students are prepared for the flipped classroom.

_____Any questions from preparatory homework? Expect students to review upcoming unit and come to class with questions.

_____'Programming' is the buzzword among middle school students. They either want to do it or are afraid of it. What does it mean? Who has their own website or blog? Who wants to write programs and/or apps? If they tried, what did they use? Discuss how these activities promote problem-solving, critical thinking, and computational thought.

_____Most people—students and adults—think programming looks like *Figure 90a* when it actually looks like *Figure 90b*:

Figure 90a-b—What programming feels like vs. what it is

_____Do students remember coding activities from previous years (*Figures 91a-e*)?

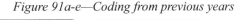

Figure 91a-e—Coding from previous years

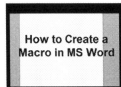

_____December will host **Hour of Code**, a one-hour introduction to programming and why students should love it. It's designed to demystify "code" and show that anyone can learn to be a maker, a creator, and an innovator.

_____This lesson has three activities:

- *Scratch*
- *Auto Hotkeys*
- *Wolfram/Alpha widgets*

Scratch

_____What is Scratch: *A free download from MIT designed to teach pre-high school students programming basics without the techie-ness. With it, students create interactive stories, animations, games, and/or music.*

_____Whether you're a Common Core school or not, these eight constructs from Standards for Mathematical Practice regarding critical thinking tie flawlessly into Scratch programming:

- ***Make sense of problems and persevere in solving them***—*Students must understand where they made a programming error and fix it.*
- ***Reason abstractly and quantitatively***—*coding requires abstract understanding.*
- ***Construct viable arguments and critique the reasoning of others***—*Coding and remixing requires students critique others' work.*
- ***Model with mathematics***—*Translate scripts to student needs, like decoding a math formula.*
- ***Use appropriate tools strategically***—*Adapt coding tools strategically to student needs.*
- ***Attend to precision***—*To get scripts to do what students want requires precision*
- ***Look for and make use of structure***—*look at available tools, scripts, blocks, options, in selecting those which facilitate student needs*
- ***Look for and express regularity in repeated reasoning***—*notice when a formula/program/script accomplishes goals.*

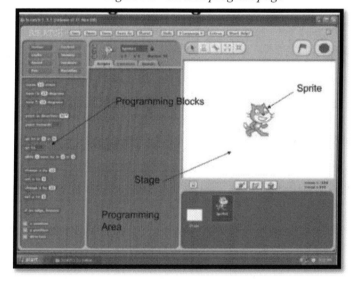

_____Students work in groups. This is a self-paced student-directed unit. Provide a quick overview. In fact, after your screen tour, students will know 90% of what is required to complete the project. As you present, encourage students to listen for the following:

Figure 92—Scratch program page

- *What is background and how is it edited?*
- *What is broadcasting?*
- *How does one build/edit a sprite, make it glide?*
- *How does one add dialogue and recordings?*
- *How does a sprite move forward/backward and/or flip?*
- *How does one automate movement?*
- *How does one wait (under control)?*

Figure 93a-b—Scratch script and result

_____Open Scratch on class screen. Point out:

- *top toolbar with tools to save/share projects*
- *toolbar above stage where students duplicate/delete/grow/shrink their Sprite*
- *small stage, full stage, presentation mode tools*
- *how to connect and activate scripts*
- *three ways to create a Sprite and add costumes*
- *blocks—scripts that change with options*
- *control options*
- *green flag to automate scripts*
- *programming categories (motion, looks, sound)—demonstrate each*
- *drop-down menus available on some blocks/scripts*
- *tabs for sprites/backgrounds that change depending upon which you're in*

_____Take questions, but remember: You aren't teaching. You're introducing. Students are explorers and risk-takers in this project.

_____Provide a list of resources to help students find answers, like those on Ask a Tech Teacher's resource pages for Scratch.

_____Before you help, students must try to solve their own problem. Here are strategies:

- *check resource list*
- *check Scratch website Task cards*
- *right-click on a tool and select 'help'*
- *check with a neighbor*
- *check Help (with Scratch's website)*

Figure 94—Scratch tools I

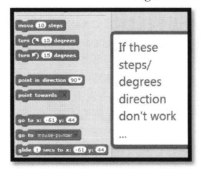

If these steps/ degrees direction don't work ...

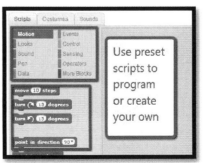

Use preset scripts to program or create your own

_____Give students time to view resource list and Task cards, experiment with tools, explore functions before beginning the project.

Figure 95—Scratch tools II

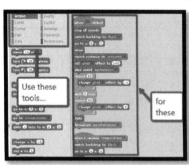 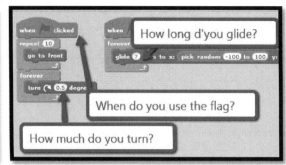

_____When students have practiced skills, have them create an account on Scratch and download a project from another 7th grader. Find a topic similar to one they will create. Explore how this student accomplished tasks; remix to suit project needs, then save remix to student portfolio (*Figures 96a-b*).

Figure 96a-b—Scratch remix

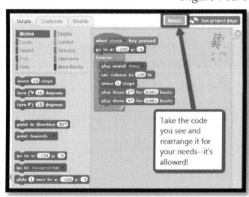 

_____Next: Students create a project aligned with class inquiry. It could support a history lesson or review a book they're reading. Give them much freedom to do in a way that works for their learning style. This is student-directed, independently-paced. *Figures 97a-d* are examples.

Figure 97a-d—Scratch projects

_____Have each student save completed projects to both their Scratch account and digital portfolio. Works-in-progress are saved to digital portfolios, and backed up to Google Apps, flash drive, or emailed home via a web-based email program.

Figure 98—Scratch embed

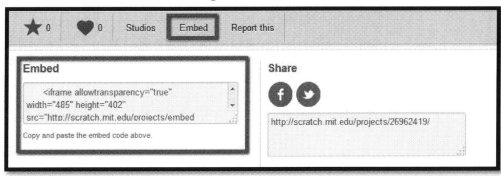

_____When project is completed, upload to Scratch, use code to embed into Blog (*Figure 98*), and write a summative blog post (*Figure 99a-b*) about the Scratch experience:

- *What did student like/dislike?*
- *Was it as easy/hard as student thought it would be?*
- *What problem-solving skills did student use/learn?*
- *How was this alike/different from robotics (if you did this lesson)?*
- *What other school projects could Scratch be used for?*

_____Use rubric (*Figure 100*) as summative assessment (zoom in to see better).

Figure 100—Scratch rubric

Category	Beginning	Developing	Proficient	Exceptional
Content area concepts (Add specific targets as needed)	___ Does not include ideas about the subject area or ideas are incorrect	___ Includes a few ideas about the subject, shows some understanding	___ Focuses on and understands important concepts about the subject matter	___ Makes important connections between subject area concepts, shows in-depth understanding
Project design	___ Did not try to make own artwork ___ No clear purpose of project or organization ___ Does not provide a way for other people to interact with program	___ Project uses artwork of others with some effort to change ___ Has some sense of purpose and structure ___ Includes way for user to interact with program, may need to be clearer or fit program's purpose better	___ Project uses original artwork or reuses imported images creatively ___ Has clear purpose, makes sense, has structure ___ Includes way for user to interact with program and clear instructions	___ Project artwork and creativity significantly support the content ___ Has multiple layers or complex design ___ User interface fits content well, is complex; instructions are well-written and integrated into design
Programming	___ Project shows little understanding of blocks and how they work together ___ Lacks organization and logic ___ Has several bugs	___ Project shows some understanding of blocks and how they work together ___ Has some organization and logic ___ May have a couple bugs	___ Project shows understanding of blocks and how they work together to meet a goal ___ Is organized, logical, and debugged	___ Project shows advanced understanding of blocks and procedures ___ Uses additional programming techniques ___ Is particularly well organized, logical, and debugged
Process	___ Student did not get involved in design process ___ Did not use project time well and did not meet deadlines ___ Did not collaborate	___ Student tried out the design process ___ Used project time well sometimes and met some deadlines ___ Collaborated at times	___ Student used design process (stated problem, came up with ideas, chose solution, built and tested, presented results) ___ Used project time constructively, met deadlines ___ Collaborated appropriately	___ Student made significant use of the design process ___ Used project time constructively, finished early or added additional elements ___ Found ways to collaborate beyond class structure

_____Comment on five student blogs, following class rules for conversations.

Figure 99a-b—Blogs about programming

_____Remind students to transfer knowledge to the classroom or home.

Code a Widget with Wolfram/Alpha

_____Widgets are free, personalized mini-apps that can do almost anything the user can program, from calculating the calories in a recipe to solving complex problems. Students can browse **Wolfram/Alpha's gallery** for a widget that fits their need and embed the code into their personal website, or build their own widget from scratch using the Builder tool. The level of difficulty will determine how long it takes so start simple during Hour of Code.

Figure 101—Wolfram/Alpha widget

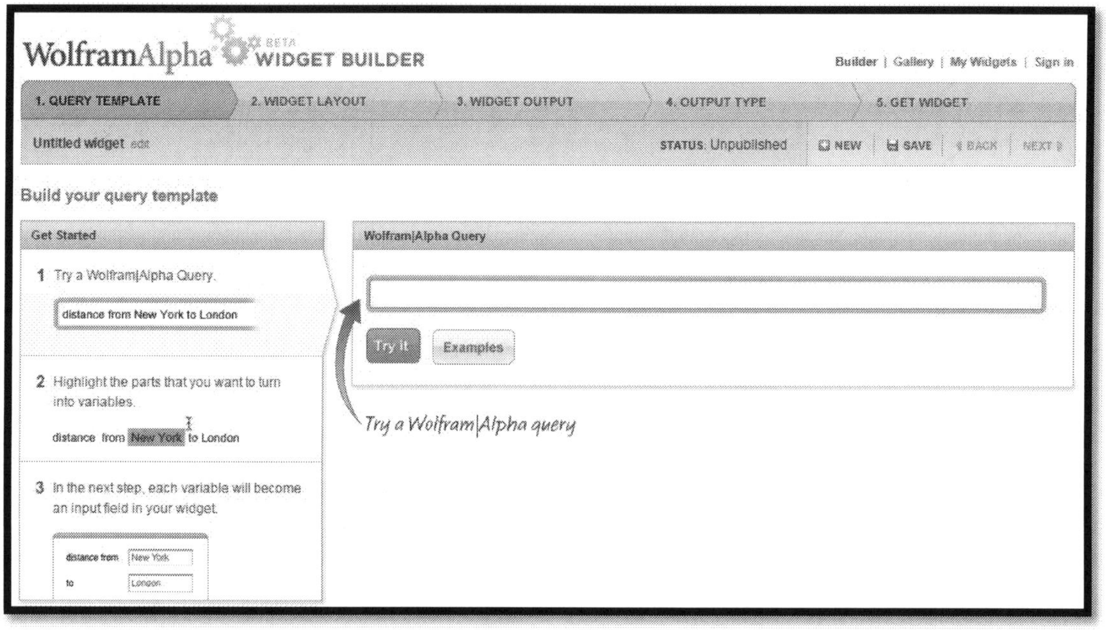

_____Here's an example students can easily create to determine their grade (*Figures 102a-b*):

Figure 102a-b—Wolfram/Alpha completed widget; 102c—embedded in blog

_____Using the Wolfram Alpha embed code, add this to the student blog (*Figure 102c*):

AutoHotkey

_____**Auto Hotkey** is a free download for the Windows platform that enables users to program a series of keystrokes to launch programs, open documents, send mouse clicks and movements—accomplish pretty much anything you want it to. This is similar to macros, but more versatile. It, however, is not intuitive. There are no menus and no friendly interface. It is a great geek-immersion experience for those students who live and breathe coding and computers. If creating scripts is a line in the sand many will not cross, this program may not be for you.

Class exit ticket: ***Using a virtual wall (like Padlet), have students add their thoughts about their coding project.***

Differentiation

- *Discuss this quote: "What is the best method to obtain the solution to a problem? The answer is, any way that works" - Richard Feynman.*
- *Discuss this quote: "Make things as simple as possible, but not simpler." – Albert Einstein.*
- *Create a Sprite from student school picture.*
- *Blog a progress report at the half-way point with screen shot (a formative assessment).*
- *Early finishers: visit class internet start page for websites that tie into classwork.*

"Each problem that I solved became a rule which served afterwards to solve other problems."

- Rene Descartes, "Discours de la Methode"

Lesson #21 Gamification of Education

Vocabulary	Problem solving	Homework
• Edugames • Flipped • Gaming • Gamification • Learning style • Reach • Scaffolding • Simulation • Virtual • Virtual world	• How do I undo? (Ctrl+Z) • My screen froze (clear a dialogue box) • I'm not a gamer (pick a simulation for non-gamers) • I'm stuck (think creatively, critically. Work as a group) • I don't understand (be an explorer and risk-taker) • Someone on my team doesn't know how to play games (help him/her)	Keyboard 45 minutes, 15 minutes at a time Review preparatory material Test out game you'd like to learn/teach and with whom
Academic Applications Science, history, language, more	**Skills Required** Familiarity with problem solving, online games, digital citizenship	**Standards** CCSS: Math.Practice.MP NETS:1a-d, 3d, 7a-d

Essential Question

How can games lead to learning?

Big Idea

Technology differentiates education in surprising ways

Teacher Preparation/Materials Required

- Gaming and simulation links available.
- Backchannel available.
- Upcoming lesson materials online to preview.
- Ensure required links are on student digital devices.
- Integrate domain-specific tech vocabulary into lesson.
- Ask what tech problems students had difficulty with.

Assessment Strategies

- Previewed required material
- Completed project
- Worked well in a group
- Completed all blog posts
- Acted as teacher as needed
- Developed effective arguments to support the game
- Completed warm-up, exit ticket
- [tried to] solve own problems
- Left room as s/he found it
- Higher order thinking: analysis, evaluation, synthesis
- Habits of mind observed

Steps

Time required: **90 minutes (or longer)**
Class warm-up: **Keyboarding on the class typing program**

_____Homework is assigned the week before this unit so students are prepared.

_____What is '**Gamification**' of education? Help students come up with 'use of game design elements in educational contexts'. What are some favorites? Do they see connections between those games and education (do they learn while having fun)?

_____Watch *Teaching with Games: GLPC Case Study* (available on YouTube)—a case study on using games in learning.

_____Games offer what nothing else can. Through these virtual worlds, students have the opportunity to impact events around them with no prejudice based on youth. Properly-selected games invoke problem-solving, critical thinking, logical thinking, and collaboration—all significant skills in Common Core Standards, ISTE guidelines, and 21st Century classrooms.

_____Common Core alludes to skills gaming (and programming) is known for, specifically (from Common Core Standards for Mathematical Practice):

- ***Make sense of problems and persevere in solving them***—*Students understand the problem, how to solve it within the constructs of the game.*
- ***Reason abstractly and quantitatively***—*Students immerse themselves in the game environment. This requires they visualize the process.*
- ***Construct viable arguments; critique the reasoning of others***—*Students interact with other players. They must which characters can assist in completion.*
- ***Model***—*Games are models of a reality students likely will never experience.*
- ***Use appropriate tools strategically***—*As with real life, there are only so many tools at a player's disposal. Determine what those are and how to use them.*
- ***Look for and make use of structure***—*Life works better with a plan.*
- ***Look for and express regularity in repeated reasoning***—*Learn the rules of the community. The ones that work can be repeated.*

_____Best practices for using games in the classroom include:

- *plan time for a learning curve*
- *have students work in groups*
- *be actively involved*
- *set behavioral expectations*
- *pick great games*
- *align goals with learning*
- *scaffold non-gamers*
- *update parents consistently*
- *demo game-ed connections*
- *if possible, invite parents*
- *make failure fun*
- *ignore unrealistic expectations on how quickly results populate*
- *differentiate instruction*
- *fit games into class schedule*
- *expect students to play games in many locations*
- *include varied assessments—reflection, blogs, discussion boards*

_____Students select a game from the list below (or one of their own) and present their case to the class as to why they can play it during class time. Include the following information:

- *Discuss academic tie-ins—show game is more than just 'play'.*
- *Discuss student engagement, intellectual motivation, and academic reach (what does game touch; how does it appeal to different learning styles).*
- *How will control be exerted? Class must remain 'in control'.*
- *Provide citations to its effectiveness.*

- *Align selected game with standards, the Big Idea, and Essential Question of lesson.*
- *Review its ease of use and scaffolding required for non-players.*
- *Review its accessibility (do students require accounts? Are accounts free?)*
- *Does game encourage peer support?*

_____Only one group can play each game. This time may be the most effective part of the unit.

_____When arguments are completed, students vote on who gets to play which game. Any students who were not involved in this selection can pick one of the remaining games.

_____This list includes varied gaming levels (search Internet for websites). Include your own:

- *Coffee Shop—run a coffee shop business*
- *CSI Web Adventures—solve crimes. learn forensics*
- *Dimension U—focuses on math knowledge*
- *Financial Football—game strategy based on financial knowledge*
- *iCivics—what it means to be part of a democracy*
- *Lemonade Stand—run a lemonade stand business*
- *Minecraft (or MinecraftEdu—fee required)*
- *Mission US—students role play historic roles*
- *Past/Present—early 1900's life as an immigrant*
- *Science simulations—lots of choices at 7th-grade level*
- *Stock Market Game—learn how the Market works as you invest your money*

_____Here are tasks students must accomplish during game play, regardless of game they select:

- *Students post a start-up blog on 1) how game connects to education standards, 2) how they will be inclusive of non-gamers, and 3) goals of unit.*
- *Students blog about 1) individual involvement, 2) connections between game and education, 3) how education was differentiated as needed, 4) where group experienced problems and how they were solved, 5) where group experienced success and why.*
- *Students participate in Discussion Board topics you as teacher choose.*
- *Students complete three self-assigned tasks (or a number that works for your group) that demonstrate game's educational applications. Share these in a blog post. For example, students may expect Minecraft to:*

  o *teach electricity*
  o *teach basic programming*
  o *measure gravity*
  o *create contour/topographic maps using randomly generated mountains*
  o *measure/evaluate area/volume or surface area*

A note: Some games require registration, software, and/or fees. If this is not an option for you, pick a different game or come up with game choices that satisfy your situation.

_____Suggestions for (free) **Coffee Shop, Lemonade Stand:**

- *Preview both. Pick one.*

- *Play simulation.*
- *Track results in a spreadsheet.*
- *Evaluate data using charts and graphs.*
- *Do a pre- and post-blog about student business knowledge.*
- *Optionally, create marketing materials—business cards, fliers, websites using tech skills already learned. Students decide what will promote their business.*

_____Suggestions for using (free) **CSI Web Adventures**:

- *Students solve crimes while learning forensics.*
- *Students can complete one-five games.*
- *Students evaluate evidence using critical thinking and online help resources.*
- *Do a pre- and post-blog about student forensic knowledge.*
- *Site includes an educator guide and a family guide.*

_____Suggestions for using (fee-based) **Dimension U**:

- *Students learn math to advance.*
- *These are a variety of multiplayer game, but can be played individually.*
- *Games are online, as an app, or downloaded.*
- *Students play as part of a school license or individually.*
- *Do a pre- and post-blog about student math knowledge.*

_____Suggestions for (free) **Financial Football**:

- *Students use financial literacy to devise game strategy, which informs their success.*
- *Teams compete by answering financial questions that earn yardage and score touchdowns.*
- *Game can be played on the web, as a download, with an app, or embedded into blogs.*
- *Site includes lessons and teacher resources.*
- *Also available as Financial Soccer.*
- *Do a pre- and post-blog about student knowledge.*

_____Suggestions for (free) **iCivics**:

- *Educates students about civics, democracy, government. For example, in We the Jury, students decide a tough case while learning what jurors discuss in deliberation room. They analyze*

evidence, weigh testimony, and use appropriate arguments to reach a fair and impartial verdict.

- *Students can play several iCivics games.*
- *Students do a pre and post blog about their civics knowledge.*

_____Suggestions for using (fee-based) **Minecraft**:

- *Students follow preset activities or their own.*
- *Students establish preliminary goals of surviving, finding food, building a shelter, and creating tools that allow for their survival.*
- *Encourages collaboration among gamers.*
- *If your school has MinecraftEdu, expect students to participate in forums, wikis, and chats—following class agreed-upon rules for social media interaction.*
- *Have students pre-blog about their knowledge of goals established for using program. When finished, blog how that knowledge changed.*
- *More resources on Minecraft available on Ask a Tech Teacher resource pages.*

_____Suggestions for **Mission US**:

- *There are four games, all focused on the impact of history on our world.*
- *There are many reflection tools provided to encourage deeper thinking. Have students include these in their blog posts.*
- *Have students pre-blog about topic-specific knowledge and then about what they learned.*

_____Suggestions for (free) **Past/Present**:

- *Requires decision-making and critical thinking skills in the study of American history.*
- *An interactive 3-D "virtual world" in which student "becomes" a fictional character caught up in big issues of early 1900s.*
- *Appeals to gamers as well as novices.*
- *Students pre-blog about their immigrant knowledge. When finished, blog what they learned.*

_____Suggestions for (free) **Science simulations**:

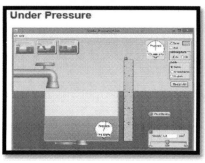

- *Lots of choices at 7th grade level. These aren't as long as other simulations, but can be tightly focused on a topic.*

- *Can be played online, downloaded, or embedded into a blog.*
- *Expect students to complete several simulations in time allotted. Have students select those that are connected thematically.*
- *Good choice for non-gamers. They will have more time to reach a comfort level with the concept of 'gamification'.*
- *Have students pre-blog about their knowledge in the area of selected simulations. When finished, blog about what they learned.*

_____Suggestions for (free) **Stock Market Game**

- *Students learn how the Market works as they invest their money.*
- *Best-suited for groups.*
- *It can be played online or with an app*
- *Site includes lots of teacher lesson plans and ideas.*

_____Expect gaming to be collaborative, where you as teacher learn with students.

_____Involve parents through student blogs and your open-door policy. Do not let them hear about 'games at school' through a child's casual comment. Make sure their introduction includes the game unit's structure, goals, and purpose. Invite them to play if/when possible.

_____When unit ends, reflect on it yourself: What did students accomplish? Did they experience the exhilarating sensation of learning for themselves rather than a grade?

_____Throughout class, check for understanding.

Class exit ticket: ***Using Twitter, Discussion Board, or student blog, post at least daily about progress on game (include #hashtag such as #stockmarketgame).***

Differentiation

- *Students have questions teacher can't answer? That's OK. Set up several students as 'Alpha Gamers'. Their job: to assist and answer questions.*
- *Some students don't like gaming? Like any unit of inquiry, some will like it better than others. Encourage student to get involved and give it a chance.*
- *Some students can't win game they picked? The goal isn't winning. The goal is learning. What have they learned? Remind them of the adage: The only failure is when you stop trying.*
- *Tie this unit in with robotics: Have students join a virtual environment that supports concepts required for robotics, i.e., Second Life.*
- *Use Science Simulations or other science-based simulations as Minecraft resources.*
- *Extend learning by exploring how to program a simulation at Gamestart Mechanic—an online game building community for students.*
- *Have students comment on three classmate posts with suggestions/ideas.*
- *Support student gaming enthusiasm with an afterschool club. Have students complete requirements and present request to Admin (if necessary).*
- *More games—Planet in Action via Google Earth.*

> **"Whether you think that you can, or that you can't, you are usually right."**
>
> - Henry Ford (1863-1947)

3 Websites to Gamify Your Math Class

Most elementary age kids I know love math, but that changes when they matriculate to middle school. If you ask seventh and eighth graders what their hardest subject is, they'll hands down tell you it's math. And that opinion doesn't improve in high school. In fact, Forbes reported that 82% of public high schoolers in the well-to-do Montgomery County Maryland failed Algebra. US News blamed math knowledge for a 33% failure rate by Oklahoma high school seniors on their exit exams.

To turn those numbers around, parents and teachers alike are looking to technology. This goes well beyond Khan Academy's online video training, into fantasy worlds of trolls and wizards, the type of activities most parents have tried to keep their kids away from. Now, they want to use their kids' native interest in online gaming to scaffold math knowledge. Here are three wildly-popular choices that have made kids choose math practice for their free time:

Dimension U

DimensionU is a collection of engaging interactive multiplayer fantasy games for grades 2-10 (some can be played solo) that focus on core skills in mathematics and literacy. Content aligns with Common Core, state standards and classroom instruction. Each game is designed with unique features to bring out distinct academic and strategic skills in students.

Dimension U is much closer to typical gaming than the usual math education fare, including edgy avatars, mystical journeys, and leaderboards. It's a little-known gem in the education tech field. Not surprisingly, Dimension U's awards have spanned a decade, including several Codies, MacWorld Editor's Choice, a Stanford Summit commendation, accolades from EdNet and Edtech, Computers for Youth, and about six more.

Land of Venn

Created by iMagine Machine for iOS and Android, in this app, kindergarten through third graders use their knowledge of geometry to stop the Evil Bookenriders from destroying the Land of Venn. To do this, players move through thirty increasingly difficult levels, becoming familiar with geometric shapes, square roots, lines, points, hierarchical relationships, and more. Players start as novices and rise through levels to become a Wizard powerful enough to defend the homeland.

Land of Venn is easy to use, with no learning curve. Content is age-appropriate, presented in an enticing manner that is irresistible to most children. Kids love the crazy characters with their funny voices, the colorful graphics, and the humor that is woven throughout the gameplay.

ProdigyGame.com

Prodigy is a free, adaptive math game for grades 1-7 that integrates Common Core or Ontario math into a role-playing game using a Pokemon-style wizardry theme. Students complete math questions to level up (become more powerful) and ultimately defeat Crios, Prodigy's main antagonist.

Based on the student's profile and an invisible diagnostic run during the preliminary tutorial, students are placed at a starting math level. As they play, question difficulty increases or decreases depending upon their answers and facility with the skills. If a student struggles with a concept, following questions will backfill the necessary skills.

As the student works through the math problems, many lessons (but not all) include virtual manipulatives to help solve the problem. These include a speaker to say the question, a hint button to provide help, detail on the required skill, and a drawing tool to work through the answer. These encourage students to build their own problem solutions in a way that works for them rather than relying on a teacher or parent.

For more detail, visit this article on Ask a Tech Teacher

Article 20 Minecraft in School

Minecraft
In school

It was lunch time on a warm spring day—the first sun of the season. Most students were outside enjoying one of the first pleasant days since the chill of winter faded. Three students came in my lab–7th graders–asking to play a program I'd never heard of called Minecraft. Their science teacher wanted them to use it as a vehicle to study minerals and geology. I knew the teacher so let them move forward and dashed off an email asking her to verify. She did.

As the students played, several 4th graders came in. "Are we allowed playing Minecraft?" Over and over. And then third graders. And fifth. To all, I said no, this was a special project for 7th grade science.

I realized I had to research this program that had so many students willing to forego the playground to sit at a computer screen with blocky retro characters who had none of the pizzazz of any other modern game. At first blush, it is about beat-em-up violence and destruction. That didn't sell me. Where was the critical thinking? The geology and minerals? I went to Common Sense Media and found it ranks Minecraft 4/5 stars with a tagline *Sandbox-style game with open online play fosters creativity.*

It goes on to say:

> *Kids can learn creative thinking, geometry, and even a little geology as they build imaginative block structures in this refreshingly open-ended mining and construction game. Given carte blanche to sculpt virtually any creation of their choice in this 3-D space, kids can try out tons of possibilities while working toward simple objectives. An option to work with others on larger building projects can help kids develop collaboration skills. Minecraft empowers players to exercise their imagination and take pride in their digital creations as they learn basic building concepts.*

Subjects covered include:
- Math: estimation, geometry, shapes

- Science: geology, rocks and minerals
- Hobbies: building

…and skills taught:
- *Thinking & Reasoning: defining problems, hypothesis-testing, problem solving*
- *Creativity: imagination, making new creations, producing new content*
- *Collaboration: cooperation, group projects, teamwork*

I'd read enough. I decided to declare Monday and Friday lunches 'Minecraft Mania'. I would watch, observe, and make sense of all the excitement.

Word got out and my lab was packed those two lunch hours—all year. As I watched my students play, I saw lots of the thinking and risk-taking we encourage in traditional educational venues. Students rattled off fifteen-digit IP addresses that allowed others to join their game, created servers to compete against each other, strategized how to reach their goals, formed alliances with other players, researched solutions on the internet, shared with each other so everyone could participate (the program requires a fee, but that didn't stop any one).

Is there something to this?

I polled my PLN and got no supporters. I might have given up, but ran across this article, *Learn to Play: Minecraft in the classroom.* And then these teaching wikis about educational uses of Minecraft, *Welcome to the Minecraft in School Wiki!* and *Gaming Educators. T*here's also an edition of Minecraft specifically for schools called MinecraftEdu.

As I was putting this review to bed, I came across ECOO 2012 who had a packed seminar on Minecraft in education. Among the benefits of playing this game:

- *peer learning*
- *sharing computers*
- *co-operative play*
- *parallel play*
- *exploring*
- *testing theories*
- *developing hypotheses*
- *negotiating social agreements*

I can't think of another educational program that does so much in so little space with so many avid followers. Can you?

Lesson #22-24 Web Communication Tools

Vocabulary	Problem solving	Homework
• Animoto • Brainstorm • Embed • GIF • Jing • MindMap • Prezi • Publish • QR code • Screencast • Screenshot • Shelfari • Voice Thread • Voki • Widget	• I don't know how to embed a tool • Where's embed code? (search screen) • I see 'share' (click that) • My typing disappeared (Ctrl+Z) • How do I undo? (Ctrl+Z) • My screen froze (clear dialogue box) • Log-in doesn't work (did you type it correctly?) • How do I save when there's no 'save' button? (try a screen shot) • I don't like the tool we're looking at (try a different one) • Which tool should I use? (which works best for your goals?) • I don't understand tool (ask teammates)	Test at least five webtools included in this lesson Come to class knowing which tool student wants to review and who will be in her/his group Keyboard 45minutes, 15 minutes at a time
Academic Applications	**Skills Required**	**Standards**
Presentations, research skills	Ability to use online tools, familiarity with problem solving, digital citizenship, keyboarding	CCSS: SL.7.5 NETS: 1a-d, 3d, 7a-d

Essential Question

How do I use technology to differentiate communication?

Big Idea

Use technology to diversify and differentiate communication so all listeners understand

Teacher Preparation/Materials Required

- Have backchannel available.
- Have student workbooks available (if using).
- Have lesson materials online to preview.
- Have web tool links easily-accessible.
- Integrate domain-specific tech vocabulary into lesson.
- Ask what tech problems students had difficulty with.

Assessment Strategies

- Previewed required material; came to class prepared
- Annotated workbook (if using)
- Worked well in a group
- Completed project; graded
- Voted on coursework poll
- Used good keyboarding habits
- Completed warm-up, exit ticket
- [tried to] solve own problems
- Decisions followed class rules
- Left room as s/he found it
- Higher order thinking: analysis, evaluation, synthesis
- Habits of mind observed

Steps

Time required: 270 minutes

Class warm-up: *Students collect in the group they will be working with for this project.*

_____Homework is assigned the week before unit so students are prepared.

_____Any questions on keyboarding?

_____Any questions from preparatory homework? Expect students to review upcoming unit and come to class with questions.

_____Discuss 'online communication'. It:

- *is a way to collaborate and publish in a variety of digital environments with varied media*
- *is a way to communicate information and ideas to multiple audiences*
- *develops cultural understanding and global awareness*
- *enables students to contribute as a team*
- *includes email, forums, blogs, and social media*
- *is a way to pose questions, elaborate on discussions, and respond to comments with relevant ideas*
- *is a way to integrate new information into views*

_____The goal of this lesson is to broaden student understanding of available communication tools. What they have used (word processing, slideshows, and desktop publishing, to name a few) is but a fraction of what is available. The good news is—many tools are intuitive to learn, free, and require nominal log-in information (suitable for pre-teen and teen users).

_____Find webtools to help students communicate in differentiated, personal ways. This list will:

- *address varied learning styles*
- *include tools students will need in 7th and 8th grade*
- *include tools students are interested in*
- *include tools the 7th grade team considers important*

_____For more ideas: Look back at options in the word processing lesson.

_____Best practices include:

- *It is OK for students and teachers to collaborate, co-learners with the same goal.*
- *Avoid web tools with too much advertising.*
- *Resist urge to 'teach'. Expect students to self-teach, using critical thinking skills and problem-solving tools honed throughout year.*

_____This lesson works best supporting a final project that requires students to collaboratively investigate, draw conclusions, share, and publish. Talk with grade-level team to identify a topic.

_____Tools that work well include (search Internet to find these websites):

- o *Alice — program a game/video in a 3D environment and embed into digital portfolio. This is a preview for 8th grade.*
- o *Animoto_— use photos and videos, mix with music and words, to create an amazing video on any topic.*

- o *Big Huge Labs — do cool stuff with digital photos like magazine covers, pop art poster, map maker, movie poster, a badge, a calendar, a picture cube, wallpaper, trading cards, comicizer, a billboard, a blog header, and more. Can be used in conjunction with another tool.*
- o *Bubbl.us — brainstorm with classmates to create a project. Can be used in conjunction with another tool.*
- o *Class Tools — includes Venn Diagrams, animated books, a fake Facebook/Twitter, and a Learning Cycle.*
- o *Comic creators — communicate with comics. See the lesson on word processing for examples.*
- o *Crossword Puzzles — formative or summative assessment.*
- o *Diagrams Online — create flowcharts, floor plans, technical drawings and more.*
- o *Glogster — create a poster; embed it.*
- o *Go Animate! — create an animated lesson to teach anything—like how to use this tool.*
- o *Scribble Maps — create personalized maps.*
- o *Prezi — organize and share ideas*
- o *QR Codes — most options free.*
- o *Goodreads — make a class library, add book reviews for next year's class, and even add QR codes with book information.*
- o *Tagxedo — evaluate words with a word cloud.*
- o *Timelines — pick from options on Ask a Tech Teacher's resource pages to create timelines online.*
- o *Voice Thread — communicate by recording with images, documents, and videos.*
- o *Vokis —create speaking avatars that communicate ideas.*
- o *Wolfram Alpha widgets — see coding lesson.*

_____Review each tool for about one minute, then give students time to sign up using Google Forms, an online calendar, or an online program like Sign Up Genius (Google for address). They will sign up for both a webtool and a presentation date. Limit the number of sign-ups per day to available class time. For example, if class is 45 minutes, limit sign-ups to two per day.

_____Review project grading rubric (*Assessment* at end of lesson) on class screen. Explain what each factor means and take student questions.

_____Students spend a class researching presentation. Use *Assessment 27's* checklist for what should be covered during the presentation. Each student will check off items and then send a screenshot to you prior to their presentation.

_____During presentation, one group member teaches while others help classmates. Teacher will observe. Students must be critical thinkers and problem solvers.

_____During presentation, students cover:

- *how to use tool*
- *how tool communicates ideas*
- *how to create a project*
- *how to troubleshoot*
- *how to embed project into blogs*
- *what students learned from tool*

_____Each presentation will take about twenty minutes. When done, student group posts an example (embed or screenshot), directions, and a reflection to their blog.

Class exit ticket: ***Send screenshot of "Am I Ready" or embedded project to teacher."***

Differentiation

- *Have students comment on three classmate posts with suggestions/ideas.*
- *Support student gaming enthusiasm with an afterschool club. Have students complete requirements and present request to Admin (if necessary).*
- *More games—Planet in Action via Google Earth.*
- *Post 'Am I ready?' sheets online as a reminder a week before presentation begin.*
- *Have students add their presentation date to class calendar.*
- *Those who finish each week can vote in PollDaddy poll and upload projects to blog posts.*

Assessment 26—Am I Ready?

Am I Ready

For Web Communications Tool Presentation

Do I know how the tool works	
Do I know the problems/trouble-shooting	
Can I embed it into wiki page	
Can I reflect on this tool	
Can I tie it into class theme	
Am I participating fully in my group	

Notes:_____

_____

_____

Assessment 27—Web-based Communication Tools

Web-based Communication Tools Assessment

Student names_____

Total points earned_____ _____

CATEGORY	Exemplary	Developing	Unsatisfactory	RATING
Knowledge of selected tool **8 points**	Demonstrates clear understanding of how to use tool including terminology and tool website. Shows evidence of preparation for both group teaching and classmate problem-solving. Understanding is student-initiated with minimal assistance from teacher. Displays enthusiasm for tool and appreciation for its part in the learning experience. *When applicable, can show class how to embed tool into blog. Knows which 'widget' to use and is able to help when classmates have difficulties.*	Demonstrates mixed understanding of tool. Shows some evidence of preparation for both teaching and problem-solving. Requires teacher assistance more than once. Displays some confidence in knowledge, enthusiasm for tool, and appreciation for its part in the learning experience. *Has some difficulty showing class how to embed completed tool into class blog or wiki page. Hasn't sufficiently prepared prior to teaching.*	Demonstrates a murky understanding of selected tool with little evidence of preparation for teaching or problem-solving. Requires substantial assistance from others to complete presentation. Displays lack of confidence in ability to make tool part in learning experience. *Unable to show class how to embed tool into class blog and/or wiki page.*	/8
Ability to teach students **4 points**	Demonstrates how to use tool in an authentic, personal, and enthusiastic manner. Uses terms class understands. Speaks slowly and clearly so class can complete steps. Provides trouble shooting and problem-solving tips (discovered as student learned to use tool).	Has some difficulty teaching students to use tool. Teaching lacks confidence and doesn't always engage students. Sometimes speaks too quickly for class to follow and some students are unable to complete project. Occasionally unable to trouble-shoot or problem-solve.	Has considerable difficulty teaching students. Teaching lacks confidence and doesn't engage students. Unable to trouble-shoot and problem-solve when asked. Students are unable to complete project.	/4
Reflection on tool's usefulness **4 points**	Reminds students how tool communicates theme with examples. Addresses student questions. Reflection on blog is authentic and original, displays thoughtful analysis, and includes goals for continued learning.	Doesn't remind students of tool's usefulness but provides examples. Is able to address some questions. Blog reflection shows insufficient original thought and incomplete itemization of goals for continued learning.	Reflection doesn't describe tool's use for class theme, shows little original thought, and does not include goals for continued learning.	/4
Group Work **4 points**	Consistently works toward group goals. Display sensitivity to feelings of others and values all members.	Sometimes works toward group goals. Is at times insensitive to the feelings of others.	Never works toward group goals. Is not sensitive to the feelings and needs of others in the group.	/4

Lesson #25-28 Differentiated Learning

Vocabulary	Problem solving	Homework
• Background • Body language • Diagram • Digital citizen • Digital native • Graphic organizer • Images • Landscape • Mind map • Portrait • Scholarly research • Visual learners • Visual organizer	• How do I open a program • Why 'save early save often'? • I'm not a visual learner (empathize with those who are) • It's confusing (ask a friend to explain why they like it) • I couldn't get on keyboarding website (try another one) • Can't I write this instead (not this time. Imagine if you HAD to use images—no text) • What can I learn about a person from their body language?	Review provided resources. Bring questions to class Review suggested tools. Select three you'd like to use for this lesson Keyboard 45 minutes, 15 minutes at a time

Academic Applications	Skills Required	Standards
Presentations, research skills	graphic organizers, mindmaps; problem solving, digital citizenship, keyboarding	CCSS: W.7.4 NETS: 1a-d, 4a-b, 6a, 6c-d

Essential Question

How can technology help communication with visual learners?

Big Idea

Students use visual communications to share ideas in a clear, succinct fashion

Teacher Preparation/Materials Required

- Have lesson materials online to preview.
- Have links for communication tools available.
- Have graphic organizers examples from past students.
- Have a mind mapping program available.
- Have backchannel tool active.
- Have student workbooks available (if using).
- Integrate domain-specific vocabulary into lesson.
- Ask what tech problems students had difficulty with.

Assessment Strategies

- Previewed required material
- Annotated workbook (if using)
- Used creativity, critical thinking
- Created three visual organizers that fulfilled requirements
- Created a blog/article
- Commented on classmate post
- Used good keyboarding habits
- Completed warm-up, exit ticket
- Joined classroom conversations
- [tried to] solve own problems
- Decisions followed class rules
- Left room as s/he found it
- Higher order thinking: analysis, evaluation, synthesis
- Habits of mind observed

Steps

Time required: **90 minutes**
Class warm-up: **Keyboarding on the class typing program**

_____**Homework assigned before start of unit so students are prepared.**

_____Any questions from preparatory homework? Expect students to review upcoming unit and come to class with questions.

_____Any questions on keyboarding homework?

_____*Figures 103a-e* are examples of visual representation of ideas students have used between kindergarten and sixth grade (if they followed the SL technology curriculum):

Figure 103a—Visual organizers in 1st grade; 103b—2nd grade;103c—3ʳᵈ grade; 103d—4ᵗʰ grade; 103e—6ᵗʰ grade

_____Discuss concept of organizing ideas visually rather than textually. What's the difference between sharing via 'text' and 'visually'? Why is a blend of both more effective?

_____For this projects, students will first determine **what information needs to be organized**. (i.e., the plot, characters, points of view from John Steinbeck's *Travel's With Charley*. Next: Students will determine the **best way to organize it**—a table (*Figure 105*)? Map (*Figure 104*)? Timeline (*Figure 108a*)? Audio (*Figure 108b*)?

Figure 104—Differentiated communication with ScribbleMaps

_____How might these differentiated approaches (per Common Core Standards):

- *build strong content knowledge via visual media*
- *respond to varying demands of audiences*
- *help to understand other perspectives and cultures*

_____Before continuing, discuss legalities of using online images. Take as much time as necessary to answer questions. This is an important and authentic topic.

Figure 105—A chart to visually represent info

Geographic Location	Characters	Plot Point	Comment
Sag Harbor	Steinbeck and his dog, Charley	Start of story	
Deerfield Mass	Steinbeck and his son		
White Mountains NY	Steinbeck and farmer		
Niagara Falls, NY	Steinbeck and Charley	Charley's vaccinations	
Chicago, Ill			
Mauston, WI			
Alice ND			

_____For this project, students work in groups. Review tools used in the past—if you used the SL tech curriculum past years. Select three from *Figures 103a-e* and *Figures 106a-e*. They'll include:

- *audio tool*
- *digital poster*
- *graphic organizer*

- *mindmap*
- *table*
- *timelines*

Figure 106a-e—More visual organizers in K-6

  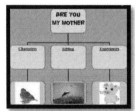  

_____Students must select a tool they've used in the past. This lesson is not about learning a new tool; rather, you want students to creatively use a tool they already understand. This may also include a tool that the student is comfortable with, but you have never used. Be open-minded; let them convince you with evidence and logical arguments that their tool is a good choice.

Figure 107—Mindmap for project

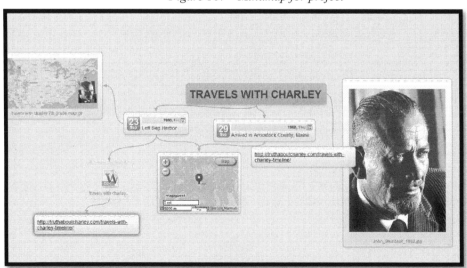

_____Students will take the same data set (say, a story they're reading like *Travels With Charley*) and present it three different ways. Then, the class will determine the best approach.

_____Divide class into groups. Organize ideas using a mindmap (see *Figure 107*):

- *What information are they conveying to readers?*
- *How can it be presented as simply as possible?*
- *How can it respond to the varying needs of audiences?*

_____Next, completed mind map in hand, each group will produce three graphic organizers from the options provided. See *Figures 104, 105, 108a-b* for samples.

_____Done? Share all three with a neighboring group. Do they understand your point? Which do they believe communicates most effectively?

Figure 108a—Timeline using Google Draw; 108b-Data communication using Voki

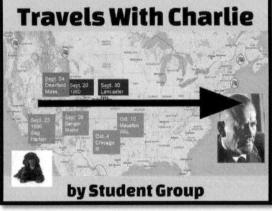

_____Remind students to save early/save often.

_____Insert all three into a blog post (or have each group member enter one and then link their post to the posts of group members. Include a screenshot of each group member post for clarity). Explain group's decision.

_____Comment on posts of three other groups and discuss why you agree/disagree with the visual organizer they selected, and how it fulfills/fails to fulfill requirements. Remember agreed-upon rules of discussion (which also apply in a social media forums like blogging):

- *express ideas clearly*
- *build on ideas of others (both author and commenter)*
- *make relevant observations*
- *bring discussion back on topic if necessary*
- *acknowledge new information expressed by others*

_____Continually throughout class, check for understanding.

Class exit ticket: **Comment on blog posts of group members.**

Differentiation

- *Try other differentiation tools if you finish early.*

Lesson #29-30 Writing/Publishing an Ebook

Vocabulary	Problem solving	Homework
• Ebook • GHO • Kindle • Novella • Point of view • Prologue • Rhetoric • Setting • Share • Tense • Theme • Voice	• I forgot to attend GHO (is it taped?) • I started novel in Word (import to Docs) • I can't think of what else to say (get help from group) • I'm uncomfortable evaluating writing (use a check list; be objective) • I don't have classmate emails (why do you need them? Use 'share') • Can't get my book ready on time (discuss with GHO group how to do this) • I lost my document (did you back up?) • I don't want to sell book (options?)	Keyboard 45 minutes, 15 minutes at a time Select ebook topic Know who will be in your critique group Know how to use critique group meeting tool
Academic Applications	**Skills Required**	**Standards**
Writing, researching, working in groups, reading	Problem solving, digital citizenship, keyboarding; familiarity with work processing	CCSS: W.7.5-7,10 NETS: 1b, 6b, 6d

Essential Question

I'm just a kid. How can I write a book?

Big Idea

With proper planning, any seventh grader can write a book.

Teacher Preparation/Materials Required

- Have publication account for ebook (if using).
- Have backchannel available.
- Have student workbooks available (if using).
- Ask what tech problems students had difficulty with.
- Ensure required links are on student digital devices.
- Have lesson materials online to preview unit.
- Have parent permission slips for virtual meeting room.
- Integrate domain-specific tech vocabulary into lesson.

Assessment Strategies

- Worked independently as well as in a group format
- Used good keyboarding habits
- Finished and published ebook
- Completed exit ticket
- Joined class conversations
- [tried to] solve own problems
- Decisions followed class rules
- Left room as s/he found it
- Higher order thinking: analysis, evaluation, synthesis
- Habits of mind observed

Steps

Time required: **90 minutes a week, every week of the semester or grading period**
Class warm-up: **Meet in critique group to discuss required topics**

This project is completed over months, ongoing language and writing skills exercise.

_____Homework is assigned the week prior to this unit so students are prepared.

_____Any questions from homework? Expect students to review unit and bring questions to class.

_____Put backchannel device on class screen.

_____Students will write and publish an ebook. Each week, they complete one of the steps and then discuss with their critique group in a virtual meeting room like Skype or another age-appropriate selection. The critique group will serve as mentor and coach. For example, if the assignment is to establish a theme (as in #3 below), each student will share **their theme**, be critiqued, and comment on the ideas of others:

- *Prepare by reading groupmates' work.*
- *Use evidence to evaluate classmate's point of view.*
- *Build on others' ideas and express their own clearly and persuasively.*

_____If using student workbooks, have them available so questions are easily accessed.

_____During critique sessions, through classmate stories, students will be exposed to all types of writing (as required in 7th grade) and open-mindedly evaluate them. They will be using reading skills associated with your school's curriculum, such as:

- *read closely to determine what the text says*
- *determine central ideas of the text and analyze their development; summarize the key supporting details and ideas*
- *analyze how and why individuals, events, or ideas develop and interact throughout text*
- *interpret words in text including technical, connotative, and figurative meanings; analyze how specific word choices shape meaning or tone*
- *analyze text structure including how specific sentences relate to each other and the whole*
- *assess how the point of view or purpose shapes the content and style of a text*
- *delineate and evaluate the claims in a text including the validity of reasoning, and the relevance and sufficiency of the evidence*

_____Once planning steps are completed (Steps 1-5 and Prologue), students will write their story.

_____About once a month, students will reflect on their story—what was easy, hard, writer's block, and research needed. This can be done in blogs, Discussion Boards, or even a Twitter feed.

_____About once a week, students comment on the written reflections of classmates.

_____Before beginning, discuss 1) difference between an amateur and professional writer, 2) what it means to be 'published', and 3) publication options (see *7: Publish!*).

_____**One more note**: Know age requirements of virtual meeting rooms students will be using. If 7th graders are too young and/or can't meet under parent supervision, suggest alternatives.

Prologue: Discuss young authors (Google for their websites):

_____Alexandra Adornetto—published *The Shadow Thief* at age 15 and *Halo* at 18.

_____Christopher Paolini—published Eragon at age 16.
_____Steph Bowe—published *Girl Saves Boy* at age 16.
_____Cayla Kluver—published *Legacy* at age 16.
_____Alec Greven—published *How to Talk to Girls* at age 9.

1:   Make decisions about how to tell story

_____1st or 3rd person? Discuss and research.
_____Present or past tense? Discuss and research.
_____Author's voice—discuss and research.
_____Genre—history, science fiction, YA? Discuss; research.
_____Topic—how do you pick a topic?

- *What is student's area of expertise?*
- *What are they passionate about?*
- *What do they have experience in/with?*

_____Be prepared to discuss these with critique group.

2:   Brainstorm content

_____Where does story occur? What fits story's characters, theme, and goals?
_____Each student shares a short summary of their story with their critique group. This reads like the inside flap of a novel—quick introduction to characters, plot, setting, and why readers should be interested. Each group member reads all summaries in preparation for meeting.
_____At critique group, each student makes suggestions based on evidence and textual information.

3:   What is the theme?

_____What is a 'theme'? Why is it important? Review several books students have read and discuss the impact of 'theme' on story's success.
_____Determine theme of student story and discuss how it will be conveyed with critique group.
_____When discussing, cite evidence to support analysis.

4:   Heroes, villains. plot, and where it happens

_____Based on the theme, determine characters, general story arc (plot), and setting.
_____Make sure characters grow from their experiences.
_____Discuss character sketches, story arc, settings with critique group. Pay attention to:

- *how the plot unfolds—episodes and character developments that make this happen*
- *how the characters change as the plot moves toward resolution*
- *whether this is a character- or plot-driven story (discuss what that means)*

_____When discussing, group members cite evidence to support analysis.

5:   Sketch out at least ten chapters of book.

_____Chapters continually increase reader interest:

- *What problem creates a crisis to be solved?*
- *What plot points make the story increasingly complex and interesting?*
- *List major conflicts and resolutions. What is the final one?*

_____Share outline with teacher.

_____When discussing, group members cite evidence to support analysis.

6:   Write the book

_____Write in any word processing program (Google Docs, Word, Notes, or another).

_____Write 1000 words at a sitting—about three pages. Let the words tumble out, based on the outline and research. Don't edit until the end. The novel must be 15,000 words (technically a novella).

_____Use proper writing conventions, relevant descriptive details, and well-structured event sequences.

_____Use domain-specific and academic language.

_____Use narrative techniques, such as dialogue, pacing, and description, to develop experiences, events, and characters.

_____Use transition words to convey sequence from one time frame or setting to another.

_____Provide a conclusion that follows from events.

_____Develop and strengthen writing by planning, revising, editing, rewriting, or trying a new approach, based on collaboration and feedback from the group.

_____Research where necessary.

_____Hints for writing:

- *Write every day even if you don't want to. Write, throw it out if no good, but write.*
- *Read—a lot. Especially in your genre.*
- *Experience life—so you can write about it. Notice the world around you. Think how you could write about it.*

_____**As student writes, share draft with critique group:**

- *Does it demonstrate command of grammar and spelling conventions?*
- *Are sentences varied for interest?*
- *Is style and tone consistent?*
- *Does plot unfold in episodes?*
- *What details carry theme?*
- *How do characters respond as the plot progresses?*
- *Are word meanings clear based on context?*

Great Writing Quotes

A book is proof humans are capable of magic. –Carl Sagan

I'm a writer. Anything you say or do may appear in a story. –Anonymous

All good writing is like swimming under water and holding your breath. –F. Scott Fitzgerald

There is nothing to writing. All you do is sit at a typewriter and bleed. –Ernest Hemingway

Writing is easy. All you do is cross out the wrong words. —Mark Twain

The road to hell is paved with adverbs. –Stephen King

Why don't you write books people can read? —Nora Joyce to her husband James

The true writer has nothing to say. What counts is the way he says it. —Alain Robbe-Grillet

It takes a heap of sense to write good nonsense—Mark Twain

It's difficult switching gears because characters have very different voices and very different ways of thinking. –George RR Martin

Write every day. –advice of all serious writers

- *Is point of view effective? Why?*
- *Does story engage and orient reader by introducing narrator/characters and organizing events to unfold naturally?*
- *Does story use narrative techniques such as dialogue, pacing, and description, to develop experiences, events, and characters?*
- *Does story use transition words and phrases to convey sequence and signal shifts from one time frame or setting to another?*
- *Does conclusion follow from events?*

_____Remind students to back up their work:

- *on a flash drive*
- *on the hard drive*
- *in the cloud*
- *by emailing a copy of the draft to themselves every time they work on it*

How to Write Ebook

1. Research young authors
2. Decide POV for story
3. Decide voice for story
4. Decide genre for story
5. Decide theme
6. Decide topic
7. Brainstorm content with writing group
8. Flesh out characters
9. Plot action
10. Research settings
11. Sketch out chapters
12. Write book
13. Review book as you write
14. Publish!

7:   **Publish!**

_____Publish student ebooks through:

- *Google Play account*
- *iBooks*
- *class Kindle account to sell books to friends*
- *PDFs that are read through Kindle or iBooks on iPads, netbooks, Chromebooks, desktop computers, other digital devices*

SELF-PUBLISHING
E-BOOKS
AUTHOR
COPYRIGHT
DISTRIBUTION

Class exit ticket: ***Using Twitter, class Discussion Board, or student blog, post weekly on individual progress. In Twitter, use a #hashtag like #7thgradeebook.***

Differentiation

- Compare Mark Twain's quote about the use of 'very' ("Substitute 'damn' every time you're inclined to write 'very;' your editor will delete it and the writing will be just as it should be") and George RR Martin's (author of "Game of Thrones") quote including 'very' three times. What do students think about that? First: Decide if this is age-appropriate in your class.
- Compare and contrast student novellas in different genres.
- Assign a student to enter virtual meeting times, publication dates, and more.
- Cost of publishing? Fund it with Kickstarter.

Lesson #31-32 Making an Ebook Trailer

Vocabulary	Problem solving	Homework
• Book trailer • Ebook • Embed • Literacies • Plug-in • Render • Screencast • Storyboard • Visualize • Webtool	• I don't know how to use the book trailer tool (you've learned other tools—try those steps) • I tried one tool and didn't like it (try another that creates book trailers) • I can't embed my trailer (take a screencast) • The webtool charges a fee (is there a free education account—or through class? Or switch tools)	Keyboard 45 minutes, 15 minutes at a time Review how to use book trailer programs Watch assigned videos Bring storyboard for trailer to class
Academic Applications Writing, videography, reading	**Skills Required** Problem solving, digital citizenship, keyboarding, exposure to video creation program	**Standards** CCSS: W.7.6 NETS: 6d, 7a

Essential Question

Why are videos better at communicating some ideas?

Big Idea

A book report doesn't have to be a document with lots of words

Teacher Preparation/Materials Required

- Have backchannel available.
- Have student workbooks available (if using).
- Expect students to bring completed storyboards.
- Have lesson materials online to preview.
- Ensure required links are on student digital devices.
- Integrate domain-specific tech vocabulary into lesson.
- Ask what tech problems students had difficulty with.

Assessment Strategies

- Previewed required material; came to class prepared
- Completed book trailer
- Shared on blog
- Commented on classmate post
- Completed warm-up, exit ticket
- Joined classroom conversations
- [tried to] solve own problems
- Decisions followed class rules
- Left room as s/he found it
- Higher order thinking: analysis, evaluation, synthesis
- Habits of mind observed

Steps

Time required: 90 minutes
Class warm-up: collect images to represent ebook

_____Homework is be assigned before starting this unit so students are prepared.

_____Any questions from preparatory homework? Expect students to review upcoming unit and come to class with questions.

_____Digital book trailers are short videos that promote a book. Their purpose is to motivate others to read the book. They are similar to film trailers that you see at the movies.

_____Why create book trailers rather than, say, a book report? How about these reasons:

- *They're comprehensive, a way to experiment with different literacies.*
- *They are a good way to get reluctant readers to read.*
- *They are good for those readers who find it hard to visualize what they read.*
- *They are a good alternative for the traditional book reports*

_____Tools for book trailers include:

- *Animoto – for iPads or as an online tool*
- *PowerPoint (any slideshow program)*
- *iMovie (for iPads)*
- *Photostory – free from Microsoft*
- *WeVideo – for iPads and as a webtool*

_____If you want to assess this activity with a rubric, there are lots of options, including this one (zoom to see better):

CATEGORY	High Performance (10)	At or Above Average (7)	At or below Average (4)	Low performance (1)
Presentation (Persuasion)	The trailer flows very smoothly and captivates the attention of the audience. It compels the viewer to read the book	The trailer flows smoothly and holds the attention of the audience. The viewer is left interested in the book.	The trailer flows reasonably but there are some transitions that need improvement in order for the viewer to be persuaded to read the book.	The scenes from the trailer are choppy and the transitions seem abrupt. The viewer may be left confused and not inclined to read the book
Content (Storyline or plot)	Key scenes or themes from the book have been creatively presented. These make the content of the book clear to the viewer	There is one key scene or theme from the book represented in the trailer. This makes the viewer generally aware of the content of the book.	An attempt has been made to depict some aspect of the book, however from the content of the book has not been made clear to the viewer.	There is no scene in the trailer that suggests that the student has read the book. The viewer also has no idea of what the book is about.
Images	Images create a distinct atmosphere or tone that matches the different parts of the story.	The images create an atmosphere or tone that match some parts of the story	An attempt was made to use images that create an atmosphere or tone but it needed more work. The choice of images is logical.	Little or no attempt has been taken to use images to create an appropriate atmosphere or tone.
Voice (Soundtrack)	The voice track is clean and fully understandable. The pace fits the storyline. The viewer is always engaged.	The voice track is occasionally too fast/slow for the storyline. The pacing is relatively engaging for the viewer	Tries to use pacing and rhythm but it is often noticeable that it does not fit the storyline. The viewer is not engaged consistently	No attempt to match the pace f the storytelling to the storyline. The viewer was not engaged
Audio (Soundtrack)	The music stirs an emotional response that matches the storyline.	The music stirs and emotional response that somewhat matches the storyline.	The music is adequate and does not distract but not much was added to the story either	The music is distracting, inappropriate or was not used.
Video Editing	Editing demonstrates a full working knowledge of the software. Many effects were incorporated and used effectively	Editing demonstrates a good working knowledge of the software. Some effects were incorporated and used effectively	Editing demonstrates a fair knowledge of the software. Limited special effects were incorporated into the video.	Editing shows a lack of understanding of the software. No special effects were used in the making of the video.
Reflection (Awareness of Audience)	Strong awareness of the audience in the design. Can clearly explain why they chose the vocabulary, audio, and graphics to fit the target audience	An awareness of the audience in the design. Can explain why they chose the vocabulary, audio, and graphics to fit the target audience	Some awareness of audience in the design. Some difficulty in explaining the choice of vocabulary, audio, and graphics for the target audience	Limited awareness of the needs and interests of the target audience.
Presentation (Interest level)	A very exciting presentation. It grabbed the attention of the viewer with suspense, humour or intrigue from the beginning.	A good presentation that used suspense, humour or intrigue well and caught the attention of the viewer from the beginning.	A passable presentation. Some suspense, humour or intrigue but no real "hook" present at the start.	Flat presentation. Little or no suspense, humour or intrigue to capture the attention of the viewer.
Presentation (Duration/length)	The presentation was the right length to keep/get the viewer involved.	The presentation was the right length to keep/get the viewer involved.	The length of the presentation was too long/short to keep/get attention of the viewer	The length of the presentation was too long/short to keep/get attention of the viewer

_____Each student will add a blog post that includes an embed of the trailer to share with classmates. If there isn't a native embed option with the tool you're using, students can take a screencast of the video as it plays and share that.

Class exit ticket: ***Watch the book trailer of a classmate. Add a comment to their blog post.***

Differentiation

- *Instead of a video, create a podcast or audio intro to student ebook.*
- *Create a slideshow of student ebook and turn it into a video.*
- *Use one of the tools students experimented with in other lessons (say, a comic creator).*
- *Early finishers: visit class internet start page for websites that tie into classwork.*

Classroom Posters

1. **10 Steps to Become a Better Geek**
2. **15 Ways to Get Your Geek On**
3. **Copyright Law**
4. **Digital Neighborhood**
5. **Email etiquette**
6. **Here's What We've Done**
7. **How to Save—4 Ways**
8. **How to solve problems**
9. **I Can't Find My File**
10. **Netiquette Rules**
11. **Popular Shortkeys**
12. **Shortkeys—Chromebook**
13. **Shortkeys—Internet**
14. **Shortkeys—iPad**
15. **Shortkeys—PCs**
16. **Steps for Internet Research**
17. **What's a Mulligan**

The law states that works of art created in the U.S. after January 1, 1978, are automatically protected by copyright once they are fixed in a tangible medium (like the internet) BUT a single copy may be used for scholarly research (even if that's a 2nd grade life cycle report) or in teaching or preparation to teach a class.

Askatechteacher©

Don't talk to strangers. Look both ways before crossing the (virtual) street. Don't go places you don't know. Play fair. Pick carefully who you trust. Don't get distracted by bling. And sometimes, stop everything and take a nap.

Askatechteacher©

EMAIL ETIQUETTE

1. Use proper formatting, spelling, grammar
2. CC anyone you mention
3. Subject line is what your email discusses
4. Answer swiftly
5. Re-read email before sending
6. Don't use capitals—THIS IS SHOUTING
7. Don't leave out the subject line
8. Don't attach unnecessary files
9. Don't overuse high priority
10. Don't email confidential information
11. Don't email offensive remarks
12. Don't forward chain letters or spam
13. Don't open attachments from strangers

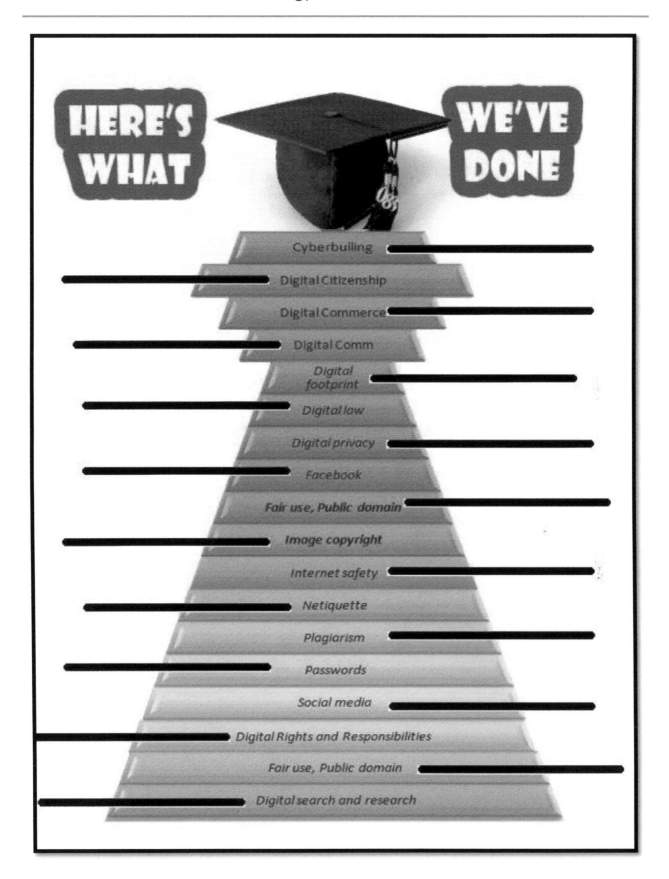

Popular shortkeys students love

Maximize window	**Double click title bar**
Quick Exit	**Alt+F4**
Date and Time	**Shift+Alt+D = Date**
	Shift+Alt+T = Time
Show taskbar	**WK (Windows key)**
Shows desktop	**WK+M**

Ctrl Key Combinations

- **CTRL+C: Copy**
- **CTRL+X: Cut**
- **CTRL+V: Paste**
- **CTRL+Z: Undo**
- **CTRL+B: Bold**
- **CTRL+U: Underline**
- **CTRL+I: Italic**

- **CTRL+P: Print**
- **CTRL+K: Add hyperlink**
- **CTRL+E: Center align**
- **CTRL+L: Left align**
- **CTRL+R: Right align**
- **CTRL+ : Zoom in Internet**
- **CTRL- : Zoom out Internet**

Fun Keyboard Shortcuts:

< + = + > = ⇔

— + >   = →

:+)   = ☺

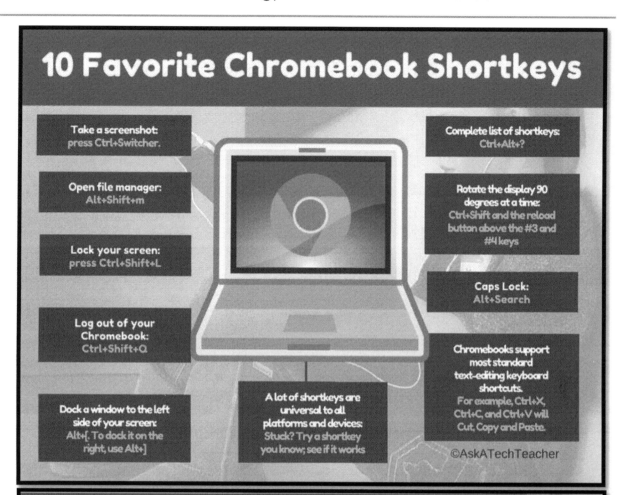

10 Favorite Chromebook Shortkeys

Take a screenshot: press Ctrl+Switcher.

Open file manager: Alt+Shift+m

Lock your screen: press Ctrl+Shift+L

Log out of your Chromebook: Ctrl+Shift+Q

Dock a window to the left side of your screen: Alt+[. To dock it on the right, use Alt+]

Complete list of shortkeys: Ctrl+Alt+?

Rotate the display 90 degrees at a time: Ctrl+Shift and the reload button above the #3 and #4 keys

Caps Lock: Alt+Search

A lot of shortkeys are universal to all platforms and devices: Stuck? Try a shortkey you know; see if it works

Chromebooks support most standard text-editing keyboard shortcuts. For example, Ctrl+X, Ctrl+C, and Ctrl+V will Cut, Copy and Paste.

©AskATechTeacher

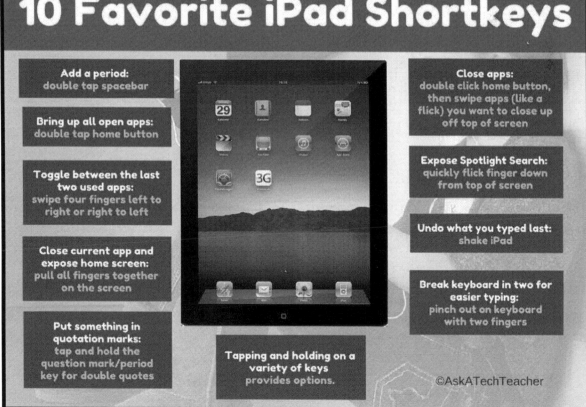

10 Favorite iPad Shortkeys

Add a period: double tap spacebar

Bring up all open apps: double tap home button

Toggle between the last two used apps: swipe four fingers left to right or right to left

Close current app and expose home screen: pull all fingers together on the screen

Put something in quotation marks: tap and hold the question mark/period key for double quotes

Close apps: double click home button, then swipe apps (like a flick) you want to close up off top of screen

Expose Spotlight Search: quickly flick finger down from top of screen

Undo what you typed last: shake iPad

Break keyboard in two for easier typing: pinch out on keyboard with two fingers

Tapping and holding on a variety of keys provides options.

©AskATechTeacher

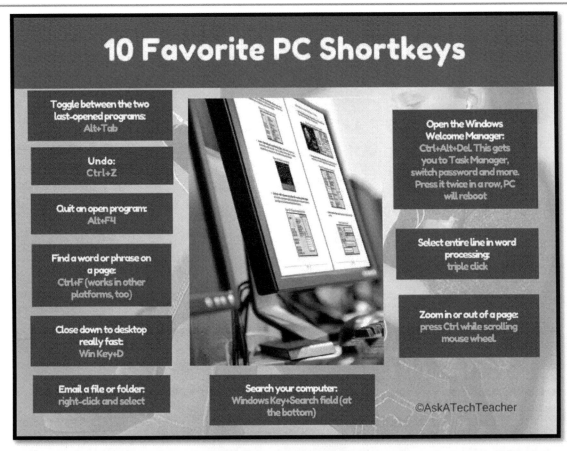

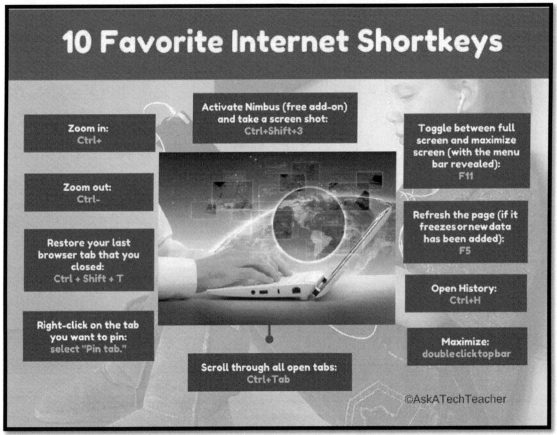

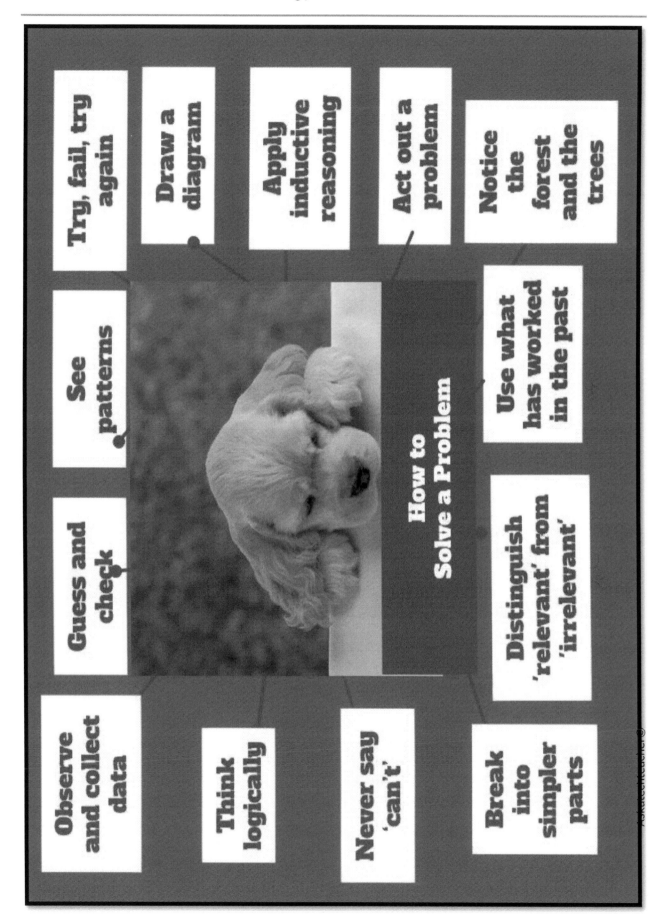

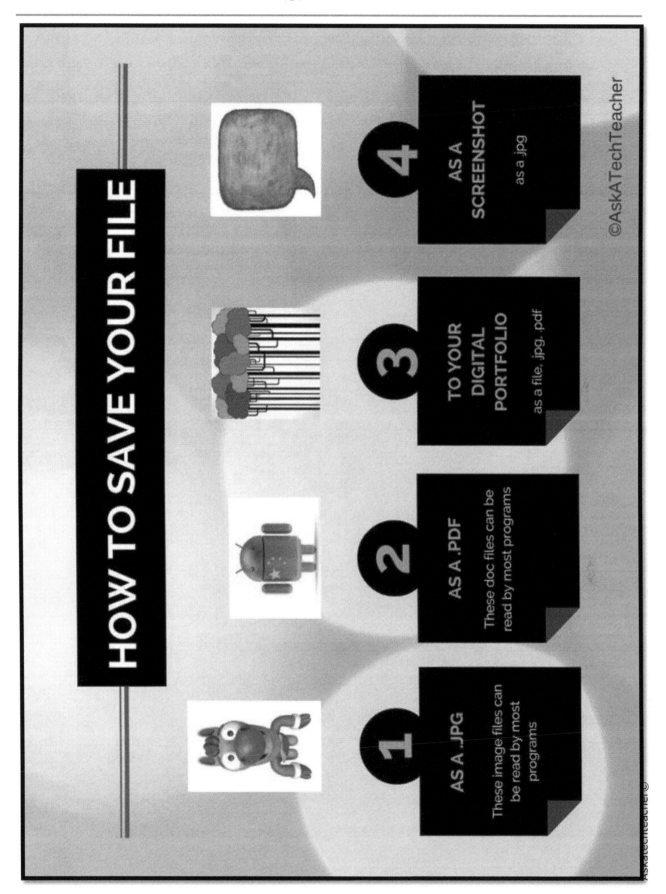

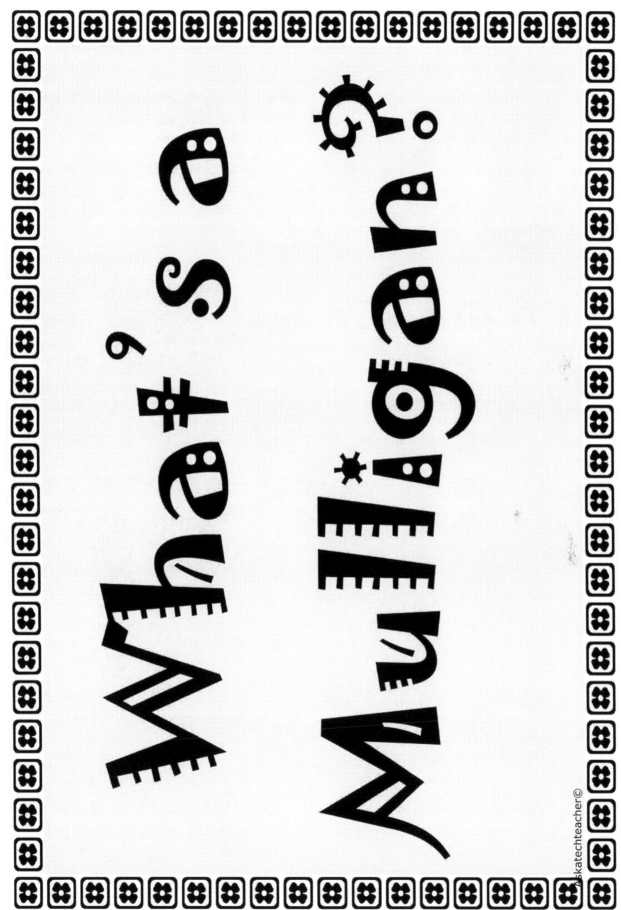

10 To become A BETTER steps GEEK

1. Use **Tech**
2. Use **it** every day--save some trees
3. Use **it** when it seems difficult
4. Use **it** in class--and at home
5. Use **Tech** now--right now
6. Use **it** instead of something else
7. Teach a friend to use **it**
8. Teach a lot of friends to use **it**
9. Make **it** your first choice
10. Keep using **it**

15 ways To GET YOUR GEEK ON

1. Be smart. Yeah, it feels good
2. That's my inner Geek speaking
3. Think. Exercise your brain.
4. Waves. Sigh.
5. Keep repeating, *People are my friends*. Like Siri.
6. Move away from the keyboard--Not.
7. Some people watch TV. I play with a Rubik's Cube
8. Be patient. I'm buffering.
9. There must be a shortkey for that
10. Life needs an Undo key
11. Leave me alone for 2 minutes and I'll go to sleep
12. Yes, I can fix your computer
13. Like a computer, I do what you tell me to
14. My RAM is full. Come back later.
15. Slow down. My processor isn't that fast

Index

Acrobat 39
Adobe Slate 127
Adobe Voice 127
Alice 184
Alt+F4 .... 95, 120
Animoto 183, 198
Annotation Tool 10, 39
Articles 14
ASCII Art 85
Ask a Tech Teacher 12
Assess 34
Assessment..6, 31, 53, 54, 55, 77, 79, 80, 81, 131, 144, 187
assessments 6
AutoHotkeys 172
Autosum 132
Avatars 39, 40
backchannel....33, 38, 40, 87, 88, 105, 116, 117, 132, 146, 147, 151, 152, 165, 183, 188, 192, 193, 197
Backchannel device 36, 40, 88, 116, 146
benchmark 77
Best Practices................................... 12
Big Huge Labs 185
Blank keyboard quiz 78, 81
Blog 36, 41, 63, 65, 67, 105, 165
Blog grading rubric 58
Blogging Rules 41, 57
Bot Battles............................... 162, 163
Bubbl.us 185
calendar.................................... 38, 42
Cartoons 123
Cell phones 106
Certificate of Completion.................... 6
chat rooms..................................... 107
Chromebook 11, 38, 39, 56, 77, 78, 82, 199
Chromebook blank keyboard............ 82
Civil War..............139, 140, 141, 142, 143, 144
Class Calendar............................... 42
Class Internet Start Page 38, 42
class rules... 26
Class Tools 185
Class warm-up....24, 27, 31, 37, 72, 88, 103, 116, 132, 139, 146, 151, 158, 165, 173, 183, 188, 192, 197
class website.................................... 44
Cloud 45
Code a Widget 171
Coding.....................13, 14, 165, 166, 167
Coffee Shop................................... 175

Comic Creators 185
Comics 123
Common Core... 5, 6, 12, 32, 41, 63, 84, 96, 133, 159
Common Core Standards 6, 30, 174, 189
Common problems 95
Compare-contrast 27, 118, 127
Content Standards 72, 103
Copyright.............. 12, 29, 60, 109, 146, 151
Copyright Law........................ 147, 199
cracking' 108
Creative Commons..................... 108, 147, 148
Creative Commons licensing....................... 148
critical thinking 138
CSI Web Adventures 175, 176
Ctr+B 95
curriculum map 6, 9
Cyberbullying.................. 104, 105, 107, 109
Data 72
date............................... 91, 95, 151
Debate.. 153
Desktop Publishing......................... 126
Diagrams 132, 185
Differentiated Learning.................. 13, 14, 188
differentiation................................ 6, 11
Digital Citizen 114
Digital citizenship 6, 12, 26, 37, 103, 105, 124, 151, 155
Digital Commerce 105
Digital communications................... 105
Digital devices 11, 38
digital economy 106
Digital footprint 104, 105, 108
Digital Law 105, 108
digital lockers 45
Digital Neighborhood 199
Digital Notetaking.......................... 44
Digital Passport............................. 152
Digital portfolio rubric..................... 60
Digital portfolios 38, 45, 60
Digital privacy 105, 108
Digital rights 105
Digital rights and responsibilities 108
Digital search and research...................... 105
digital tools 37
Dimension U............................ 175, 176, 179
Discussion Board 46, 175
Domain 151
Double click 91, 95
Dropbox 45

DTP 9
Ebook.......................13, 14, 122, 192, 197
Edugames 173
Email 28, 46, 47, 106, 107, 199
Escape...95
essential question 6
Evernote 43, 45, 84, 117
Evidence Board...........................25, 36, 38, 48
evidence of learning 138
Exit a program 91, 95
Exit Tickets...27, 31
Extension...151
Failure 88, 100
Fair use...105, 109, 147
Financial Football.............................175, 176
Find My File 199
flash drive 169
Flipped Classroom..................................9, 48
Formative assessments 77
Games...9, 85
Gamification..173
Gamification of Education 13, 14, 173
Gaming 173
GIF 183
Glogster 110, 185
Gmail...47
Go Animate! 185
Google Apps 36, 38, 42, 44, 45, 46, 49, 50, 51,
    84, 85, 115, 125, 169
Google Classroom 47, 48, 49
Google Docs 66, 120
Google Earth ..9, 13, 14, 132, 139, 140, 141, 142,
    143, 144, 145
Google Forms 27, 31, 87, 92, 185
Google Maps.......................34, 142, 143
Google Play 196
grammar 112
Graph 132
Graphics...9, 188
grit 100, 101
Habits of Mind............................11, 29, 30
hacking 108
Haiku Deck..127
Hardware 9, 53, 54
hardware quiz...................................36, 37
headlining 70
Hits 151
Hoaxes...147, 149
home row,...75
homework 6, 37, 72, 88, 104, 117, 133, 147, 152,
    159, 166, 184, 189, 193, 197
Hour of Code...166
https..109
hunt 'n peck 74
iAnnotate 10, 39

iCivics 175, 176, 177
image copyrights.........................105, 147
Images 15, 17
iMovie 198
Important Keys Quiz 78
IMs...106
Inquiry...................................7, 10, 11, 85
inquiry-based projects 76
internet images.............................153, 189
Internet Research 199
Internet Safety.........................105, 109, 152
Internet Search 152
Internet Start Page 61
iPad 38, 39, 55, 77, 86, 91, 119, 120, 124, 199
ISTE 7
Keyboard.....................................9, 79, 85
Keyboarding 9, 12, 27, 33, 72, 79, 84, 88, 103,
    116, 132, 139, 146, 151, 158, 165, 173, 183,
    188, 192, 197
Keyboarding Challenge 79, 83
Kindle 196
Lab Rules...28
Land of Venn...179
Learning style 173
Lemonade Stand......................................175
Linoit 31
literacy 5
LiveBinders 43
Mac 39
Math87, 88, 96, 132, 133, 158, 165, 173, 179, 181
menu 24, 91, 95
Mindmap 183, 190
Minecraft 97, 175, 177, 181, 182
Mission US 175
Model..............................159, 167, 174
mouse hold..37
Mouse Skills 9
MS Word...120
Mulligan 72, 75, 88, 100, 199
Mulligan Rule 75
National Educational Technology Standards.5
Netiquette 105, 109
Netiquette Rules 110, 199
Notability..........................10, 39, 44, 77
Notable 10
online calendars.......................................65
Online presence 105
Online Reputations 108
Outlining...116, 119
Padlet...............31, 40, 61, 62, 91, 105, 117, 152
PARCC 86
Passwords 105, 109, 188
Past/Present...175
personal responsibility 104
Photo sharing 66

Photostory 198
Plagiarism 105, 149
Podcasting..66
Polls 31
Portfolio..35
Posters..6, 10, 11, 199
posture...33
PowerPoint 119, 126, 198
Presentations 84
Problem solving ..24, 36, 72, 88, 89, 92, 103, 116, 132, 139, 146, 151, 158, 165, 173, 183, 188, 192, 197
Problem Solving Board 88, 90, 91, 92, 93
ProdigyGame.com...................................180
Programming......................13, 14, 161, 165, 166
Public domain 105, 108, 109, 148, 149
QR code..183
quotes...88, 89, 153
QWERTY 75
Reliable Websites 153
Report Cards..138
Research Skills 156
Right-click..24
risk takers 10
robotics............. 26, 158, 159, 160, 162, 170, 178
Round Robin Story..................................129
Rubric.........................42, 58, 59, 60, 93, 134, 137
rules...109, 112
Science simulations.................................175
Scope and Sequence 6, 13, 26
Scratch 166
screen..183
screencasts.....................................50, 183
Screenshots.................................39, 50, 183
ScribbleMaps....................................143, 189
Search Shark..155
Serialized novel.....................................122
sharing.............................32, 36, 41, 63, 103, 126
shortkeys....................75, 76, 77, 85, 89, 205
Simulation..173
Slideshows 127, 133
smartphone 10
social bookmarking 66
Social media.............................103, 105, 109
Socrative 31, 40, 105, 117, 147, 152
software..7, 11
spam...47, 107
speed quiz...77
spelling...124
Spreadsheet Skills 133, 134
Spreadsheet summative 135, 137
Spreadsheets 13, 45, 50, 126, 128, 132, 133, 134
Standards for Mathematical Practice....96, 167
Stock Market Game 175, 178
Storyboard 124

Stranger Danger 105
Student blogging agreement......................57
Student website 50
Student workbooks 12, 39
Surface tablet 39
syllabus..26
Symbaloo...................................43, 61, 62
table 131
Tagxedo...185
taskbar...95
tasks...133
Teacher Training 87
Teacher Web, ...45
Team Challenge 83, 85
Technology Curriculum............................5, 6
Texting...............................47, 106, 108, 113
Timelines......................................185, 189, 191
Tomorrow's student.................................8
Transfer of knowledge.........................26, 34
Twitter 33, 36, 40, 41, 43, 45, 50, 66, 69, 105, 109, 110, 111, 112, 113, 117, 121, 147, 152, 193
Twitter Novel.......................................121
Type to Learn 77
Virtual Wall...................................25, 31, 40
Virtual world 173
Visual organizers 189
Vocabulary 9, 24, 32, 36, 51, 72, 88, 103, 116, 132, 139, 146, 151, 158, 165, 173, 183, 188, 192, 197
Voice Thread..................................183, 185
Voki...183
warm-up 10
Web Communication Tools............. 13, 183, 187
Web Tools 65
webpage...65
website address 153
Website grading rubric 59
Weebly...50
weekly lesson 6
WeVideo 129, 198
Widgets 171, 183, 185
Windows 39, 95
Wix 50
Wolfram/Alpha 166, 171, 172, 185
Word...32, 120
Word Processing 13, 14, 116, 131
Wordpress 50
Writing36, 58, 59, 60, 72, 112, 113, 116, 122, 123, 146
writing skills 111, 113
Writing with Art...............................124, 125
Writing with Audio.................................125
Writing with Music 127
Zoho Docs..133

Certificate of Achievement

THIS ACKNOWLEDGES THAT

HAS COMPLETED THE HIGHLIGHTED 7TH GRADE TECHNOLOGY SKILLS:

- Coding/Programming
- Differentiated learning
- Digital tools in the classroom
- Digital citizenship
- Gamification of education
- Keyboarding, summative
- Google Earth
- Internet search and research
- Making an ebook trailer

- Online image legalities
- Problem solving
- Robotics
- Spreadsheets
- Web communication tools
- Slideshows, summative
- Word processing options
- Writing and publishing an ebook

Signatory

Signatory

Which book	Price (print/digital/Combo)
K-8th Tech Textbook (each)	$25.99-35.99 + p&h
K-8 Combo (all 9 textbooks)	$248-450 + p&h
K-8 Student workbooks (per grade—tech or kb)	$199/550/1500 (room/school/district)
35 K-6 Inquiry-based Projects	$31.99/25.99/52.18 + p&h
55 Tech Projects—Vol I,II, Combo	$18.99 /$35.38–digital only (free shipping)
K-8 Keyboard Curriculum—3 options	$20 and up + p&h
K-8 Digital Citizenship Curriculum	$29.95/25.99/50.38 + p&h
CCSS—Math, Language, Reading, Writing	$26.99 ea/80 for 4–digital only (free shipping)
K-5 Common Core Projects	$29.95/23.99/48.55 + p&h
Themed webinars	$8-30
Weekly tech webinars	Free or $99 per year for 180+ per year
Summer PD classes (online—for groups)	$795
Summer tech camp for kids	$179 + p&h
College credit classes (online)	$497 and up
Digital Citizenship certificate class	Starts at $29.99
Classroom tech poster bundles	Start at $9.99
PBL lessons--singles	$1.99 and up
Bundles of lesson plans	$4.99 and up (digital only)
Tech Ed Scope and Sequence (K-6 and 6-8)	$9.99 and up (digital only)
New Teacher Survival Kit	$285-620+ p&h
Homeschool Tech Survival Kit	$99 + p&h
Mentoring (30 min. at a time)	$50/session
169 Tech Tips From Classroom	$9.99 (digital only)
Consulting/seminars/webinars	Call or email for prices

Free sample? Visit Structured Learning LLC website

Prices subject to change

Email Zeke.rowe@structuredlearning.net

Structured Learning
Premiere Provider of Technology Teaching Books to the Education Community

Pay via PayPal, Credit Card, Amazon, TPT, pre-approved school district PO